# Serving the
# Public Interest

# Serving the Public Interest

## Profiles of Successful and Innovative Public Servants

Norma M. Riccucci, Editor

Advancing excellence
in public service . . .

*M.E.Sharpe*
Armonk, New York
London, England

The EuroSlavic fonts used to create this work are © 1986–2012 Payne Loving Trust.
EuroSlavic is available from Linguist's Software, Inc.,
www.linguistsoftware.com, P.O. Box 580, Edmonds, WA 98020-0580 USA
tel (425) 775-1130.

**Library of Congress Cataloging-in-Publication Data**

Serving the public interest : profiles of successful and innovative public servants / edited by Norma M. Riccucci.
    p. cm.
  Includes bibliographical references.
  ISBN 978-0-7656-3529-7 (hardcover : alk. paper) — ISBN 978-0-7656-3530-3 (pbk. : alk. paper)
  1. Government executives—United States—Biography. 2. Public administration—United States—Case
studies. 3. Leadership—United States—Case studies. 4. Political leadership—United States—Case studies. I.
Riccucci, Norma.
  JK723.E9S48 2012
  351.73092′2—dc23                                                          2011042046

Printed in the United States of America

The paper used in this publication meets the minimum requirements of
American National Standard for Information Sciences
Permanence of Paper for Printed Library Materials,
ANSI Z 39.48-1984.

IBT (c)   10   9   8   7   6   5   4   3   2   1
IBT (p)   10   9   8   7   6   5   4   3   2   1

# CONTENTS

# PREFACE

In 1995, I published a book, *Unsung Heroes: Federal Execucrats Making a Difference*, which profiled high-level public servants who made significant, positive contributions to the lives of American citizens. That book presented the experiences of six high-ranking career federal administrators operating in a vast number of policy domains, ranging from the environment to global affairs. This tradition of providing biographical profiles to examine the actual work performed by high-ranking officials has been favorably received in the field of public administration.

When Richard Stillman became editor-in-chief of one of leading professional journals in the field, *Public Administration Review*, he established an "Administrative Profiles" series aimed at continuing this important tradition of providing rich, in-depth, and balanced examples of the work performed by high-level public servants—at every level of government as well as the nonprofit sector—and the factors that contribute to their effectiveness in a setting that is immensely political. While appointed officials were included in this series, elected officials were not. The American people often overlook the fact that it is not just the people we elect to government office who make social and political decisions about how this country is run.

This reader presents the collection of profiles for classroom use. Administrative profiles are an important instructional tool in public administration classes on, for example, leadership, management, ethics, organization theory, and general public affairs and policy. The profiles also present positive images and role models to students preparing for careers in public service or to those already working in government and nonprofit organizations; they are instrumental as the public administration community endeavors to grow the next generation of public service leaders. Through biographical profiles as well as stories told by the public administrators themselves, examples of effective management and leadership in government as well as nonprofit institutions help to inspire and revitalize the mission of public service.

## ACKNOWLEDGMENTS

I wish to extend my sincere gratitude to Richard Stillman, who, as editor-in-chief of *Public Administration Review* (*PAR*), launched the administrative profiles series from which this reader emanates. His commitment to public service as expressed through this series is commendable and laudable. Many thanks also to his managing editor Jos Raadschelders and logistical editor Sheri Castleman for all their invaluable assistance. I am also indebted to my colleagues who were instrumental in the publication of the administrative profiles appearing in *PAR*. They include Terry Cooper, University of Southern California; W. Henry Lambright, Syracuse University; Hal Rainey, University of Georgia; and Hindy Lauer Schachter, New Jersey Institute of Technology.

Finally, I offer my appreciation to Harry Briggs, executive editor of M.E. Sharpe, and the staff of the American Society for Public Administration, in particular Matt Rankin, for their invaluable help in bringing this book to fruition.

# INTRODUCTION

## The Making of Effective Public Servants

There is a surfeit of studies in public administration on effective management and leadership of public and nonprofit institutions. In particular, studies abound on attributes of effectiveness and productivity at the macro as well as micro levels of organizations. But, who exactly are the actual administrators, the leaders of these programs and organizations, and what specifically contributes to their success? There is relatively little research profiling the administrators who have made significant contributions to the public through their work in government at every level as well as through nonprofit entities.

This reader seeks to fill this gap by presenting a series of profiles on public servants who are committed to promoting the public interest. From revamping the organizing structure of the IRS to bringing Nazi criminals to justice, public servants such as those profiled here have devoted their lives to providing more effective and efficient services to the American people and, in the latter case, to bringing justice to victims of one of the most evil atrocities in the history of humankind.

### THE SIGNIFICANCE OF ADMINISTRATIVE PROFILES

There is a time-honored tradition of profiling persons who are exemplary practitioners of public administration. For example, Doig and Hargrove (1990), in *Leadership and Innovation*, provide stories of public servants whose management and leadership skills served to impact the economy or society in some major way. In *Exemplary Public Administrators*, Cooper and Wright (1992) offer "character" studies of public servants, seeking to identify, through an examination of ethical behaviors, exemplars of virtue or morality in the public service. Riccucci's (1995) *Unsung Heroes* profiles high-level career administrators in the federal government who have made extraordinary contributions to citizens throughout the world. Most recently, King and Zanetti (2005), in *Transformational Public Service*, bridge theory with practice to illustrate how public servants have advanced the goals of democracy, inclusiveness, and social and economic justice.

There are a number of benefits to using biographies, storytelling, or case studies. For one thing, they are an extremely effective way to link theory with practice. We know that public servants engage in policy making and they make important contributions through their participation. Case studies provide us with actual or tangible instances of how and why they participate, as well as the various factors that help to explain their success. Studying the actions, behaviors, and political environments of public servants can provide a rich analysis of the actual factors and circumstances that contribute to their effective and innovative performance.

As Cooper and Wright (1992, xii–xiii) point out, profiles of exemplary administrators provide "instructive and inspirational role models both for preservice students considering careers in public service and for working administrators in a field that often feels maligned and demeaned by the public and the media." Administrative profiles, they go on to say, also serve as "an effective means for projecting a more positive image of public service to the citizenry."

## WHAT ARE THE CHARACTERISTICS OF EFFECTIVE PUBLIC ADMINISTRATORS?

From the existing literature on effective public managerial performance (see, for example, Rainey 2009; Agranoff 2007; Agranoff and McGuire 2003; Denhardt 1993; Perry 1989, as well as the books outlined above), a number of characteristics of effective performance can be identified, including, for example, political skills, management and leadership skills, experience, strategy, and personality.

Public servants operate in highly politicized environments, requiring the ability to maneuver within the environment by networking and building coalitions with political actors, including interest groups, government agencies, the media, and other important stakeholders. Political skills are obviously critical for successful performance of public servants.

In addition, management and leadership skills contribute to effective performance in government and nonprofits. Such skills include, for example, the ability to communicate clearly, plan, organize, foster transparency, listen, and set realistic goals. Motivating staff and exhibiting fairness and understanding are also key. Experience refers to the environment (e.g., public, private, nonprofit) within which the administrator acquired most of her or his experience. It is not uncommon to find that those persons committed to public service acquire most of their experience in some capacity of public service.

The specific strategy the administrator relies upon is also important for effective performance. This includes, for example, coalition building, networking, empowering stakeholders, partnering, or fostering organizational change. Finally, personality or personal attributes such as honesty, inspiration, loyalty, energy, and patience can influence the efficacy of public administrators.

It should be stressed, however, that while there may be some commonalities between and among the administrators profiled here, there is no one best way to manage, lead, or administer. That is, this reader does not seek to prescribe attributes of effective public servants but rather to foster a better understanding of administrative behavior and the complex environments within which these administrators operate.

Finally, it should be noted that the profiles are presented in the order in which they were originally published in *Public Administration Review*.

## REFERENCES

Agranoff, Robert. 2007. *Managing Within Networks: Adding Value to Public Organizations.* Washington, DC: Georgetown University Press.

Agranoff, Robert, and Michael McGuire. 2003. *Collaborative Public Management: New Strategies for Local Governments.* Washington, DC: Georgetown University Press.

Cooper, Terry L., and N. Dale Wright. 1992. *Exemplary Public Administrators: Character and Leadership in Government.* San Francisco, CA: Jossey-Bass.

Denhardt, Robert B. 1993. *The Pursuit of Significance: Strategies for Managerial Success in Public Organizations.* Belmont, CA: Wadsworth.

Doig, Jameson W., and Edwin C. Hargrove. 1990. *Leadership and Innovation.* Baltimore, MD: Johns Hopkins Press.

King, Cheryl Simrell, and Lisa A. Zanetti. 2005. *Transformational Public Service.* Armonk, NY: M.E. Sharpe.

Perry, James L. 1989. The Effective Public Administrator. In *Handbook of Public Administration,* ed. James L. Perry, 619–627. San Francisco, CA: Jossey-Bass.

Rainey, Hal G. 2009. *Understanding and Managing Public Organizations.* 4th ed. San Francisco, CA: Jossey-Bass.

Riccucci, Norma M. 1995. *Unsung Heroes: Federal Execucrats Making a Difference.* Washington, DC: Georgetown University Press.

# Serving the Public Interest

# ELMER BOYD STAATS AND THE PURSUIT OF GOOD GOVERNMENT

## KATHE CALLAHAN

Elmer Boyd Staats devoted 65 years of his life to making government more productive, more transparent, and more accountable. His service to our country spanned the Roosevelt, Truman, Eisenhower, Kennedy, Johnson, Nixon, Ford, Carter, Reagan, and George H. W. Bush administrations. Ever an optimist, at the age of 91, he continues to believe in the goodness of people and in an honest and effective national government. While he was the comptroller general of the United States from 1966–81, he routinely dealt with issues of fraud, waste, corruption, and criminal behavior (Frederickson 1992). However, Staats's objective—and that of the General Accounting Office (GAO) under his leadership[1]—was to advance good government. He had no desire to restrict the GAO's role in searching for fraud and corruption, although he had ample opportunity to do so during his tenure. Although the GAO continued to conduct audit reports, Staats introduced a new element to the task of ensuring government accountability: program evaluation. Instead of focusing solely on compliance studies and audit sheets, he took a more proactive approach and chose to focus on making government more honest and effective.

If Elmer Staats stands for one thing, it is good government. In reflecting on Staats's service to our country, a senior GAO manager referred to him in 1981 as "a pragmatic agent of good government" who viewed GAO audit reports as "a way to achieve results rather than simply hitting someone over the head" (Mosher 1979, 174). Staats was a strong advocate of public service and constructive change, and he worked tirelessly to improve the performance and integrity of government throughout his career. As the current comptroller general, David M. Walker, said, "In addition to his record of remarkable achievements over a lifetime, Elmer is widely considered one of the finest public servants of our time—a man who is admired as much for his intellect and ability as for his decency and devotion to the public good" (GAO 1987).

Elmer Staats's apartment in Chevy Chase, Maryland, is a testament to his lifetime of service. The walls of his living room are lined with photographs of former U.S. presidents, each inscribed with a sincere message of friendship and gratitude for years of dedication and service to our county. In addition to the photographs of presidents are numerous photographs of vice presidents and prominent senators, and again, each is inscribed with a message that reflects admiration and appreciation. The walls are also covered with numerous awards, plaques, and medals reflecting his significant contributions to our country. When asked about his collection of awards and honors—in particular, the signed photographs of presidents Truman, Eisenhower, Kennedy, Johnson, Nixon,

From *Public Administration Review,* 66, No. 2 (March/April 2006): 160–166. Copyright © 2006 American Society for Public Administration. Used by permission.

Ford, Carter, Reagan, and George H. W. Bush—Staats shrugged his shoulder as if to suggest it was no big deal and said, "My bosses."[2]

There are numerous well-written accounts of Elmer Staats's life and accomplishments (Frederickson 1992; Krusten 2004; Mosher 1979; Walker 1987). Mosher's book, *The GAO: The Quest for Accountability in American Government,* is perhaps the most comprehensive of them all and provides a highly detailed account of the GAO and Elmer Staats's role as comptroller general. Rather than attempt to summarize his career, which would be difficult to do in this limited space, this profile will focus on organizational change and the transformation of the GAO that took place under his leadership.

## KANSAS ROOTS AND THE EARLY YEARS

Elmer Staats was born to Wesley Forest and Maude Goodall Staats on June 16, 1914, in Richfield, Kansas. He was one of eight children, and his early life was spent on a farm in the Kansas Wheat Belt, making him a son of the prairie. He was valedictorian of the 1931 graduating class of Sylvia High School in Sylvia, Kansas. In 1935, he graduated Phi Beta Kappa from McPherson College, a private liberal arts college founded by members of the Church of the Brethren, in McPherson, Kansas. He went on to receive a master's degree in political science and economics from the University of Kansas and a doctorate from the University of Minnesota in 1939. In 1940, he met and married Margaret Shaw Rich, the daughter of Congressman Robert Fleming Rich of Pennsylvania. They were married for 52 years and raised three children: David, Deborah, and Catharine (Frederickson 1992; Walker 1987).

As a young man, Staats was shaped, as were many young people of his generation, by the Depression. Times were tough and jobs were hard to come by. He didn't always envision a career in the public sector. He took "jobs along the way," as he put it. He spent a short period of time as an intern for the Kansas Legislative Council and then held a position with the Public Administration Service in Chicago. After completing his coursework at the University of Minnesota, he was offered a fellowship at the Brookings Institution. Those early years in Washington sounded like good years. Staats was completing his dissertation on the administration of social security. He, along with 17 other fellows, lived at the Brookings Institution. " We received $30 a month, room and board—and a squash court." It was during these early, exciting years in Washington that he met his wife. She was a graduate of Brown University and was in Washington visiting her father. It was love at first sight, as he explains it. "I met her in April, we were married in September."

Staats began his government service in 1939, during the Roosevelt administration. He started his career in the Bureau of the Budget when there were 35 people on staff. Over a span of 25 years, he advanced from management analyst, to section chief, to assistant to the director, to executive assistant to the director, to assistant to the director, and ultimately, to deputy director of the bureau (Frederickson 1992). He came to work for government at a time when Americans generally regarded a career in the public sector as a noble calling. He left at a time when bureaucrat bashing was the norm.

As he progressively advanced through the ranks at the Bureau of Budget, he was recognized by his colleagues and the administration for his work ethic, loyalty, and optimism. In 1966, President Lyndon B. Johnson appointed Staats to head the General Accounting Office as comptroller general of the United States. At the swearing-in ceremony, President Johnson referred to Elmer Staats as a "builder, not a doubter" and advised him to remember the kind words that were said about him at the ceremony, as they would likely be the only kind words he would hear for the next 15 years (Mosher 1979). Having spent a quarter-century in the Bureau of the Budget, Staats was able to draw on his many years of government experience as he led the GAO during a period of dramatic change and national turmoil. As an "outsider," he had limited knowledge of the internal operations of the agency and few personal contacts within the GAO, yet he knew many people on Capitol Hill and certainly understood the political and bureaucratic environment of Washington. Uncertain as to the expectations the president had for him as comptroller general, he asked the president what he thought the job entailed. Johnson responded, "Congress passes a law and I sign it, and I want you to make sure the laws and programs are carried out as both the president and Congress intended" (Mosher 1979, 172).

## GENERAL ACCOUNTING OFFICE

The GAO is an independent, nonpartisan agency that works for Congress and is the government's accountability watchdog. According to Staats, "[The] GAO is first and foremost a problem-solving organization." The GAO serves Congress and the American people by keeping a close eye on virtually every federal program, activity, and function. "Its highly trained evaluators examine everything from missiles to medicine, from aviation safety to food safety, from national security to social security" (Kruston 2004, 1). Or as Mosher put it, "The GAO is, among other things, a picture window on a moving vehicle traversing a rapidly changing landscape" (Mosher 1979, xvii).

In many ways, the GAO is unique. According to Mosher,

> The uniqueness of the GAO stems in part from its legal and official status in the U.S. government. It is an arm of the Congress, from which it receives its powers, responsibilities and resources. But it is also independent, even of Congress, in the exercise of some of its powers and in its choice of the majority of its projects and the conduct of virtually all of them. This independence, which the GAO treasures, is enhanced by the nature of the appointment and tenure of its top leaders. The comptroller general and the deputy comptroller general are both—like many other high federal officials—appointed by the president with the consent of the Senate; but unlike most other officials except judges, they have long terms (of fifteen years) and are almost irremovable. Although most of the GAO's work concerns the executive branch, it is not responsible to it. Its potential scope is almost as broad as that of the government itself. (1979, 2)

Through a variety of oversight and inquiry activities such as program reviews, program evaluations, financial audits, legal opinions, and investigations, the GAO holds executive agencies and individuals accountable for their actions and outcomes. Since its establishment on July 1, 1921, the GAO's focus has been government accountability. Although the agency has always worked for good government, its mission and organization have changed a great deal since 1921. In the early years, from its establishment through World War II, the GAO was defined by its focus on legal compliance and voucher checking. This period often is referred to as the "Era of the Accountant." From 1945 to 1966, priorities shifted to consolidation and contracts—the "Era of the Economist" (Mosher 1979). To outsiders, the GAO, as John Rourke described it, had "the image of dusty ledgers, armbands and green visors" (1978, 453). In fact, one of Staats's earliest memories of the GAO reflects this image. "What sticks out in my memory," he reflected, "is the rows of desks, face to face, with dozens of employees doing voucher audits." Those green visors and armbands gradually disappeared under Staats's leadership. Accountants soon shared office space and assignments with social scientists, computer professionals, health care experts, policy analysts, and information-management specialists.

## TRANSFORMING THE GAO

The 1960s to the late 1970s was a time of great turbulence and change. President Johnson aggressively pushed for dramatic changes in domestic programs—in particular, civil rights, urban development, education, health, and welfare. Momentum for policy change was overshadowed by unrest over civil rights and an unpopular war. Vietnam, civil rights, and the assassinations of John F. Kennedy, Martin Luther King, and Robert Kennedy fueled protests on college campuses across the country. Civil unrest was high during the summer of 1967, and race riots broke out in major cities from California to New Jersey. Trust in government was eroding as the horrors of war were televised in living rooms across America; this was followed by the gradual unfolding of the Watergate scandal.

Fortunately, the transformation of the GAO under Elmer Staats's leadership was far less turbulent than the times. Elmer Staats's appointment as comptroller general "in no way resembled the turmoil that often accompanies political transition in the executive branch" (Mosher 1979, 173). He was a respected administrator, and his nomination was greeted enthusiastically in Congress and in the press. When the Senate Committee on Government Operations held hearings on his confirmation, he was said to be "eminently qualified" with a "long and distinguished career." According to one of the senators on the committee, no one came to the job "better equipped than Elmer Staats" (Mosher 1979, 72). The committee voted unanimously for his confirmation, and two days later, he was confirmed by the Senate.

When Staats first arrived at the GAO, he was shocked by the lack of organization, in particular the fragmentation and duplication of effort. In 1966, the GAO, as he saw it, was essentially three separate agencies: One agency addressed international concerns, another defense concerns, and another civilian concerns. Each "agency" had its own priorities, processes, and procedures, and communication among the three was weak at best. Staats knew that changes were in order, but he did not want to rush into things or jump to conclusions. "I didn't go in with a plan. I knew what my responsibility was. The question was how to implement it."

Staats was instrumental in transforming the GAO from a relatively narrowly focused, accountant-dominated organization concerned with budgets and the bottom line into a multidisciplinary organization concerned with the much broader issues of program evaluation, managerial effectiveness, and accountability. Though his efforts began quietly and grew slowly, Staats's focus was improving the GAO's internal planning processes, expanding its relevance to Congress, and addressing issues of accountability and program effectiveness.

Staats is widely recognized for increasing the GAO's relevance to Congress. He is credited with a dramatic increase in the number of reports prepared for Congress. It is estimated that in 1966, when Staats first starting working at the GAO, 8 percent of the agency's work was prepared for Congress. When Staats left in 1981, that number had increased to between 40 percent and 50 percent. Staats shared an interesting story about this turnaround and his initial assessment of the GAO's output. When he was first assessing what the GAO actually did, he asked one of his senior staff members, "How much of our work is for Congress?" The staff member replied that he didn't know. Staats asked the staff member to "go and look at the reports prepared in the last five years and let me know how many were prepared at the request of Congress." Staats's proactive approach in focusing on the congressional customer allowed him to broaden the scope of the GAO audits to better serve Congress and the American people.

## SLOW AND STEADY WINS THE RACE

Staats knew he did not want to make any major changes until he got a feel for the organization and the people. He visited all the regional offices, 8 to 10 at the time, to meet the staff and talk with them about the issues they were addressing. He used this as an opportunity to assess the professional qualifications of the field staff and to identify employees with leadership potential. He built on the background, expertise, and loyalty of the staff who were there, and he promoted from within. "I deliberately didn't bring in outsiders, not even secretaries. It was a wise decision—they didn't feel like they were going to be replaced." Staats also knew several big retirements would be coming soon, and he waited to fill those key positions with competent professionals who would help him broaden the scope of the GAO and increase its relevance to Congress.

When it came time to hire new staff, the entry- and mid-level recruitment policy shifted. The recruitment of staff was broadened from the traditional disciplines of accounting and law to include program evaluation, engineering, and systems analysis. Staats set a recruitment goal: Fifty percent of the new hires would be from the newly identified fields. He also established a task force on women and minorities. He wanted not only to recruit more women and minorities but also to address the disparity in pay and advancement opportunities. In addition, Staats created a variety of professional development and training opportunities for his staff. He said one of the most rewarding aspects of his job "was seeing the organization change and seeing people develop professionally."

Staats created an opportunity for staff growth and development by establishing the Office of Congressional Relations (OCR). He selected four to five talented young employees to staff this office and to work more closely with Congress and congressional committees. These young people were to be the eyes and ears of the GAO. They were to stay abreast of congressional issues through day-to-day interaction with committee members. As comptroller general, Staats found himself testifying before Congress on a regular basis—at least three to four times a week on different subjects. He was a regular, and they soon got to know him on the Hill. Staats admitted that it was nearly impossible for him to know all the details of the reports that were issued, and he found himself relying more and more on the OCR staff. Staats had confidence in his staff, and he would take them with him when he testified. In doing so, he gave his staff an idea of the expectations of Congress, and he "let Congress know that intelligent people were working for them." In time, the OCR staff joined him in testifying before Congress.

Staats introduced a variety of initiatives to recognize and reward his staff. Award ceremonies were held on a regular basis, and it was not uncommon to have the Marine Corps Band play at these celebrations. When Staats came on board, there was one award given on an annual basis, and that was for longevity—not necessarily something to strive for. Under Staats's leadership, there were numerous opportunities for staff to be recognized for their contributions to the organization; the highest honor was the Comptroller General's Award. Once or twice a year, he would bring the regional staff to Washington for two to three days of training and socializing. Staats felt this was essential to building a strong and unified agency. He also introduced a weekly newsletter, *GAO Management News*, which acknowledged professional and personal milestones. The staff joked that the newsletter was more for the comptroller general than the staff because "we know better than you what's going on."

The changes in structure and workforce evolved over a period of four to five years. Staats was remarkably honest about his incremental approach: "I didn't know enough in the beginning to do basic reorganizing. I needed to think through, with the staff that was there, how to proceed and bring about change. I knew what we needed to do and they knew what would work and what wouldn't work. They were not resistant to change. They knew change had to be made." He went on to say, "Changing an institution is a very difficult thing to do. I needed to bring the staff with me to help me think it through. I decided the course, but they would tell me the pros and cons, they alerted me to the trouble I might encounter along the way."

Mosher remarked on Staats's ability to bring about change with minimal resistance:

> This writer has sensed in the GAO little of the attitude common within many executive agencies that their political boss will be around only two or four or, at the outside, eight years, and the subordinates can wait him out before their programs can be seriously modified or damaged. In the GAO there is more of an inclination to understand and respond to the boss; where there are differences, to search for acceptable compromises; but certainly to satisfy him in his perceptions of purpose, even when they are not in full agreement. The impact is considerable. The Comptroller General's subordinates read and study his directives and other internal announcements, his testimony, his speeches, and his articles with care. (1979, 346)

Reflecting on the transformation of the GAO under his leadership, Staats remarked, "Change— you can't force it on people. You need to explain exactly what you want to accomplish and bring the organization with you. We continually explained what we wanted to achieve and where we wanted to go. We had endless discussions. Many staff members criticized our efforts and the amount of time spent talking. In the end, it was worth it in the consensus that was achieved."

## CHANGES IN STRUCTURE AND WORKFORCE

Within the GAO, Staats practiced a participatory management style, often relying on task forces to study job processes and organizational issues. He flattened the hierarchical structure of the GAO by replacing it with a committee and subcommittee system that reflected that of Congress and the agencies, bureaus, and departments of the executive branch. In doing this, the issues and divisions at the GAO were easily aligned with the legislative and administrative structures (Frederickson 1992, 221). Staats reorganized the agency along functional lines, with divisions responsible for areas such as logistics and communications, manpower and welfare, federal personnel, and compensation.

One of his big concerns was how to assess the priorities for GAO work. There were many pressing issues confronting the agency, but there was no way to classify or prioritize every issue put before them:

> One of the frustrations I had with the staff was how do you decide priorities. Initially, I had a hard time reaching consensus. One Saturday morning I came up with this list of 37 issue areas. A week later I tried them out on the staff and it went down pretty well. They seemed to like it. All the areas were areas where there were problems and all were auditable. It was a good way to decide what the priorities were going to be. The heads of the divisions were to outline what they thought needed to be done. It was a way to nail down what their priorities ought to be. We involved all the senior staff in these areas. It did a lot to crystallize what the issues were and audits were conducted around these areas.

Staats relied on his experience at the Bureau of the Budget to develop the issue areas. A lot of the issues he was confronting at the GAO were similar to the ones he had worked on at the bureau.

Staats remarked that the identification of the 37 issue areas, and the resulting ability to establish agency priorities, was one of his greatest accomplishments at the GAO. Eventually, the internal structure of the organization was framed around these issue areas.

## SEEKING AN OUTSIDE PERSPECTIVE AND ENHANCING THE GAO'S VISIBILITY

Staats valued and welcomed the expertise and insight of people outside the organization. He introduced several initiatives that enabled him to enhance the visibility of the GAO and to obtain insight from experts outside the organization. The Educators' Consultant Panel was one such initiative. Staats invited presidents and deans of major universities to serve on this panel to provide a different, broader perspective on some of the issues the GAO was addressing. The use of consultants in this manner was somewhat new and different, and Staats welcomed a different perspective as the scope of the agency grew. The wisdom and insight of professionals from different fields enabled the GAO to look at problems and issues from multiple perspectives.

> The Consultant panel would meet quarterly. My staff would lay out what they were doing and these people would respond. They'd come in on Friday morning and we'd go through Saturday. We had a topical agenda. My staff would present and then the consultants would ask questions. It generated a lot of discussion. We wanted to get the reaction of very different, senior people—like university presidents. It was another way for us to get our ideas understood and accepted.

The Educators' Consultant Panel also furnished an opportunity for Staats and his staff to get the word out that the GAO was more than an accounting agency. Staats worked tirelessly to increase the visibility of the GAO. He felt the more people understood what the GAO did, the more successful he would be at bringing about change. "It was never a secret what we were trying to do. I wanted everything out in the open." The educators' panel also helped with staff recruiting efforts. As the university presidents and deans learned more about the GAO, they were able to communicate this knowledge to their students and faculty. Staats reported, "We had a hard time explaining why graduates would want to come and work at GAO," and through this panel they were able to increase the visibility of the GAO and recruit some top-notch candidates.

Staats also revived the Joint Financial Management Improvement Program (JFMIP), which he felt had been underutilized by his predecessor, Joseph Campbell. Campbell was known as a rather insular comptroller general, and he continually stressed the appearance of independence by the GAO's auditors. He went so far as to discourage his employees from joining external professional organizations, such as the Federal Government Accountants Association, and from socializing too much with the employees of other government agencies; consequently, he had little interest in the JFMIP, which would have required his auditors to interact with people outside the GAO. Established in 1948, the JFMIP is a joint undertaking of the GAO, the Office of Management and Budget (OMB), the Office of Personnel Management (OPM), and the Department of the Treasury. During its first 25 years, the program operated without any permanent staff, and most of its work was conducted by staff from the GAO. In 1969, Staats established the office of executive secretary and four years later, created the office of executive director with a small, fulltime staff that could provide continued leadership (Mosher 1979, 221). Senior administrators from the GAO, OPM, OMB, and Treasury would meet on a quarterly basis to brainstorm and discuss ways to improve financial-management practices.

The JFMIP assisted a number of individual agencies in the development of innovative projects in the area of financial management. For example, in 1971, the JFMIP met with 10 different agencies, including the Federal Bureau of Investigation, National Science Foundation, Peace Corps, and U.S. Information Agency, to emphasize the need for managing programs in terms of performance and cost, as well as to assist them in the design of an accounting system to meet those management needs. In addition, they sponsored seminars and training programs, held annual conferences and awards ceremonies, and helped establish programs of financial management at universities—most notably, the Institute for Applied Public Financial Management at American University. The JFMIP provided a unique perspective across agencies, and the group realized that many of the problems the agencies confronted were common problems. Perhaps the most important role of the JFMIP was symbolic: It was an institutional expression of the efforts of the federal government to promote accountability and improve financial-management practices.

## A CONVERGENCE OF FORCES

At the GAO, an important factor that helped bring about organizational change was that many people within the organization felt the need to change. The external environment was right; so was the internal environment. Accountability was an emerging topic. Educators at Columbia University were working with the Carnegie Corporation to explore the subject of accountability in government. Staats, along with members of Congress, attended one of the first conferences, held in Williamsburg, Virginia, at which the researchers from Columbia wanted to discuss this notion of government accountability with high-ranking officials. "The concept of three-way accountability kept coming through the discussions—that is, financial accountability, what they called managerial accountability, and program accountability. This helped a great deal in sharpening my own thinking on the subject."

At the same time, Congress was questioning the efficacy of the antipoverty programs implemented as part of Johnson's Great Society program. Domestic spending had shot up, and Congress found it needed more information about how well government programs were performing. In 1967, amendments to the Economic Opportunity Act of 1964 directed the GAO to examine antipoverty programs to determine their efficiency and the extent to which they were carrying out their objectives. Of particular concern to Congress was the funding arrangement for the antipoverty programs. Federal dollars bypassed city government and went directly to the community agencies implementing the various programs, such as job training, Head Start, and Meals on Wheels. As Staats recalled, "The law that established this funding arrangement was expiring and it was very controversial whether it was going to be extended. A senator suggested [the] GAO should determine if this was an effective way to disburse funds. We had to fish or cut bait. . . . It was kind of a shock to the organization."

The GAO had six to nine months to conduct the evaluations and prepare the reports. The contacts that Staats had developed through his continual efforts to make the GAO more visible and more relevant came in handy. He called on universities and other organizations that had experience in program evaluation and hired top-notch program consultants. As he said,

> We had to bring in some fresh blood. A lot of shoe leather went into this. It was a pretty good test to see if we could do it. The question was how do you start? What test do you apply? Well, of course, you go back to the statute and committee reports. That is where you always start on an audit of a program. Then you go to the agencies and see how they interpreted their mandate and then you go to their appropriations reports. All these things play a part

in defining the objectives of a program. The antipoverty programs dealt with some very sensitive issues. We submitted reports on each one and Congress was quite positive. We weren't saying, "Do away with this program"—we emphasized change—changing priorities, changing program emphasis.

The GAO prepared more than 60 reports. During its reviews, the office examined a number of programs aimed at fighting poverty. It found that some had shown progress but needed management improvement, whereas others had produced limited success, and still others had achieved less than expected given the amount of money spent on them. The GAO concluded that although the antipoverty programs had moved ahead in four years, their administrative machinery needed substantial improvement. The reports on the antipoverty program were generally well received.

## CONCLUSION: STAATS AS A ROLE MODEL FOR 21ST-CENTURY PUBLIC ADMINISTRATORS

Elmer Boyd Staats occupies a special place not only in the GAO's history but also in establishing the foundation of improved government accountability and fiscal responsibility that is so important to the sound functioning of our government. In reflecting on the change that transpired under his leadership, he made it sound quite simple. As we all know, however, transforming a large, bureaucratic organization is far from easy. Staats demonstrated a unique mixture of integrity, fairness, respect, energy, innovation, patience, and perseverance as he introduced a series of changes that transformed the GAO from a narrowly focused, accountant-centered organization to a multifaceted organization dedicated to improving government performance and making government more honest and effective.

Successful change requires a well-orchestrated, integrated design that responds to the internal and external needs of the organization. It requires the ability to frame the issues, build coalitions, and communicate a vision. In Staats's own words, it is about "setting your goals and incrementally bringing them about." It's about communicating effectively and continually. It's about hiring right: bringing in high-caliber people, providing them with the tools to do their jobs effectively, and rewarding them for a job well done. He also says it requires "strategy—goals for yourself and the agency—it's about a plan of action. I'm not sure a strategy implies that you have it laid out so clearly. It's more evolving and incremental. It's specific actions you take to achieve interim goals."

Staats introduced change incrementally and was flexible in his approach, listening to his staff and outside experts. He wanted to ensure the staff bought into the vision of change before moving forward. "It wasn't that I didn't want to make changes. Instead of rushing things, I took my time. I knew I had a long-term appointment." His 15-year appointment offered opportunities for change that other public managers, because of their short appointments, do not experience. He was able to move slowly, be adaptive in his approach, and build trust.

The biggest obstacle to organizational change is usually found within the organization: the people working there. Change inevitably engenders conflict as individuals and groups compete for resources, positions, and recognition. Resistance to change is common when people are uncertain about expectations. Change in routine practices and procedures undercuts people's ability to perform with confidence and success. As change emerges, camps form consisting of supporters, opponents, and fence sitters. Fortunately for Staats, he mostly had supporters. He did have a few opponents and fence sitters, and as a result, change was uneven. Supportive division directors steadily advanced while resisters dragged their feet. The opponents and fence sitters were encouraged to see the merits of the proposed changes. Staats invited employees who questioned what was going on to serve on task forces so that they could become part of the change process. In this way, change was not forced upon them—they became part of the change as they were included in the decision-making process. As a result, they became supportive of the new direction the GAO was taking. Staats acknowledged that this prolonged the process, but the consensus and support were well worth the time invested.

Staats demonstrated loyalty to a staff that had demonstrated loyalty to the agency. He deliberately promoted from within. He took concrete steps to diversify the workforce and promote women and minorities. He flattened the organization, convened and utilized a variety of task forces and panels, and enabled the GAO to be more responsive to Congress. He embraced the input of professionals outside the organization, and in doing so, he encouraged creative responses to the broad range of issues his staff faced every day. It sounds simplistic to point out that successful change requires an investment in training and job development, but that is exactly what he did. He created opportunities for personal and professional development, and he recognized and rewarded performance.

Mosher (1979) summarizes the transformation that took place at the GAO, much of it during Staats's tenure:

> Since World War II, the change in the GAO's attitudes and approaches have generally, though not always, been in certain common directions:
>
> - From frugality in expenditures toward effectiveness;
> - From audits for legal compliance toward reviews of management;
> - From suspicion of and hostility to the executive branch toward cooperation and collaboration;
> - From individual transactions toward systems and problems;
> - From a punitive approach toward a corrective approach;
> - From nearly total independence toward interdependence with Congress;
> - From concerns about the past to concerns about the future;
> - From concentration on auditing in itself toward devolution to executive agencies; and
> - From strictly financial matters toward costs and results of programs. (225)

Staats created an organizational identity through the development of a shared vision. This vision was based on the historical foundation of the GAO and the legislative intent of its establishment. The 1921 Budget and Accounting Act transferred auditing responsibilities and accounting and claims functions from the Treasury Department to a new agency. The GAO was set up because federal financial management was in disarray after World War I and wartime spending had driven up the national debt. Congress saw that it needed more information and better control over expenditures, and the act made the GAO independent of the executive branch and gave it a broad mandate to investigate how federal dollars are spent. "In looking at the 1921 Budget Act you see what the framers of the original legislation had in mind and it was very close to what I wanted to do at GAO." Elmer Boyd Staats, an extraordinary public servant and champion of good government, molded the GAO into an organization that was true to its legislative intent and responsive to contemporary demands. In addition, he ensured the integrity, professional competence, and nonpartisan position of the GAO for future generations.

## NOTES

1. Throughout this article, the GAO is referred to as the General Accounting Office, as it was known under Staats's leadership. On July 7, 2004, the GAO officially changed its name to the Government Accountability Office.

2. All direct quotations of Elmer Staats appearing in this article are drawn from a personal interview conducted by the author.

## REFERENCES

Frederickson, H. George. 1992. Elmer B. Staats: Government Ethics in Practice. In *Exemplary Public Administrators: Character and Leadership in Government,* edited by Terry L. Cooper and N. Dale Wright, 214–40. San Francisco: Jossey-Bass.

General Accounting Office (GAO). 1987. *Elmer B. Staats: Comptroller General of the United States 1966–1981.* Oral History Series. Washington, DC: GAO. http://archive.gao.gov/t2pbat19/134346.pdf.

Krusten, Maarja. 2004. Working for Good Government since 1921. Washington, DC: Government Accountability Office. http://www.gao.gov/about/history/introduction.htm.

Mosher, Frederick C. 1979. *The GAO: The Quest for Accountability in American Government.* Boulder, CO: Westview Press.

Rourke, John T. 1978. The GAO: An Evolving Role. *Public Administration Review* 38 (3): 453–57.

Walker, Wallace E. 1987. Elmer Staats and Strategic Leadership in the Legislative Branch. In *Leadership and Innovation: A Biographical Perspective on Entrepreneurs in Government,* edited by Jameson W. Doig and Erwin C. Hargrove. Baltimore: Johns Hopkins University Press.

# 2

# LEADERSHIP AND THE TRANSFORMATION OF A MAJOR INSTITUTION

## Charles Rossotti and the Internal Revenue Service

### HAL G. RAINEY AND JAMES THOMPSON

When Charles Rossotti was approaching the end of his five-year term as commissioner of the Internal Revenue Service (IRS) in late 2002, the agency held a reception for him at the IRS headquarters building at 1111 Constitution Avenue.[1] Representatives of numerous authorities and groups praised Rossotti, including members of Congress, a member of the IRS Oversight Board,[2] the secretary of the Treasury, the president of the National Treasury Employees Union (NTEU, the major union for Treasury and IRS employees), and representatives of tax professionals' groups (such as tax accountants and other tax-preparation professionals). As these testimonials ended, Robert Tobias, who had been president of the NTEU during most of Rossotti's tenure, asked another guest, "How often do you think you will hear such sincere praise, from every group or authority with which he dealt, for an agency head who led a major, challenging reorganization of that agency?"[3]

Such an outcome would have seemed improbable five years earlier. Shortly before Rossotti became commissioner in late 1997, Senator Bob Kerrey told him that he was glad Rossotti owned a dog, because if he took the IRS job, he would need a friend. Kerrey drew a diagram showing all of the authorities, stakeholders, and critics who would be trying to give Rossotti orders, each with an arrow pointing toward a bull's-eye clearly representing Rossotti (Rossotti 2005, 48–49). Later, Rossotti would have a team collect all of the recommendations for improvements to the IRS advanced by six congressional committees and multiple oversight organizations and advisory committees. When the number of recommendations totaled 5,000, he stopped counting. Rossotti thus assumed leadership of what is arguably the most unpopular and controversial agency in government, an organization with about 100,000 employees spread across the nation—120,000 during tax season—that each year handles more than 240 million tax returns and collects about $2 trillion in taxes. Adding to this complexity, as the bull's-eye analogy shows, a chorus of critics keeps close watch, usually with skepticism (Rossotti 2005, 17).

The agency had problems to match its vast size and complexity, and for decades, controversy and legislative action had focused on them. For years, critics had claimed that IRS managers aggressively required their subordinates to maximize the taxes they extracted from citizens and to intensify the enforcement actions to do so. According to some IRS employees, a swinging pen-

From *Public Administration Review,* 66, No. 4 (July/August 2006): 596–604. Copyright © 2006 American Society for Public Administration. Used by permission.

dulum complicates these pressures: Congress and critics press the IRS to show less aggression toward taxpayers, but when tax revenues start to fall, the pendulum swings to the other extreme, and the same authorities and critics call for the IRS to step up tax collection and increase revenues. Around the time of Rossotti's swearing-in, the pendulum was swinging toward the protection of taxpayers. The Senate held widely publicized hearings at which taxpayers told shocking stories of abuses by IRS agents or extremely frustrating and stressful mishandling of their tax situations. Some IRS employees testified about the encouragement of excessively aggressive tactics and abuses by other IRS managers and employees. Investigations later found many of these allegations to be false or exaggerated, but Rossotti knew that all too often, faulty IRS procedures imposed hardships on taxpayers. Fueling the criticism, during the late 1980s the agency had undertaken a very expensive modernization of its woefully obsolete information technology (IT) system, only to abandon the initiative about a decade later in what one member of Congress condemned as a "four billion dollar fiasco."[4]

Each year, IRS employees would send out more than 100 million notices to taxpayers, usually telling them they owed more taxes. In response to these notices and for other reasons, citizens often needed to question IRS employees by phone. An unacceptably high proportion of their calls would go unanswered, and far too often the advice and information that IRS representatives gave them was inaccurate. Years of criticism and complaint led Congress to authorize a reform commission in 1996, which resulted in the U.S. Internal Revenue Service Reform and Restructuring Act of 1998 (RRA 98). This act mandated major reforms at the IRS that Rossotti would be charged with implementing. Anyone taking on such responsibility faced high risks. Rossotti and other IRS leaders recognized that they would have to implement the reforms while still administering the tax system effectively; a serious breakdown in revenue collection during the changes could be disastrous for the nation. The modernization would be like repairing an airplane while flying to a new location.

Rossotti actually influenced important provisions of RRA 98 because he saw many organizational problems at IRS. While Treasury Department executives were recruiting him for the job of commissioner, he had begun to think about a plan for addressing these problems. Rossotti and other IRS officials proposed reforms that the legislators incorporated into the act. One of these reforms focused on the organization's structure. Rossotti regarded the IRS's structure as a fundamental source of its problems. During the 1950s, scandals had led to reforms that removed from the IRS any political appointees other than the commissioner and otherwise insulated the agency from improper political pressure. Rossotti acknowledged that these reforms allowed the IRS to become "one of the world's most honest tax administration agencies," but they also posed problems (Rossotti 2005, 149).

The agency adopted a geography-based structure that went largely unchanged until RRA 98. In this structure, 33 district offices and 10 service centers processed all types of taxes within their geographic areas. A complex matrix of regional directors and assistant commissioners overlay this structure, but the 33 district directors held highly prestigious positions and exercised considerable autonomy. Rossotti felt this dispersed and fragmented structure was justifiable during earlier times—before advances in information and communications technology—but judged it obsolete for the late 1990s and beyond. Among other problems, this structure assigned IRS representatives to tax cases on the basis of where they were, not what they knew. That is, IRS agents might be assigned to work on the taxes of a corporation in their region even though they did not really understand the business or its industry.

Rossotti also saw this structure as hampering change and coordination. The problems with the phone services arose in part because there were multiple phone service operations in different regions, operating independently with no central policy or coordination. The questions that

IRS phone service representatives had to answer could be very complex, and with the immense intricacies of the tax code, no one could answer all of the possible questions. The fragmentation of the structure, however, prevented the sharing of expertise across regions.

The structure made it more difficult to address the daunting challenges of modernizing the IRS's archaic computer and information system. Facing some of the most demanding information-processing responsibilities of any existing organization, the IRS had to retain records over time of every transaction with every taxpayer in the nation. A massive master file of these records had fallen into obsolescence. Programmers had coded it in a computer language that had become outmoded, and they had repeatedly jury-rigged it to accommodate the numerous changes in the tax code.[5] The programmers who understood the intricacies of the master file were retiring. This master file had to be moved into a modernized database in a way that involved painstaking, time-consuming work. Data moved slowly in and out of the file; data updating taxpayer records was entered twice a week from the obsolete technology of computer tapes, flown from processing centers around the nation to a main processing center in Maryland. IRS agents inadvertently created problems for taxpayers because they were working with records for which updated information had not yet been entered into taxpayers' records in the master file.[6] Because of the problems with the master file and for other reasons, IRS employees devised dozens of special systems and databases for specific tasks, further complicating the coordination of information.

The IRS faced many other challenges in improving its IT capabilities. For example, RRA 98 directed the IRS to have 80 percent of tax returns filed electronically by 2007, so IRS employees had to work toward that IT objective, as well as many others. The IRS had 15 independent IT departments, and the chief information officer had very limited authority over them (Rossotti 2005, 207). Rossotti regarded the fragmented organizational structure as aggravating these problems of coordination. He saw reorganizing the IRS as integral to reforming the way the agency carried out its business and coordinating its IT resources with that way of doing business. He and others emphasized this point by labeling the IT initiatives "business systems modernization."

## LEADING CHANGE

Treasury Department executives and other leaders sought out Rossotti because he had a strong background in private business and significant knowledge and experience in organizational management. He had been the chief executive officer of American Management Systems, a large consulting firm specializing in the modernization of large data systems. This managerial experience showed as he moved into his new position at the IRS.

### A Plan

Refreshingly, Rossotti never made much use of the now-hackneyed term "vision," but he had one. He realized that, even with support, he had to have a plan. He and the Treasury Department executives developed a conception of the transition to a new IRS in a report titled *Modernizing America's Tax Agency*. This plan included a new mission statement, a revision of the mission statement that the IRS had used. The new one emphasized service to taxpayers and helping them understand their responsibilities. In the *Modernizing* report, Rossotti embraced a new approach to taxation that emphasized service, support, and information for honest taxpayers rather than the threat of being caught and penalized for noncompliance. Because most taxpayers comply with the tax laws, he argued, compliance could be enhanced by support, outreach, and education for taxpayers to increase their voluntary compliance and the accuracy of compliance.[7]

Critics in the press, some IRS employees, and others argued that the IRS could not fulfill its tax-collection duties while being nice to taxpayers. Rossotti, however, contended that the IRS could balance enforcement with service. He pointed out that business firms have to achieve a similar balance all the time because they cannot sell their products at any price customers want, but they still have to provide good customer service.

Rossotti, together with other leaders at the IRS, undertook a comprehensive set of reforms aimed at achieving this balance. In addition to the new operating divisions described below, they put in place a "balanced measures system" (BMS) for measuring the agency's performance. The BMS assessed customer satisfaction, employee satisfaction, and business operations results.[8] They also undertook innovative steps in human resource management and other aspects of the structures and processes of the IRS.[9]

### Leadership, Ideas, and the Plan: Four New Operating Divisions

Rossotti's concerns about the IRS's organizational structure led to the most lasting change in the agency. The modernizing plan proposed reorganizing the agency into four new "customer-oriented" operating divisions. The new divisions, which "stood up" in October 2000, replaced the 50-year-old structure of geographic districts and regions. Layers of management were reduced by half, top jobs were redefined, and managers were assigned new roles through a competitive process.

Rossotti based the idea for the operating divisions on the way many large private sector financial institutions are organized. Many of these institutions have one operating division to provide retail banking services to individuals and another division to serve small businesses that have needs distinct from those of retail customers, such as payroll and business taxes. Still another division serves large and medium-sized corporations, which have different needs than the customers of other divisions. The new IRS structure involved four new operating divisions, each oriented to serving a particular type of taxpayer.[10] This structural redesign supported the increased emphasis on service and support for taxpayers. As discussed earlier, it also removed the district directors and their high levels of autonomy.

## LEADERSHIP AND THE REFORM LEGISLATION: RRA 98

### RRA 98: Advantage Rossotti

The act carried provisions that supported the change initiatives. It directed the IRS to adopt a structure oriented to types of taxpayers, to "eliminate or substantially modify the existing national, regional and district structure," and to "establish organizational units serving particular groups of taxpayers with similar needs." This mandated the structural redesign that Rossotti and his colleagues had proposed. This authorization of the restructuring in the legislation headed off objections that opponents might have raised. And the change would have opponents—at least some of the managers in the old structure who had to compete for jobs in the new one could be expected to resist, as could attorneys in the Treasury Department who might question any change (Rossotti 2005, 77).

### A Five-Year Term

The short tenure of most political appointees in the leadership of government agencies impedes successful change. The people in the agency can simply wait them out if they want to resist the change. The RRA 98 legislation allowed Rossotti a five-year term of office, and this gave him significant advantages in following through on change initiatives. Former Deputy Commissioner Robert Wenzel commented,

> There were career people in headquarters that basically said, "Well, we'll wait out this commissioner because there will be another one coming down the road some time. Today is different . . . the five-year format doesn't allow that to happen."[11]

## RRA 98: Disadvantage Rossotti

As the bull's-eye analogy shows, multiple authorities and groups sought to influence the IRS, often at cross-purposes. Rossotti had to struggle with "micromandates" from Congress and other authorities. For example, the White House sometimes simply announced that the IRS would follow new procedures, such as providing telephone service around the clock (Rossotti 2005, 129–30). In addition, past IRS leaders had sometimes made hasty assurances in response to pressures, that later they could not fulfill. These quick-fix announcements, followed by inadequate action, bred more skepticism toward the IRS. One very troublesome version of these pressures came from the RRA 98 in the form of the "10 deadly sins." The legislation contained a provision that required IRS employees to be fired if they committed any of 10 broadly defined offenses, such as violating any provision of the 83,000-page IRS manual. The offenses had always been forbidden, but the provision for immediate firing made IRS employees feel vulnerable and led to a slowdown in enforcement actions. Employees pointed out to Rossotti and other leaders that they felt they might be mired in an investigation for months if a disgruntled taxpayer decided to make an unwarranted allegation (Rossotti 2005, 158–59).

Actually, RRA 98 also tightened some of the required procedures and clearances for enforcement actions. This simply made it harder and slower to take them. Evidence indicates, however, that the deadly sins provision accounted for much of the falloff in enforcement because IRS leaders had to spend time and resources reassuring worried employees (Rossotti 2005, 158–59). At the same time, other critics, complaining that Rossotti's shift toward more customer service would weaken enforcement, pointed to the slowdown as evidence of such weakening.

## IMPLEMENTING THE REFORMS

### Confronting Resistance

The RRA 98 legislation provided support for the reforms but also for those who resisted them. Any major change prompts resistance, but the IRS leadership had to contend with a legacy of skepticism and criticism. Many employees faced with the new structure and new procedures felt uncomfortable, especially in view of the 10 deadly sins and other worrisome developments. Some of the managers who had been successful in the old structure resented losing their positions and having to compete for new ones. Aggravating such concerns, according to Rossotti, was an atmosphere of distrust of management among IRS employees and distrust of IRS headquarters by managers and employees in the regions.

Rossotti recounts that observers and stakeholders expressed doubt that the IRS could really change or that it could serve as an effective tax-collection agency while emphasizing service. Former IRS commissioners and commentators in the media, for example, expressed doubts about the new emphasis on service. Representatives of the Office of Management and Budget (OMB) resisted providing resources to support the reforms; they had sought repeatedly to halt funding of the small taxpayer-assistance offices that the IRS operated. The OMB representatives felt that the assistance offices did nothing to increase revenue collected and thus should be closed. Many IRS employees shared similar doubts. Rossotti describes how, in one of his many meetings with employees, some sarcastically challenged his emphasis on service; one referred to taxpayers as "adversaries," and another complained that "All we're doing is making it easy for the deadbeats to get away with not paying" (Rossotti 2005, 105).

## Building Support for Change

Successful change leaders build support internally and externally through communication and participation. Rossotti provides a textbook illustration of this process.

## Communication

Upon taking office, Rossotti opened the normally closed door of the commissioner's office, propped it open with a doorstop, and gave instructions that the doorstop was to stay in place to keep the door open (Rossotti 2005, 54). He thus took a symbolic action to emphasize his commitment to "open and honest communication," both internally and externally, which he saw as necessary to counteract the "death spiral of distrust" into which IRS had fallen (Rossotti 2005, 88). He constantly met with every type of person or group associated with the IRS. Internally, he resolved to talk with "every key person" who had a stake in the modernization plan, and he did so. He consulted senior IRS executives and was pleasantly surprised to find them receptive to reform. He conducted a videoconference with Robert Tobias, the NTEU leader, as well as all of the union chapter presidents. He and Wenzel assembled about 600 field managers and union representatives—the first assemblage this large in the history of the agency—and, with efforts to enliven the meeting to distinguish it from the traditionally dry IRS meetings, talked to them about the theme of "mission possible." They sought to counteract the skepticism that many failed changes at IRS had engendered and explain the modernization plan. Rossotti also made videotapes about the modernization plan and circulated them. He traveled frequently to meet with groups of employees, such as those who had referred to taxpayers as "adversaries" and "deadbeats." The IRS conducted tax problem-solving days, at which IRS employees would meet with taxpayers who came in for help with tax problems. Rossotti attended many of these and sat with IRS representatives and taxpayers to hear firsthand about the challenges that frontline IRS personnel and taxpayers faced and to observe closely what the basic work involved.

In communicating externally, Rossotti continued his endless series of meetings with senators and representatives, with associations of tax-preparation professionals, with former IRS commissioners, and with other authorities and groups. He invited external stakeholders, such as staff members from congressional committees, to attend problem-solving discussions at the IRS. He described meeting rooms so full of people from outside the IRS that participants stood against the walls. He recounts efforts to avoid responding to problems by offering quick fixes or hasty reassurances that the IRS could not fulfill. For example, at one point, the president convinced Congress to authorize tax refunds to stimulate the economy (and for electoral benefits, one can safely assume), and the IRS faced the challenge of computing these refunds and mailing the huge volume of checks. Other complications—the events related to 9/11 and the anthrax episode in Washington, D.C.—had already burdened the IRS and threatened the agency's ability to conduct a timely and effective tax season. Rossotti balked at congressional demands that the refunds be sent out on a very tight schedule. He said he could not promise such a response because the IRS employees were already stretched thin. In one of the packed meetings, a congressional staffer arrogantly threatened reprisals (such as filing charges with the Inspector General) if Rossotti did not comply with demands for rapid processing of the tax refunds. Rossotti simply stated that he could not honestly and responsibly promise to meet the congressional demands.

In interviews, those who worked with him attested to Rossotti's commitment to open and honest communication. Nancy Killefer, assistant secretary of the Treasury at the time, described Rossotti's attempt to open up the organization:

> What Charles has tried to do is invite in the outside, . . . to open up the organization to its stakeholders, to invite them into decision-making processes, . . . to view them as part of the organization, not . . . "we versus them."

Deputy Commissioner Wenzel affirmed Rossotti's success in changing this aspect of the IRS culture:

> In meetings . . . before a decision would be made in going forward, the question would come up, "Well, have you talked to the outside stakeholders to get some of their input in this?" If the answer was yes, and it was described who they were, then we went forward. But if the answer was "No, I haven't done that yet," then he would say, "Well why don't we take a little bit longer here and make sure we touch that base and get some input?"

Dave Mader, assistant deputy commissioner during this period and a key executive in the modernization process, added the following observation:

> One of the hallmarks of this reorganization is that Charles said this needs to be transparent. It needs to be transparent both inside and outside the organization. . . . He said, "We're going to involve everybody. Everybody's going to be engaged. We don't have anything to hide. We'll get a better product by making it transparent and inclusive." He drove that philosophy throughout the whole organization.

### Participation

According to those involved in the events, Rossotti's time at the IRS involved teams, groups, and participation to an extent exceeding anything observed up to that time in the agency. The most noteworthy use of participation involved two dozen "design teams," which worked out numerous details of the design of the new IRS and the implementation of the modernization plan. Rossotti, Wenzel, and a Modernization Steering Committee assembled the 24 teams with a heavy emphasis on broad participation; they included people from all levels and many different subunits and geographic locations.

One of the key challenges in developing effective participation involves convincing the participants that the process is genuine and that leaders have a sincere interest in the participants' views and a sincere intent to follow up on participants' proposals. All too often, participation efforts end up convincing employees only that the process is phony and the leaders are trying to co-opt or manipulate them. Rossotti's and other IRS leaders' interaction with the teams was exemplary in this respect. The design teams met periodically with the entire Modernization Steering Committee, which Rossotti chaired. Robert Wenzel said that rarely in the old IRS would employees from so far out in the field and so far down the hierarchical ranks actually meet with the commissioner. He said that you could see on the faces of the participants that they found meeting face to face with the commissioner emotionally moving.

### Participation and the Union

Apart from including many different employees in the teams, Rossotti invited the leadership of the NTEU to have a say in appointments to the teams. Robert Tobias, the NTEU leader at the time, pointed out that the union could have seriously impeded the modernization and reorganization efforts if it had felt the need to oppose them. Tobias described this decision to involve the union in appointing the teams as a masterstroke because it encouraged the union to buy in to the change process and support it.[12] The positive comments about Rossotti offered by Tobias and his successor, Colleen Kelley, indicate that Rossotti achieved one form of effective participation through a good working relationship with the union leadership.[13]

### Participation and Partnering of Insiders and Outsiders

Rossotti made a strategic decision to bring in outsiders such as consultants and new executives and professionals, break down the agency's insular culture, and promote openness and transparency. He asked for the authority to hire new people, and RRA 98 authorized the IRS to hire 40 "critical-pay" personnel.[14] This gave the IRS streamlined authority to hire new people rapidly at salaries that were high by the standards of the federal government. Rossotti paired these newcomers with experienced insiders. He chose Robert Wenzel as his deputy commissioner. Aware that Wenzel had led a task force on improving service to taxpayers, Rossotti opened up a dialogue with him about change at the IRS and later asked Wenzel to serve as his deputy commissioner. Thus, Rossotti partnered himself with a highly respected, very experienced insider.

Rossotti also paired executives when he hired critical-pay executives for major positions. For example, two of the heads of the new operating divisions were private sector executives whom Rossotti talked into joining the IRS to take critical-pay positions. Both of these executives had a long-term IRS insider as their primary deputy. Another of the new division heads was a long-term IRS executive who had a newly hired critical-pay executive as his deputy. The two people who headed up the organization of the design teams were experienced and respected IRS career executives. In his book, Rossotti emphasizes the importance of finding change-oriented insiders who knew how things worked and could help guide effective improvements (Rossotti 2005, 176). In this way, Rossotti linked internal experience and knowledge with new ideas from the outside.[15]

## PARTICIPATION AND COMMUNICATION: THE LISTENER AND THE ANALYST

For effective participation and communication to happen, leaders need to display sincere attention to participants and show responsiveness to them. By all accounts, Rossotti excelled at this.

### A Sincere Listener

Rossotti convinced many of the people with whom he worked that he communicated sincerely and effectively and that he valued participatory decision making. Colleen Kelley, the current head of the NTEU, noted his openness to new ideas and how carefully he listened:

He will revisit issues. He doesn't say, "I made the decision and its mine, and nobody's going to change my mind." He's very open. He's a good listener; he's an excellent listener; he's open to new ideas, so it's not about him having . . . preconceived notions and that he won't listen to evidence, because he does.

### Intellect and Analytical Ability

Rossotti became an IRS legend for his keen intellect and analytical ability. In interviews, executives and professionals referred to him as "a genius," "incredible," and "superhuman." One former IRS executive called Rossotti a "management genius" but also said that he was "an analyst's analyst." Others also attested to his extraordinary ability to cover large volumes of information rapidly and with analytical insight. In meetings with the design teams, according to participants, Rossotti constantly displayed this combination of careful listening and analytical acumen. Rossotti came to the meetings with detailed knowledge of the extensive "pre-read" material that had been circulated. According to a vice president at Booz Allen Hamilton, the consulting firm that facilitated these meetings and the reorganization process,

> He would read the entire document; he wouldn't be someone who delegated and let a staff person read it. He would listen very empathetically. So we would have the team come and say, "Here is the work in the past month," in a two- to four-hour session depending upon where we were. And he politely let them go for the first two hours and maybe ask a question or two and get the sense for his group and then he would say, "I think I got your message and I like it. Let me ask a question on page 115 . . ."

After the long meetings, he would go home for the weekend and return the next week with a detailed written response to the design team's presentation at the meeting. These white papers always reflected his careful attention to the teams' reports and his thoughtful, often challenging consideration of major issues raised in the reports and the meetings.[16]

### Poise in the Bull's-Eye

Those around him saw Rossotti carrying out his role under pressure, scrutiny, and criticism with a high level of energy, skill, and commitment. He never responded to the pressures with rancor or discouragement. In his book, he rejected some of the criticisms of him and of the IRS as inaccurate, but he displayed respect for all participants and stakeholders and a tolerance of their perspectives. When a top IRS executive praised Rossotti, we asked him to identify Rossotti's main attribute that justified such admiration. The executive said, "He is never down."

### CONCLUSION: THE SUCCESS OF THE REFORMS

In his book, Rossotti describes constraints on resources to support the reforms. He says that he verified that Treasury Department executives and other authorities provided "enough aligned forces" to support fundamental change. But he also expresses regret that he never brought up the budget increases he would need to support the change. He thus indicates that the budget constraints hindered the transformation efforts. This raises the question of just how successful the reforms and changes have been and what factors, such as resource constraints, have influenced their effectiveness. Without question, some changes succeeded. The new structure with the new operating divisions has endured. In testimony before Congress, Rossotti's successor said that this structure needed no change.[17] He also noted that the IRS's services to taxpayers had improved markedly, according to measurable indicators and recent audits that show continuing improvement in those indicators (GAO 2005, 28ff).

Rossotti, relying on long-term career IRS leaders, successfully consolidated the telephone service operations; an impressive operations center in Atlanta receives hundreds of thousands of calls each day and routes them to centers around the nation. The proportion of calls answered rapidly, with accurate responses to taxpayers' questions, has gone up significantly. Rossotti substantially enhanced the taxpayer-assistance offices. By 2003, the IRS had achieved significant increases on performance measures of service and compliance activities. An employee morale survey showed an increase of about 20 percent in employee "engagement" over two years earlier. Electronic filing of tax returns increased. Customer satisfaction surveys have shown substantial improvement, with respondents who filed electronically reporting about a 20 percent higher level of satisfaction than those who did not. One nationally publicized news report pointed out that the IRS was receiving customer satisfaction ratings higher than those of McDonald's.

Rossotti describes continuing complications with contracting for computer and IT improvement throughout his tenure, but in congressional testimony, Rossotti's successor pointed out that the first phase of updating the master file had been completed and other advances achieved. The IRS Web site is now impressive and a valuable resource for taxpayers and tax professionals (Bozeman 2002). In addition, one should note that every tax-collection season has proceeded effectively.

On the other hand, some developments call into question whether Rossotti and his colleagues achieved a lasting commitment on the part of the IRS and its stakeholders to balance taxpayer service, code enforcement, and tax collection. The new commissioner has proposed closing down taxpayer-assistance centers to devote more resources to enforcement. In statements made near the end of his service and in his book, Rossotti emphasizes major problems with the tax code and the tax system that the leadership and management of the IRS cannot fix by itself: collecting the massive amount of revenue that large corporations and wealthy individuals shelter from taxes in abusive schemes, reforming the tax code to eliminate unhealthy complexities, and inducing political authorities such as the president and the OMB to support investments in technology and staffing to make the nation's tax-administration system as effective as it needs to be.

These remaining challenges—and the apparent emphasis of the current IRS leadership on enforcement over service—suggest that Rossotti's goal of achieving balance between the two commitments has not been fully achieved, and that what has been achieved may not endure. In his book, he concludes that one of the lessons learned from this major reform initiative is that change in any large organization has limits set by constraints in its broader context. The leaders and employees of the IRS cannot fix the tax code or the tax system by themselves; political leaders must support the necessary reforms.

These contextual forces may limit the success of Rossotti's reforms, especially in relation to the high goals that he and his colleagues set. Criticism of government in general—and the IRS in particular—is an industry in the United States. Some critics will continue to question Rossotti's actions. The substantial progress and success achieved during his tenure are undeniable, however, as is his influence on those who worked with him. Most Americans pay their taxes honorably and want an IRS and tax system that are fair and effective. Some Americans will continue to despise taxes and vilify the IRS, as well as support radical alterations to the tax system, including outright abolition of the income tax. Even they, however, should acknowledge that the nation owes gratitude and honor to those who, as Rossotti and his colleagues did, work diligently and innovatively to make and keep the U.S. tax system one of the most honest and well managed in the world.

## NOTES

1. A longer and more detailed version of this article is available from the authors.

2. The Restructuring and Reform Act of 1998, described later in this article, established the oversight board.

3. Robert Tobias is now a Distinguished Adjunct Professor in the School of Public Affairs at American University.

4. Barry Bozeman's authoritative report on the struggle to modernize information technology at the IRS points out that, although the IRS did experience severe frustrations and failures, criticisms of the agency's efforts were often overstated. He points out that IRS employees and contractors used much of the IT hardware and software purchased and developed during this period in later applications, improvements, and modernization efforts. In interviews, IT executives in the IRS praised the Bozeman report, noting that it addressed the problems and failures but was also balanced and fair (Bozeman 2002).

5. It is hard to explain all of the complications with the IT challenges at the IRS. For example, programmers at one point might have faced a new requirement to keep a record of the zip code of each taxpayer. They might plug this number into some space in the computer records that was originally created for recording tax information. Keeping track of many such changes and carrying out a process for transferring the data to a modernized database involved many time-consuming complications.

6. For example, a taxpayer might send in a check to pay more taxes as instructed by an IRS employee and later receive another notice demanding the payment. The IRS employee may have generated the additional notice because he or she had not received the updated information about the taxpayer's payment in a timely fashion. Then the taxpayer might call to inquire why he or she had received the notice after sending a payment, but it would take so long for an IRS phone service representative to answer that the taxpayer would give up. Or the taxpayer might get an answer from an IRS representative, but the taxpayer's most recent information was still not available in the file because of the slow data-entry process.

7. Rossotti, in *Modernizing America's Tax System*, credits the influence of Malcolm Sparrow. In his book *Imposing Duties: Government's Changing Approach to Compliance* (1994), Sparrow criticizes the dominance of a distrustful, coercive, enforcement-oriented approach to compliance in such government programs as tax administration, law enforcement, and environmental protection. This approach assumes that compliance depends on the threat of being caught and penalized. Sparrow advocated measures to support and increase voluntary compliance.

8. When Rossotti took office, the IRS already had under way an initiative to develop performance measures built on the concept of the balanced scorecard, and Rossotti supported this effort because of its consistency with the modernizing plan and its principles. In an influential 1992 *Harvard Business Review* article (and later, a book), Robert Kaplan and David Norton advanced this approach to assessing organizational effectiveness, which had a wide influence in business and government. They argued that for long-term success, a business must assess and achieve customer satisfaction, training and motivation of employees, and excellent financial returns through effective business operations. The assessment system measures each of these dimensions. Rossotti saw the framework as applicable to the IRS and supported the development and adoption of the BMS—balanced measurement system—for both organizational and individual-level performance evaluations. The BMS included measures of customer satisfaction, employee satisfaction, and business results (indicators of the quantity and quality of work performed, such as case closures and cycle times). The expansion of performance assessment to include measures of customer satisfaction, of course, accords with the modernizing plan's emphasis on improved taxpayer support and service. Thus, the IRS leadership sought to coordinate changes in different systems—in this case, coordinating the assessment system with the change in orientation to taxpayer service.

9. For more description and analysis of these reforms and changes, see Thompson and Rainey (2003).

10. The Wage and Investment Division handled the returns of individual taxpayers. The other divisions included Small Business/Self-Employed, Large and Mid-Size Business, and Tax Exempt/Government Entities.

11. Obviously, one answer to the short-tenure problem involves providing an executive with a fixed, reasonably lengthy term of office. Such an arrangement has pros and cons. The cons include weakening the political control of the bureaucracy and the accountability of agency executives to political officials. Still, the IRS case appears to illustrate the viability of the alternative.

12. Interview with Robert Tobias.

13. In interviews, some participants in the IRS reforms during this period voiced different views. One person reported that some union chapter presidents had serious criticisms of the IRS reforms but did not wish to express them openly because they were loyal to the IRS and did not want to contribute to bad publicity for

the organization. One executive told us he thought that involving the unions in appointing the teams sometimes allowed team members who were not well qualified to contribute to the teams' work. One high-level IRS executive commented, after Rossotti's departure, that he felt Rossotti had given too much to the union.

14. For more description and analysis of this critical pay program, see Rainey (2001).

15. These approaches contributed to a sense of the value and effectiveness of most of the critical-pay newcomers, a sentiment that IRS insiders expressed repeatedly in interviews. Of course, many of the interview respondents were supporters of the modernization process and Rossotti's leadership, as well as higher-level executives and managers who often avoid negative comments and take a positive orientation. Nevertheless, again and again in interviews, they said that they felt the critical-pay executives and professionals brought valuable new perspectives to the work of the IRS and were valuable additions to the organization.

16. The consultant described the process as follows:

> When very difficult issues surfaced up under which there was a conflict between his executive team and the design team, he would often go away over the weekend and write a white paper ranging from two pages to ten pages long that dealt with the issues at hand and what his perspective was. Now those white papers were seminal and sometimes he exerted a heavy hand and said this is what I really expect as a direction and other times he'd raise them as questions.

An extended version of the present article, available from the authors, discusses at greater length the involvement of this consulting firm in the reorganization process. Some critics contended that the firm's services were expensive and that the money would have been better spent on enforcement. Many of the IRS executives we interviewed, however, considered the involvement of the firm essential to the success of the reorganization.

17. Testimony of Mark W. Everson, Commissioner of Internal Revenue, before the Annual IRS Restructuring and Reform Act of 1998 Joint Congressional Review, May 20, 2003.

## REFERENCES

Bozeman, Barry. 2002. *Government Management of Information Mega-Technology: Lessons from the Internal Revenue Service's Tax Systems Modernization.* Washington, DC: IBM Center for the Business of Government.

Kaplan, Robert S., and David Norton. 1992. The Balanced Scorecard: Measures That Drive Performance. *Harvard Business Review* 70: 71–79.

Rainey, Hal G. 2001. *A Weapon in the War for Talent: Using Special Hiring Authorities to Recruit Crucial Personnel.* Washington, DC: IBM Center for the Business of Government.

Rossotti, Charles O. 2005. *Many Unhappy Returns: One Man's Quest to Turn around the Most Unpopular Organization in America.* Boston: Harvard Business School Press.

Sparrow, Malcolm. 1994. *Imposing Duties: Government's Changing Approach to Compliance.* Westport, CT: Praeger.

Thompson, James, and Hal G. Rainey. 2003. *Modernizing Human Resource Management in the Federal Government: The IRS Model.* Washington, DC: IBM Center for the Business of Government.

U.S. Government Accountability Office (GAO). 2005. Financial Audit: IRS's Fiscal Years 2005 and 2004 Financial Statements. Washington, DC: Government Accountability Office. GAO-06–137. www.gao.gov/new.items/d06137.pdf [accessed March 29, 2006].

U.S. Internal Revenue Service (IRS). 1999. *Modernizing America's Tax Agency.* Washington, DC: U.S. Department of Treasury, Internal Revenue Service. www.irs.gov/irs/article/0,,id=98170,00.html [accessed March 29, 2006].

# 3

# LEADERSHIP WITH AN ENDURING IMPACT

The Legacy of Chief Burtell Jefferson of the
Metropolitan Police Department of Washington, D.C.

## BRIAN N. WILLIAMS AND J. EDWARD KELLOUGH

Leadership has many meanings and evokes many images. Fundamentally, it involves the ability to inspire others to work toward the accomplishment of an organization's mission. In this sense, it is an essential ingredient of effective management. Leadership typically requires a willingness to address the most difficult and challenging tasks that confront an organization. The best leaders are constantly learning and developing new skills and abilities. They demand much from those around them, but no less than they demand of themselves. They communicate effectively, they promote trust within their work groups, and they have an understanding or vision of where they want to take their organizations. Moreover, effective leaders—through coaching, mentoring, teaching, serving as role models, and conceiving and implementing innovative programs—develop and encourage others. In essence, they grow other successful leaders (Blunt 2004).

These are the characteristics of Burtell Morris Jefferson, one of the founders of the National Organization of Black Law Enforcement Executives (NOBLE), who in 1978 became the first African American chief of the Metropolitan Police Department of Washington, D.C.[1] He served honorably in that position until his retirement in 1981. Jefferson left an impressive legacy, not only in the policing procedures and practices he put into place but also in the progress he made in facing and overcoming discriminatory practices that for decades had kept black officers from progressing in their careers. He mentored and encouraged the development of an unprecedented number of young African American officers, as well as officers of other races, who later assumed leadership positions in law enforcement agencies across the country. Those officers, in turn, have promoted the growth of subsequent generations of leaders. In a sense, Jefferson's story is their story: Their success was made possible by his own.

Jefferson's career illustrates how many small decisions made over the course of a number of years can have a profound impact on officer growth and development, police practices and procedures, and organizational change and development. He stands as a testament to the long-term impact of equal employment opportunity and affirmative action. His appointment shows clearly how such a policy can produce dramatic change. Jefferson's actions as chief show how a commitment to fairness, openness, and equality of opportunity can make a significant difference.

From *Public Administration Review,* 66, No. 6 (November/December 2006): 813–822. Copyright © 2006 American Society for Public Administration. Used by permission.

## THE JOURNEY

Burtell Jefferson was born in Washington, D.C., on March 14, 1925. Educated in the segregated schools of the District of Columbia, he graduated from Armstrong High School in 1943. After graduation, he entered the segregated U.S. Army, where he served three years. His military service included tours of duty in the Philippines and New Guinea during World War II. After an honorable discharge, Jefferson, with assistance provided under the GI Bill, enrolled in Howard University's School of Engineering. Soon, however, he opted to leave the school in order to find employment that would provide more than the subsistence level of income offered by the GI Bill.

In 1948, the realities of segregation and discrimination meant that career options for black men were extremely limited. Jefferson recalls that difficult period: "At the time, the only fields of financial stability available to me were teaching, the United States Postal Service, and the fire and police departments. I believed that police work would be most challenging."[2] Jefferson sat for and passed the Metropolitan D.C. Police Department's entrance exam, was found physically fit for duty, and successfully passed a face-to-face interview with members of the department's interviewing board. As a recruit in the Metropolitan D.C. Police Academy, he completed 16 weeks of training. Classes covered the D.C. Code, the U.S. Code, traffic regulations, the law of arrest, firearms training, physical fitness, and all departmental regulations. On September 16, 1948, he was appointed to serve as a patrolman in the overwhelmingly black Ninth Precinct of the Metropolitan D.C. Police Department.

Employment as a sworn officer by no means meant that Jefferson was free from the ravages of racism. Indeed, his professional journey was largely shaped by deeply entrenched discriminatory practices. Jefferson notes that at that time, black officers could account for no more than 10 percent of the positions in the department, although African Americans made up 35 percent of the population of the district, according to the 1950 Census. Speaking of the difficulties confronting black officers, Jefferson recalls,

> African Americans were assigned to specific duties, precincts, and assignments. . . . When I began working in the department, the opportunity for growth [for blacks] was very limited. . . . Promotional exams were used for advancement and for assignments to specific positions. Eligibility was based on a "suitability for promotion" rating, given *before* each exam, which was provided by your supervising officer—typically a white officer. African Americans were given low suitability ratings, which prevented them from scoring high on the overall exam. This practice caused many [black] officers to refuse to take the examination for promotion because the low "suitability for promotion" rating ensured that they would not have a high ranking on the overall list for promotion.

This reality of limited opportunity for African American officers was reinforced by the organizational structure and culture that pervaded the Metropolitan D.C. Police Department at that time. In that regard, Jefferson points out that

> . . . in the entire agency, there were six African American detective sergeants, six motorcycle officers, one uniformed lieutenant, and no African Americans were assigned to ride in scout cars.[3] When an African American sergeant retired, he was replaced by another African American. None were assigned to "downtown" precincts or to an "all white precinct." Out of 13 precincts, four were considered "all white" based on the makeup of the citizens residing there.

Despite the many obstacles that were erected to discourage black officers, Jefferson pushed forward in his career. From 1948 until 1951, he worked as a patrolman in the overwhelmingly black Ninth Precinct. In 1951 and 1952, he worked as a special investigator assigned to the U.S. Attorney's Office. From 1952 until 1960, he was assigned to the Morals Division, which was charged with the investigation of gambling, narcotics, and prostitution exclusively in minority neighborhoods and communities. It was during this time, in 1958, that he rose to the position of detective on a probationary basis.

In 1960, his probationary status as a detective ended. He was promoted to precinct detective and assigned to the Robbery Squad. While serving as a precinct detective, Jefferson and a black colleague, Detective Sergeant Tilmon O'Bryant, developed the idea of holding a covert "study class" for black officers, modeled after the departmentally sanctioned and socially accepted study class that was available to aspiring white officers. As Jefferson remembers,

> The first session was held at my home. The practice grew and continued over approximately 10 years. We obtained and assembled information and material not normally available to [black] officers seeking promotion. The first study group consisted of 13 [black] officers. Ten of them were promoted on the next examination.

Although the examination questions were based on materials and assignment experiences not typically available to black officers—many questions were about administrative matters—Jefferson was able to successfully tutor many young officers. This strategy helped immeasurably in assisting blacks in overcoming the artificial and discriminatory barriers that had been erected to stifle their professional growth and development.

In 1963, Jefferson was promoted to detective sergeant and supervisor of the Robbery Squad. Five years later, in 1968, he was promoted to lieutenant and platoon commander of the Fifth District. A year later, Jefferson was named community relations coordinator for the Fifth District. This assignment allowed him to establish what are now referred to as "community-oriented policing practices," which enabled officers within the district to routinely interact and collaborate in a positive way with community residents, local business leaders, and community-based organizations. According to Jefferson,

> The assignment required that I work closely with the Model Cities Commission, Roving Leaders, Youth Opportunities Services, and other community-based organizations. In response, I established a neighborhood community center and several community-oriented programs to improve relations between citizens and the police department, like the Neighborhood Scout Car Program. This program required the officers in those cars to meet and become familiar with business owners and citizens in their assigned areas. This promoted trust and openness among police and citizens.

This prescient and far-sighted practice reflected Jefferson's understanding and appreciation for community and organizational dynamics.

After two years of serving in this capacity, Jefferson was promoted in 1971 to captain and watch commander of the Fifth District. Soon after, Jefferson earned the distinction of becoming the first African American in the history of the Metropolitan D.C. Police Department to be assigned to command a major squad, the Robbery Squad. As captain and commander of the Robbery Squad, he reorganized the unit into six divisions, each responsible for investigating a specific category of robbery depending on the location, type of premises, or circumstances involved. This innovation led to a significant increase in the number of arrests and closed a number of criminal cases. His efforts were recognized and rewarded with a promotion to inspector and commander of the Third District. This was his second promotion in 1971, and with it, Jefferson joined his study class co-architect, Tilmon O'Bryant, in becoming the second of only two African American inspectors in the Metropolitan D.C. Police Department.

As a result of his leadership and his impact on reducing the crime rate in the Third District (a decline of 13 percent), President Richard M. Nixon awarded Jefferson a Presidential Citation in 1972. This national acclaim was followed by a promotion to deputy chief in 1974. As part of that promotion, he was designated chief of detectives in charge of one of the four divisions of the D.C. Police Department—the Criminal Investigation Division—and became the first African American in the history of the department to head a division. In 1976, Jefferson was promoted to assistant chief of field operations. This position was the number two position in the department, and it was the first time that an African American had been appointed to that rank. While serving in that capacity, the department experienced an unprecedented 22-month decline in crime, and Washington, D.C., was cited as one of the safest major cities in the United States.

On September 16, 1977, Jefferson was appointed acting chief of police for the Metropolitan D.C. Police Department. On January 13, 1978, after nearly four months as acting chief and nearly 30 years of serving the District of Columbia, Jefferson became the 23rd chief of police of the department and its first African American chief.

## THE ESSENCE OF LEADERSHIP: A POSITIVE IMPACT ON ORGANIZATIONS AND CAREERS

Early in his tenure as a supervisor, Jefferson's primary challenge was to find effective strategies to promote change within the Metropolitan D.C. Police Department. His objective was to transform the department by dismantling discriminatory policies and practices and enhancing the equality of opportunity. Central to this challenge was the need to overcome resistance to equality of opportunity among white officers in leadership positions in the organization. Jefferson drew on his own deep resolve, dedication, and sheer determination to push this objective forward despite his segregated surroundings. As Jefferson describes the situation,

> When I first came to the department, they had certain patrol beats that blacks were assigned and certain areas where they did not allow blacks to patrol. . . . No blacks could drive in the scout cars. . . . They put cars out of service [white supervisors took the cars off the streets] rather than have blacks drive them. . . . They didn't try to justify this; it was a long-standing practice, and this kind of thing sent a message to me and probably all other black officers.

Not only was it a challenge to constantly motivate himself in such circumstances, but as he ascended the ranks, Jefferson worked hard to motivate other marginalized officers to stay productive in the face of their second-class status within the department and their extremely limited opportunities for professional growth. The personal reflections of former Metropolitan D.C. police officers and executives who served with Jefferson—Marty Tapscott, Clay Goldston, and Isaac Fulwood—illustrate the kinds of challenges that black officers faced. Tapscott, a former assistant chief of the Metropolitan D.C. Police Department, retired from the department to become chief of police for the Flint (Michigan) and Richmond (Virginia) Police Departments. He recalls,

> I came on at the end of '59. . . . D.C. was my first job. . . . When I took my physical, I didn't know hay fever was a point of rejection. . . . I had hay fever as a youngster, and I

told them . . . so they looked at my throat. I had never had a throat problem in my life, but all of sudden I had inflamed tonsils. . . . They said, "Well, you got to take them out to be considered for employment." So I took them out, and they hired me. You know I wasn't even aware at the time of the fact that this was a way of controlling the numbers [of blacks]. As a matter of fact, if I knew the police department was so racist in the way they handled black officers, I probably never would have considered working there. I didn't know that when I was employed I couldn't work with white officers. You couldn't ride in a car. You couldn't work in the station. The only job available to you was walking the beat as a patrol officer and primarily in the black neighborhoods. . . . It was pretty hard to work in that type of environment.[4]

Goldston, a former assistant chief of the Metropolitan D.C. Police Department who went on to become director of public safety for Catholic University, describes a particularly insidious practice that helped keep many black officers from being considered for promotion. Goldston reports,

My first day on the job was February 10, 1958. . . . A lot of times we, the black officers, worked the streets, predominantly in the black community, on liquor and gambling. When we would make an arrest the white officer who helped process the case would be listed as the arresting officer and the black officer would be listed as the complainant. That was an obstacle, because when they would start tallying up your arrests you would never show up as the arresting officer. If you complained they would say, "Go down and look on the book, I don't see your name anywhere as the arresting officer." . . . I can remember in roll call Burtell Jefferson, he was a precinct detective at that time, and I remember him bringing it up. And I think probably by him bringing it up . . . things started to change.[5]

Fulwood, a former chief of the Metropolitan D.C. Police Department and current commissioner of the U.S. Parole Commission, provides further insight into the frustrations of many black officers and the sense of hopelessness that they felt. According to Fulwood,

Back in '64 was when I went to the department. . . . The organizational culture was one to make everybody conform. . . . You have to stick together. You know it is only the people in blue. . . . But it was a culture [for black officers] of, "You are here, but you are not a part of it." . . . It was a culture of, "You are not good enough to ride in the car. You are not important so we are not going to give you the kind of experiences that we give everybody else." . . . It was obvious from how they treated us that they had no respect for us and tried to take away our dignity. A lot of guys just stood there and didn't say anything. I said, "We need to say something about this kind of behavior. This is not acceptable." They said, "Hey, you are fighting an uphill battle with no where to go."[6]

The difficulty of overcoming the entrenched pattern of racist and discriminatory practices can hardly be overstated. Such practices extended well beyond the confines of the police headquarters and precinct houses. They directly affected African Americans and other marginalized populations served by the Metropolitan D.C. Police Department. The damage caused by this discriminatory behavior cut deep and left a lasting scar on the psyche of African American officers and citizens. Clarence Edwards, a native Washingtonian, former police chief of the Montgomery County (Maryland) Police Department, and past national president of the NOBLE, found his own opinions directly shaped by personal experience. Edwards remembers,

I had grown up in Washington, D.C. and during that time there were very few black police officers. I think they had three slots in the whole city for detective sergeants that would be of color. The only way you could get promoted to that rank was if one of them retired or died. Other than that, if you were in criminal investigations you basically were going to be locked in as a detective with no place to go in terms of promotion. Initially, I didn't choose to become a city police officer because I was well aware of the fact that there was little hope for you to do anything other than walk a foot beat . . . I really never thought I would ever become a police officer, as a matter of fact. I had a bad experience with a white D.C. police officer during my childhood. My brother and I were walking to Sunday School. We attended a church near our home, but you had to go through a predominately white neighborhood to get there. On this Sunday morning, an officer happened to see my brother and me as we were walking to church and he asked us what we were doing in this neighborhood. We told him that we were heading to church. He said we weren't moving fast enough and proceeded to kick me in my behind. That left a pretty nasty taste in my mouth about police officers and the Metro D.C. Police Department.[7]

Goldston and Fulwood, who both speak to the impact of discriminatory practices on the morale of African American officers, provide further understanding of this perception. According to Goldston,

I never thought that I would reach any high rank because like I said, you just didn't see it. You know with the atmosphere at the time you felt that it was impossible. . . . For a long time, blacks weren't supervisors on the street. When a black would get promoted they would use plainclothes and the reason you would stay in plainclothes was because you wouldn't have the amount of authority that someone in uniform would have. . . . A sergeant on the street had the stripes. He was uniformed and he ran the streets. He had a lot of authority, and so blacks for the most part didn't get uniform assignments until the mid- to late 60s.

Similarly, Fulwood recalls,

The thing that racism has, and the capacity it had at that time, is the ability to take away your hope. It could take away your desire to achieve—to be successful. So you would give in to the system and the system would kick you in the head. That is what it did for a number of guys. There were some people in the precinct who were college educated. You know, black guys who were well educated. Very bright, but they lost their desire.

In the late 1950s and early 1960s, in spite of these limitations and his lack of formal authority because of race and rank, Jefferson pushed hard to make improvements. He envisioned a time when opportunity would be extended to black officers, and he constantly pushed blacks to prepare themselves for that time. Jefferson was able to lead effectively because of his own high standards, his generosity and encouragement of others, and his positive outlook. This approach is reflected in the following statement made by Goldston:

You knew your chances for advancement were very slim. . . . So you tried to associate yourself with people who were looking to move up in the police department and one of my control officers was Burtell Jefferson. . . . I was sort of under his guidance. I was in his first study class. He kept encouraging us that things would get better and told us that what we should do was be in a position when things did get better that we would be able to take advantage of that opportunity.

These sentiments are echoed by Fulwood:

The first time I ran into him [Burtell Jefferson] in a meeting he said to me, "Things are not going to always be like this. You guys have got to study. If you don't study, you can't use race as a crutch. You've got to first study and be prepared. Once you get preparation, then you can say race is an issue if you don't get promoted." You know, he was right. You first have to be prepared. He used to talk about that all of the time. He said, "You can't get motivated by allowing this man to steal your hope. You know you got to always be hopeful that we can get this thing turned around."

By the 1970s, opportunities were indeed beginning to open up for blacks in the D.C. Police Department. This is evident in the comments of Robert Stewart, Leonard Cooke, and Rodney Monroe, all officers whose career in law enforcement began in the department from the late 1960s to the late 1970s. Stewart, former chief of police of the Ormond Beach (Florida) Police Department, former interim chief of the Rutgers University–Newark Public Safety Department, and current interim chief of the Camden (New Jersey) Police Department, recalls,

I started out in Metro in 1969. . . . If I remember correctly, I think Burtell was an inspector. At that time I don't think he was my commanding officer, but ultimately he became the commander of the 3rd District where I worked. . . . I try to give credit where credit is due. Jerry Wilson probably helped support the reform movement in the D.C. Police Department. But Jefferson really led the charge in terms of getting black guys in particular to think about getting prepared for promotions and advocating equal opportunities for assignments to minorities. . . . People began to see that the funnel in the D.C. Police Department at the executive levels was wider now and that there were going to be more opportunities than we had in the past. The number of [black] groups studying for promotions increased exponentially.[8]

Cooke, former chief of the Portsmouth (Virginia) and Eugene (Oregon) Police Departments, past national president of NOBLE, and current director of the Virginia Department of Criminal Justice Services, recollects,

My appointment date was in January of 1970. In 1972 or 1973 we received our first black sergeant assigned to our precinct. . . . When we got him, we felt kind of liberated because at least we felt we would get a fair shake. Now, that sergeant still held us accountable as well, but that sent a message to us that we were going to get a fair shake and there wasn't going to be that much disparity going on like it had been. . . . I am not sure if that would have taken place without the previous efforts of Burtell Jefferson and Tilmon O'Bryant.[9]

These perspectives are shared by Monroe, former assistant chief of the Metropolitan D.C. Police Department, former chief of the Macon (Georgia) Police Department, and current chief of the Richmond (Virginia) Police Department. Monroe reminisces,

I started my career with Metro in March of 1979. Burtell was the chief at that time. I was in D.C. when Chief Jefferson was appointed. That told me that that was the police department I wanted to be a part of. You know, you had the Capital Police, U.S. Park Police, Prince George's County Police, Montgomery County Police, but at that time, D.C. was the only one that had a black chief. . . . I just admired the leadership within the department. It felt good to look and see someone like you. You felt like you had an opportunity to do things, an opportunity to be involved in things, an opportunity to get promoted. It was just a good feeling. . . . Burtell Jefferson, Ike Fulwood, Marty Tapscott, Rodwell Catoe, Maurice Turner—these guys were true pioneers. . . . They made sure that people like myself, Richard Pennington [future New Orleans superintendent and Atlanta police chief] and others wouldn't be denied opportunities. . . . I heard the stories about them not being able to ride in cars with other people. How they were disrespected. Those were some tough times for them.[10]

As Jefferson rose to more senior levels and ultimately to the chief's position, the challenge of providing equal opportunities for African American and other marginalized officers became more pressing for him. By leveraging his rank and the formal authority and platform that accompanied it, he began broadcasting his vision to a broader audience. This is reflected in his 1977 essay "Policies for Increasing the Number of Black Police Executives," which is included in Herrington J. Bryce's volume *Black Crime: A Police View*. In that essay, Jefferson notes,

The modern police department places increasing emphasis on professionalism and efficiency. These goals can be reached only through advanced technical training of a select group of officers with the best managerial aptitudes and leadership abilities. . . . The opportunity for assignment and training for favored staff functions has been systematically denied blacks. Lack of knowledge and experience in these critical functional areas have been effective bars to promotion. Discriminatory assignment and promotion practices largely account for the dearth of black executives in staff level and command positions. (1977, 131)

To remedy this problem, Jefferson argued that police leaders would have to lead the way. He encouraged chief executives of law enforcement agencies to take proactive and creative steps in designing personnel policies to combat the stifling impact of racism and discrimination, which pervaded local law enforcement agencies and were often reflected in their practices and policies. He concluded, "This problem will continue unless our chief executives make an honest and determined effort to develop effective affirmative action and career development programs" (Jefferson 1977, 132).

In particular, Jefferson advocated the adoption of a management intern program for all police departments. Such an arrangement would provide deserving officers, irrespective of race or gender, the opportunity to be taught, coached, and mentored and ultimately the chance to gain the experience and training necessary to effectively function at all levels within a department. Jefferson consistently stressed hard work and high performance. He encouraged an optimistic outlook and focused on extending opportunities.

Jefferson's professional journey reflects the changing landscape and realities of American society in general, as well as the changing institutional arrangements that influenced American law enforcement agencies such as the Metropolitan D.C. Police Department from the 1940s to the 1970s. From the more segregated and hostile realities of the early years of his career—which led to the establishment of study classes, a clandestine strategy to survive in a hostile and challenging work environment—to the relatively inclusive arrangements that surfaced during his later years as chief, Jefferson was able to take what his professional life presented him and make the most of it, not only for himself but also for others. Among other activities, he participated in the department-sanctioned Law Enforcement Education Program at American University from 1969 to 1972 and the FBI Academy's National Executive Institute in 1976. At every stage, he touched the lives of other officers in positive ways. He worked tirelessly to ensure that opportunities within the Metropolitan. D.C. Police Department would be available to all who were qualified, regardless of race, ethnicity, or sex. Minority and female officers too numerous to count progressed in their careers because of Jefferson's efforts to overcome and eliminate discriminatory barriers. Table 3.1 lists a few of the officers (black and white) who benefited directly from Jefferson's work in forging a path of equal opportunity.

## JEFFERSON'S LEGACY OF LEADERSHIP

What has been the impact of Jefferson's efforts? What is his legacy of leadership within the law enforcement community? When asked these questions, Jefferson simply replied,

> I hoped to make our department one of the best in the nation. I hoped to provide growth opportunities previously denied to African Americans and other minorities to make them ready to replace me as chief or capable of becoming chiefs in other departments. During my tenure, the organizational culture was one of complete integration, promotional opportunities, and professionalism. Many female officers felt they had been overlooked for opportunities. Therefore, I created a task force to examine and address their unique concerns. I hope to be remembered for working to remove barriers that hampered minority officers, thereby making the playing field level for all and allowing every officer to rise to his or her maximum ability.

Questions about Jefferson's legacy are perhaps best answered, however, by those who knew him, worked with him, and followed the path he helped to clear. Comments from his contemporaries and his successors bring to light a richer understanding of the impact that Jefferson had, not only on the careers of numerous minority officers but on policing in general. For example, Fulwood notes,

> In 1964 when I came to Metro, race was major. It was major throughout my career. The environment of the Metropolitan Police Department was very conscious of race, and one that dampened your spirits. But when Burtell Jefferson started to get elevated and became chief of detectives, one of the things he said to the people was that there were blacks who weren't getting certain assignments. So, he brought some of the cameras in [brought more attention to the problem] and asked, what is the justification? They couldn't justify it. . . . To me, Jefferson has got to be the all time affirmative action person. I mean he broke it wide open. . . . He was able to change the landscape so that the playing field would be level. . . . He understood that change had to be made. He understood how that change had to be in an institution that he came up in. He saw the problems, and yet he was not a part of the institution, but was in the institution. Sometimes, that is something that we don't get. . . . His impact went nationwide, it had to go nationwide. He was a member of IACP [International Association of Chiefs of Police]. He was a member of the major organizations of city chiefs. . . . The mayor used to take him to the Big City Mayor's meeting. He spoke about his vision of law enforcement, wrote about it, put it in place. . . . I stood upon Jefferson's shoulders. He blessed me with opportunities that were previously denied to us.

Table 3.1

## Law Enforcement Executives Who Benefited from Burtell Jefferson's Leadership

| Name | Agency Affiliation(s) |
| --- | --- |
| Carl Alexander | Chief, Danville (Illinois) Police Department, 1999–present<br>Chief of Police, Veterans Administration Hospital, Danville, Illinois, 1991–99 |
| David Bostrom | Director of Public Safety, Wilmington, Delaware, 1997–2000* |
| Al Broadbent | Vice President for Security, Amtrak Corporation, 2004–present<br>Assistant Chief, Metropolitan D.C. Police Department, 1998–2004 |
| Rodwell Catoe | Professor of Justice and Administration, Northern Virginia Community College, 1994–present<br>Assistant Chief, Metropolitan D.C. Police Department, 1991–94* |
| Lenny Cooke | Director, Virginia Department of Criminal Justice Services, 2002–present<br>National President, NOBLE, 2000–01<br>Chief, Eugene (Oregon) Police Department, 1998–2002<br>Chief, Portsmouth (Virginia) Police Department, 1992–98 |
| Kim C. Dine | Chief, Frederick (Maryland) Police Department, 2002–present*<br>Assistant Chief, Metropolitan D.C. Police Department, 2000–02* |
| James Forney | Director of Public Safety Director, Catholic University, 2003 |
| Isaac Fulwood | Chief, Metropolitan D.C. Police Department, 1989–92<br>Commissioner, U.S. Parole Commission, 2004–present |
| Clay Goldston | Deputy Chief, Metropolitan D.C. Police Department, 1981–84*<br>Director of Public Safety, Catholic University, 1984–95 |
| William Harrison | Chief, Capitol Heights (Maryland) Police Department, 1991–2002 |
| Melvin High | Chief, Prince Georges County (Maryland) Police Department, 2003–present<br>Chief, Norfolk (Virginia) Police Department, 1993–2003<br>Assistant Chief, Metropolitan D.C. Police Department, 1991–93*<br>Special Assistant to the President, NOBLE, 2005–present |
| William McManus | Chief, San Antonio (Texas) Police Department, April 2006–present<br>Chief, Minneapolis (Minnesota) Police Department, 2004–06<br>Chief, Dayton (Ohio) Police Department, 2002–04<br>Assistant Chief, Metropolitan D.C. Police Department, 1998–2001 |
| Rodney Monroe | Chief, Richmond (Virginia) Police Department, 2005–present<br>Chief, Macon (Georgia) Police Department, 2002–05<br>Assistant Chief, Metropolitan D.C. Police Department, 1998–2001 |
| Ronald Monroe | Chief, U.S. Government Printing Office Police Department, 2005*<br>Assistant Chief, Metropolitan D.C. Police Department, 1999* |
| Richard Pennington | Chief, Atlanta (Georgia) Police Department, 2002–present<br>National President, NOBLE, 2005–present<br>Superintendent, New Orleans Police Department, 1994–2002 |
| Sonya T. Proctor | Chief of Police and Security, Amtrak Police Department, 2004–present<br>Acting Town Administrator and Chief, Bladensburg (Maryland) Police Department, 2003–04<br>Deputy Director, Maryland Crime Control and Prevention Office, 2000–03<br>Interim Chief, Metropolitan D.C. Police Department, 1997–98<br>Assistant Chief, Metropolitan D.C. Police Department, February 1997 |
| Charles Samarra | Police Chief, Alexandria (Virginia) Police Department, 1990–2006<br>Assistant Chief, Metropolitan D.C. Police Department, 1988–1990* |
| Reginald Smith | Police Chief, Howard University Campus Police Department** |

*(continued)*

Table 3.1 *(continued)*

| | |
|---|---|
| Robert Stewart | Interim Chief, Camden (New Jersey) Police Department, February 2006–present<br>Interim Chief, Rutgers University–Newark Public Safety Department, May–September 2005<br>Chief, Ormond Beach (Florida) Police Department, 1992–97 |
| Ross Swope | Chief, U.S. Supreme Court Police Department, 2002–present |
| Marty Tapscott | Chief, Richmond (Virginia) Police Department, 1989–96<br>Chief, Flint (Michigan) Police Department, 1986–87<br>National President, NOBLE, 1985–86<br>Assistant Chief, Metropolitan D.C. Police Department, 1979–86 |
| Lawrence Thomas | Interim Police Chief, Howard University Campus Police Department** |
| William Tucker | Assistant Chief, Prince Georges County (Maryland) Police Department, 2003–05<br>Chief of Public Safety, Georgetown University, 1988–2003<br>Chief of Public Safety, University of Pittsburgh, 1980–88 |
| Maurice Turner | Chief, Metropolitan D.C. Police Department, 1981–89<br>Assistant Chief, Metropolitan D.C. Police Department, 1979–81* |
| Robert White | Chief, Metropolitan Louisville (Kentucky) Police Department, 2003–present<br>Chief, Greensboro (North Carolina) Police Department, 1998–2002<br>Assistant Chief, Metropolitan D.C. Police Department, 1997–98<br>Chief of Police, District of Columbia Housing Authority, 1995–97* |
| Jimmy Wilson | Chief, Virginia State University Police Department, 2002–present<br>National President, NOBLE, 2002–03<br>Chief, Suffolk (Virginia) Police Department, 1997–2002 |

*Denotes approximate tenure.
**Denotes tenure unknown; efforts to track the exact or approximate dates were unsuccessful.

Fulwood's perspective is shared by Cooke, who recalls,

> During my first six- or seven-year stretch [1970–77] . . . the highest ranking [black] officers were Burtell Jefferson and Tilmon O'Bryant. They were downtown and you really didn't see those [black] managers out in the precincts as much. After a while, you started seeing that [command-level diversity at the precinct level] happen. I said to myself, that doesn't happen by flicking your fingers. That is management. That is vision. That is leadership. There is no question about Burtell's lasting impact on Metro D.C. . . . I take my hat off to him because I know that he had a challenge there. To start promoting this whole issue of diversity within Metro D.C. at that time was really tough.

Yet another observer, Monroe, notes,

> When you think about Metro D.C. over the years, everything revolves back to Chief Jefferson. He was the first black chief. He brought about that needed change. . . . I started in 1979, and that was inside of one year of him being there. . . . I mean everywhere you looked, you saw blacks reflected in leadership throughout the department. . . . To young guys such as myself, that was very comforting. From what I understand, that wasn't always the case. . . . I didn't see all of the struggles that those individuals who had gone on before had gone through, but you know some of the older ones reminded you of it.

Comments by former Metro D.C. officers and subsequent chiefs of other agencies—Robert Stewart, William Harrison, Sonya T. Proctor, and Carl Alexander—also speak to Jefferson's impact on local law enforcement in Washington, D.C., as well as nationally. According to Stewart,

> Jefferson's legacy to me is the number of African Americans who came out of that department who have gone on to hold law enforcement CEO positions elsewhere. . . . Not only did we come out of D.C. but we all got at least one if not two promotions in D.C., very largely because of his efforts. Whether that was direct or indirect, he created an environment where it was possible for us to seek these positions and attain these positions. He was the first chief that I know of in America who really had the opportunity to allow for the growth of African American promotions from within. There were other black chiefs, but many of them were in environments where they just could not, for political reasons, allow many minority promotions. Jefferson took advantage of the changing politics in Washington to create that kind of growth. In some of the larger departments, blacks trickled into the executive ranks. Very often by trickling in you don't have a peer group to depend on and matriculate with. . . . We had an explosion of people who moved into the executive ranks, which meant you had your own support group. . . . Metro D.C. has turned out to be very fertile ground and I think Jefferson had a lot to do with cultivating it. . . . In a way, you can see how his work in changing the department for the better has benefited other agencies across the country.

Stewart's view is shared by Harrison:

> I retired from the Washington D.C. Metropolitan Police Department in 1991. I then served as Chief of the Capital Heights, Maryland Police Department from 1991 through 2002. . . . I am not sure if others spoke to you about how he impacted undercover operations. . . . To my knowledge, he was the first chief [in D.C.] to put in a structure for undercover officers. He set up a system where they rotated out every two years. This system helped to minimize the potential for corruption.[11]

Like Harrison and Stewart, Proctor and Alexander provide their assessments of the direct impact of Jefferson's legacy of leadership on policing in the district and beyond. According to Proctor,

> D.C. has had a tremendous influence on policing across the country. People [former Metro D.C. officers who are appointed chiefs of other agencies] bring to their new agencies what they have been exposed to in their old agencies. I think you will find that a lot of the policies that are in place in a lot of these new places [police agencies] can be traced back to our nation's capital.[12]

Similarly, Alexander says,

> I started out in Metro D.C. in 1969 and retired in 1990. We [African Americans and other previously marginalized officers] had one of the best all-around experiences. Burtell put into place a system. We were mentored. Our assignments were changed frequently so we could get the full exposure to law enforcement. These things helped prepare us for the challenges associated with being a chief. I think those agencies that hired us benefited from our experiences and Burtell's leadership. I see that as one of the legacies of Burtell Jefferson.[13]

## CONCLUSION

Frances Hesselbein raises the question, "How do we develop the leaders our organizations require for an uncertain future?" (1998, 7–9). Burtell Jefferson's leadership offers an example of one approach. Jefferson was able to build support for change and grow other leaders through his coaching, mentoring, and commitment to high quality and performance. His personal and professional actions reflected the prescience and innovativeness that Doig and Hargrove (1990) consider essential for effective leadership. He could see opportunities and possibilities that were on the horizon. Moreover, he was willing and able to share his vision with others and encouraged them to position themselves for that new day. This ensured a generation of future leaders who were well-prepared to accept new opportunities.

Table 3.1 provides only a partial list of the black and white officers who benefited from Jefferson's efforts to provide equal opportunity for advancement, regardless of race or gender. Jefferson struggled to cultivate and transform the Metropolitan Police Department's internal environment, structures, policies, and practices. He created an environment that made possible the training, development, and nurturing of minority law enforcement executives who went on to lead their own departments across the country. The direct and indirect beneficiaries of Jefferson's efforts, such as current Atlanta police chief Richard Pennington and former Metropolitan D.C. police chief and current U.S. parole commissioner Isaac Fulwood, have mentored other new chiefs, such as Ronal Serpas of the Metropolitan Nashville (Tennessee) Police Department and Rodney Monroe of the Richmond (Virginia) Police Department, respectively. These outcomes may not have been possible without Jefferson's early efforts. The many decisions he made throughout his career and, ultimately, his appointment as chief of the Washington, D.C. Police Department set in motion a cascade of efforts and decisions that have indeed had an enduring impact on policing in the United States.

Speaking in South Africa in 1966, Senator Robert F. Kennedy said,

> It is from numberless diverse acts of courage and belief that human history is shaped. Each time a man stands up for an ideal, or acts to improve the lot of others, or strikes out against injustice, he sends forth a tiny ripple of hope, and crossing each other from a million different centers of energy and daring, those ripples build a current that can sweep down the mightiest walls of oppression and resistance.

Such has been the impact of Chief Burtell Jefferson of the Metropolitan Police Department of Washington, D.C.—an exemplary public servant who overcame adversity and injustice through personal and professional excellence, patient determination, and integrity. He envisioned and built support for change. Jefferson was able to convey his virtues and values to bring out the best in others and to leave a positive legacy for law enforcement and other leaders to follow. He generated numerous ripples—indeed, waves—of hope that converged into a powerful current whose effects are still being felt today.

## NOTES

1. The Metropolitan Police Department of Washington, D.C. is commonly referred to as the Metro D.C. Police Department, and the Metropolitan D.C. Police Department, or simply Metro P.D. by the person's interviewed for this project. Consequently, these references are used interchangeably.

2. This and all subsequent quotes from Jefferson are drawn from a personal interview conducted on October 10, 2005.

3. A "scout car" is a police cruiser.

4. Interview with Marty Tapscott, May 25, 2005.

5. Interview with Clay Goldston, May 25, 2005; subsequent quotes from Mr. Goldston are also from this interview.

6. Interview with Isaac Fulwood, September 28, 2005; subsequent quotes from Mr. Fulwood are also from this interview.

7. Interview with Clarence Edwards, August 30, 2005.

8. Interview with Robert Stewart, August 23, 2005; subsequent quotes from Mr. Stewart are also from this interview.

9. Interview with Leonard Cooke, April 6, 2006; subsequent quotes from Mr. Cooke are also from this interview.

10. Interview with Rodney Monroe, March 9, 2006; subsequent quotes from Mr. Monroe are also from this interview.

11. Interview with William Harrison, former chief of the Capital Heights (Maryland) Police Department, June 6, 2006.

12. Interview with Sonya T. Proctor, former interim chief of the Metropolitan D.C. Police Department; former chief of the Bladensburg (Maryland) Police Department; former deputy director of Maryland's Crime Control and Prevention Office; and current chief of police and security for the Amtrak Police Department, June 7, 2006.

13. Interview with Carl Alexander, former chief of police for the Veterans Administration Hospital in Danville, Illinois, and current chief of the Danville Police Department, June 8, 2006.

## REFERENCES

Blunt, Ray. 2004. *Growing Leaders for Public Service.* 2nd ed. Washington, DC: IBM Center for the Business of Government.

Doig, Jameson W. and Erwin C. Hargrove, eds. 1990. *Leadership and Innovation: Entrepreneurs in Government.* Baltimore: Johns Hopkins University Press.

Hesselbein, Frances. 1998. *The One Big Question.* J-B Leader-to-Leader Series. San Francisco: P.F. Drucker Foundation.

Jefferson, Burtell. 1977. Policies for Increasing the Number of Black Police Executives. In *Black Crime: A Police View,* edited by Herrington J. Bryce, 131–39. Washington, DC: U.S. Department of Justice, Law Enforcement Assistance Administration, National Institute of Law Enforcement and Criminal Justice.

# 4

# QUALIFIED TO LEARN THE JOB

## Donna Shalala

### BERYL A. RADIN

There are many ways to document the career of an exemplary public administrator. Traditionally, one would focus on the career progress of a public servant who chooses to stay within the confines of a public sector organization throughout his or her years of service. That individual might be a generalist administrator who moves between organizations employing a set of technical skills (such as personnel, budgeting, or information management). Alternatively, that individual might be a policy or program specialist who performs a variety of functions but always in a defined sector (such as education, transportation, or defense).

But there are other career paths as well. In an era when individuals are less likely to stay within a single organization for an entire career, some of the assumptions that we once made about public sector jobs have changed. A significant number of individuals who are beginning their careers with master's degrees in public administration or public policy are likely to move in and out of jobs without ever exiting the public sector, but at least some of them will also move between career public service jobs, jobs in the private sector, and other positions that might involve political appointments. The blurring of lines between the sectors has provided opportunities for individuals to call on skills that have not always been associated with public sector work.

Donna Shalala's career provides an example of a progression that might be useful to others who are attempting to develop a career strategy. This profile illustrates several related themes. First, it suggests that there is not always a clear separation between the skills employed by career and political officials. Second, it illustrates a career strategy that is quite different from that found in classic human resources textbooks. As Shalala puts it,

> With one exception, I have always taken jobs where the consensus was that I wasn't qualified for the job. So it's always an uphill climb. I was not taking skills from one place and applying them to another. It was always a new uphill climb and I was always a little over my head. I like to ask not whether one is qualified for the job, but whether one is qualified to *learn* the job.

---

As this profile will illustrate, Shalala's career departs from the view that the functions of politics and administration are separate—that both elected and appointed political leaders determine policy, whereas career administrators manage the implementation of those policies (Ingraham and Ban 1986).

Hugh Heclo's classic work *A Government of Strangers* (1977) depicts the two groups as very different from one another. Political figures are transient and have a short time frame, and their roles are dependent on their competencies and interests rather than organizational perspectives. Bureaucrats, by contrast, have enduring careers and are characterized by loyalty to programs and institutions rather than particular leaders. Paul Light (1987) describes the situation as one in which "political appointees and career civil servants operate in two different worlds. Whether appointees intend to stay the average eighteen months or eight full years, they look for the immediate return. Theirs is the short-term perspective." Some observers have suggested that political appointees should rely on their careerists when assuming office (Michaels 2005, 7–9); however, it is rare to suggest that political appointees may actually have some of the same attributes—in terms of expertise and knowledge of programs and institutions—that careerists exhibit.

Yet, as Norma Riccucci notes in her book *Unsung Heroes* (1995), the line between career and political appointees is often blurred as top career officials take on important leadership positions. She comments that despite this blurring, there are notable differences between the two sets of government staffers (5). Her model of organizational effectiveness for top career officials (whom she calls "execucrats") includes political skills, management and leadership skills, situational factors, experience in government, technical expertise, strategy, and personality. Though this skill set is not unique to this group of officials, they are often likely to exert influence as indirect—rather than direct—participants. Riccucci's portrait of top career officials is somewhat different from the description of both career and political officials offered here. This profile of Donna Shalala looks at her role from a perspective that argues that blurred roles can also be developed by political appointees. It does so by focusing on her entire career, not simply those periods of her career when she was formally in government service.

The traditional literature tends to focus on careerists adopting characteristics that are normally associated with political appointees. Rarely is the relationship one in which political appointees adopt characteristics associated with careerists. Like Riccucci's framework, it suggests that a political appointee can combine attributes of both career and political figures. Yet Shalala has never been in public service as a career official; her experience has only been as a political appointee. But her behavior in the various jobs that she has held indicates that she is informed by many of the same skills, conceptual frameworks, and literatures that are usually associated with career public servants. At the same time, she has approached her career in a way that is very different from that of a high-level career official. This profile seeks to review a career of a woman who has been able to respond to quite unpredictable opportunities.

## WHO IS DONNA SHALALA?

Donna Shalala's career is not easy to characterize. Most *PAR* readers know her as a Clinton administration cabinet official—the longest-serving secretary in the history of the Department of Health and Human Services (HHS)—as well as a subcabinet official, assistant secretary for policy development and research in the Department of Housing and Urban Development (HUD) during the Carter administration. If she is known to the public administration community beyond that, she is known as a university president (of Hunter College of the City University of New York, the University of Wisconsin–Madison, and currently the University of Miami).

These two streams of her career—public service and university leadership—are not unique. Others have moved back and forth between the academy and public service (current defense secretary Robert Gates likely will do the same). What is unique about Shalala's career is that she is also a student of public administration. When she thinks about running an organization, she focuses not only on the substance of the work done by that organization but also on the processes of that challenge, and she uses academic and conceptual frameworks drawn from the literature of public management and public policy. This is a characteristic of her career path, not simply the ways that she has operated in a specific position.

Thus, it is the confluence of these strands that makes her unique but also questions some of our traditional views about the difference between political and career officials. Balancing these two approaches to leadership is often difficult, and not everyone has agreed with her choices. During a recent presentation on health policy in Washington, D.C., Shalala joined her successor at HHS, Tommy Thompson, to discuss ways to move beyond the current impasse on health policy. Thompson had been briefed about the status of the issues and rattled off a range of statistics to support his position. By contrast, Shalala stepped back from the current situation and explicated a range of issues that had to be confronted in that policy area. Her presentation called for balancing the fiscal, equity, implementation, and political perspectives in health policy design, as well as the need to find ways to build public support for a complex policy area; she alternated between analytical and advocacy perspectives.

## A CAREER DEVELOPMENT: RESPONDING TO OPPORTUNITIES

Shalala was born in Cleveland, Ohio and received a baccalaureate in history from the Western College for Women. During her undergraduate years, she participated in American University's Washington Semester Program, during which time she "fell in love with Washington." She notes that she has always been interested in the interface between politics and policy, but she confesses that she was not "quite conscious at the time of what kind of career [she] was going to have."

After finishing her undergraduate studies, she joined the Peace Corps and spent two years teaching English in Iran. When she returned to the United States, she enrolled in the PhD program at the Maxwell School of Citizenship and Public Affairs at Syracuse University. Her career goals at the time involved journalism. She notes that "it never occurred to me that I was going to have a long academic career rather than a journalism career."

While at Syracuse, she began to focus on issues of school politics and finance. Working with faculty members Stephen K. Bailey and Alan K. Campbell, she and several other students were Carnegie Foundation fellows who responded to the availability of funds to study the politics and finance of schools. As with many other occurrences in her career, she was able to take advantage of the target of opportunity afforded her by those resources.

When she completed her PhD, she knew that she wanted to live in New York City and sought a job as a journalist there. Most of Shalala's colleagues at Maxwell took a more traditional academic path and made different career choices. She went to the *New York Times*, but they weren't interested in hiring her. Her move into an academic job (first at Baruch College, then at Teachers College and the Political Science Department at Columbia University) continued her pattern of responding to opportunities. At Teachers College, she continued her work on the politics of education and finance. She received a Spencer Foundation fellowship that sought to identify political scientists and economists and get them interested in education policy. At Teachers College, her job was to help develop a PhD program for students who were getting their degrees in political science and education from the graduate faculty at Columbia.

She developed a collegial relationship with a number of the people in the Maxwell program and some at Columbia. These individuals continued their relationships with Shalala over the years; they included John Callahan (former assistant secretary for management and budget at HHS), Astrid Merget (now the dean at Indiana University's School of Public and Environmental Affairs), and Susan Fuhrman (one of the first individuals to receive the Teachers College PhD in education politics and school finance and the recently appointed president of Teachers College).

In 1975, Shalala found herself in the middle of what many viewed as a crucial period in the history of New York City. The city government was on the brink of financial collapse and had to restructure its debt through the Municipal Assistance Corporation—known as Big MAC—headed by financier Felix Rohatyn. The recognition of the financial problems of the country's biggest city came just after a new Democratic governor, Hugh Carey, had taken office. Carey needed help putting his budget together and was faced with the reality that all of the known individuals with budget expertise were either Republicans or had worked for Republicans. One of the faculty members at Maxwell knew that Shalala was one of the few Democrats who actually understood the state budget. She served on Carey's budget transition group but declined an invitation to join his administration. She had been awarded a Guggenheim fellowship and was planning to take a year off to write.

When the city fiscal crisis hit, Carey asked Shalala to be his appointee to the Big MAC board. She was the only individual on that board with expertise in state government and finance matters. She also was the only academic, and about 20 years younger than the rest of the board members. As she describes the experience, Shalala notes, "It was fabulous. I got to work with people from Wall Street. They didn't know anything about state government and I didn't know anything about Wall Street."

Her doctoral dissertation served her very well in that situation. New York City's fiscal home rule had been revoked by the state of New York. Her doctoral dissertation focused on the New York State constitution and the financial arrangements between New York State and New York City. Shalala found that "it was like seeing your substantive area played out."

In 1977, Shalala's affection for Washington, D.C., had an opportunity to reemerge. But instead of seeing the city through the eyes of a student, she returned as a subcabinet official. She had returned to Columbia the year before (after the Guggenheim fellowship), received tenure, and thought it was time to try something new. Her political contacts in New York paid off, and she had a choice between going to the Department of Housing and Urban Development as an assistant secretary for policy development and research or going to the White House to work on the domestic policy staff. She chose the HUD position.

As she recalls those years, Shalala notes that this experience was the first time she had been "inside" government. She found the job hard but very rewarding. HUD, like most cabinet departments, was characterized by turf fighting, often between program units and staff roles. She did not always come up on the winning side of those battles, but she did learn how a federal agency operates from the inside. Patricia Harris, then HUD secretary, gave Shalala extensive administrative authority, allowing her to chair the executive review board for Senior Executive Service reviews and other administrative tasks. She learned how cabinet departments were organized, both through her experience at HUD and as a participant in the transition to the newly established Department of Education. In addition, she learned how to use discretionary money as a resource, as her unit did not have a lot of formal power. She surrounded herself with first-rate deputies whom she drew from the academic world and Capitol Hill. These were individuals who had strong reputations and skills. When Secretary Pat Harris moved to head the reorganized Department of Health and Human Services, she asked Shalala to come with her, but the assistant secretary chose to stay at HUD.

Harris's replacement was Moon Landrieu, the mayor of New Orleans, whom Shalala had known when he was head of the U.S. Conference of Mayors during the fiscal crisis in New York City.

Shalala chose to leave HUD before the 1980 presidential campaign took off at full speed. She assumed that she would go back to a teaching job but didn't want to limit herself to the field of education. Rather, she wanted to teach public policy, and she was close to accepting a position at the Kennedy School at Harvard when she received a phone call from former federal education official Harold Howe II asking whether she would be interested in the Hunter College presidency. The search for the Hunter presidency had been difficult, and the search committee was looking for a new candidate. At the time, Shalala had a conversation with former Treasury secretary Michael Blumenthal, who told her that if she was ever going to be a cabinet officer, she needed to get administrative experience. Though Blumenthal's advice focused on administrative experience in the private sector, he acknowledged that a university presidency could fit the bill.

Returning to New York meant that Shalala could draw on her contacts within the political world of the city. Because the appointment process to the Hunter presidency did not follow traditional rules, she was faced with a situation in which faculty and staff were skeptical about her. For some, the Hunter presidency should not have been filled by a white woman. She notes that her experience at HUD had taught her how to listen and how to analyze situations. She took her time in scoping out the situation, and she employed her analytical skills to figure out what was going on, what was needed, and how her connections could be tapped to facilitate an agenda that would respond to the concerns of the Hunter community. She took care in identifying top staff whom she thought would be strong. Although she was the major decision maker in this situation, she actually adopted the techniques of a policy analyst: She defined the problem, formulated alternative ways to deal with it, thought about those who were involved in (or could influence) the decision, collected data to assess approaches to address the problem, and moved to a decision point.

Her Wall Street connections provided her with information that allowed Hunter to float bonds for a new building. Once the building program began, she hired staff who shared her perspective. These included a provost and deans. Most of these individuals were older and more experienced than she was, and she comments that "they taught me a lot in the process."

Her strategy was to do a survey soon after arrival and learn what everybody's priorities were—a technique that she would use in future situations. She learned that the Hunter community wanted the buildings to be clean and the facilities safe. She concentrated on fund-raising, brought visibility to the institution, and improved Hunter's financial position. The new buildings that were constructed (it is estimated that 500,000 square feet of facilities were built during her years at Hunter) allowed the institution to realize its building plan, which had been delayed by the city's fiscal crisis.

Shalala comments, "I cut a deal with the faculty. If we could get 90 percent occupancy of the classrooms, I'd give them a faculty club and private offices. We were able to get people to teach from morning to night and absolutely transformed the place. It energized the institution and reflected its reality that it was a big commuter school with a very good faculty. Many of the students could have been admitted to any school but they were new immigrants and many were poor. This introduced me to a complex, multiethnic setting."

Shalala's strategy at Hunter focused on issues that are not always at the top of a change agenda. Because the school was unionized, she was not able to do much about salaries, and some thought that was the most important agenda item for change. But she could focus on such issues as safety, space, and new facilities, as well as the recruitment of minority faculty. As a former faculty member, she could empathize with the concerns of the faculty. But she was an outsider in the sense that she had not been a dean or provost. And she was able to use the political environment because she had participated in it.

The strategy that Shalala employed during her seven years at Hunter was similar to the approach that she took when she assumed the job of chancellor at the University of Wisconsin–Madison. She conducted a survey of the public and found that the Wisconsin citizenry was concerned about three issues. First, they thought that the campus was too liberal. Second, they thought that the university did not pay adequate attention to the needs of undergraduates. Third, they wanted the sports teams to be competitive. As Shalala comments, "I don't know if I ever changed their minds about the campus being too liberal, but I certainly changed their minds about undergraduates. Now it is hard to get into Madison because the best kids don't want to go to the Ivy League but to Madison. We raised the standards and changed the undergraduate experience. By chance, I had the opportunity to turn around the sports teams."

Though she was new to Wisconsin, Shalala developed political relationships in the state. The campus was not known for its positive relationship with the legislature, so Shalala worked hard to establish those links. She went up to the legislature frequently and talked to them. She constantly traveled the state and talked to citizens, as well as newspaper editors and editorial writers. Her identity as a Democrat did not limit these efforts, and her relationship with a Republican governor was generally productive. The powerful faculty on the campus was happy that someone was handling the politics for the university. As at Hunter, she was able to appoint very capable and talented deputies. Both her provost and the dean of the graduate school were able to work effectively with the faculty.

The election of Bill Clinton as president provided Shalala with the opportunity to become a cabinet official. One might have assumed that she would move into the Department of Education, given her expertise in education policy and her experience in higher education. But she surprised some people by accepting the job of secretary of health and human services. Though she had been a board member of the Children's Defense Fund, she was not acknowledged for her involvement in health and social services issues. But she was a friend of both Hillary and Bill Clinton and known for her intelligence and energy. At the time she entered the HHS, that department consumed 40 percent of federal spending.

Because of delays in the appointment process, Shalala relied on careerists during her first months on the job. Throughout the eight years of her tenure as HHS secretary, she continued to work closely with career officials. It was rare to have meetings that were limited in attendance to political appointees. Many meetings held in her big office were attended by a wide range of careerists at all levels, as well as political appointees, and she enjoyed opportunities to engage all of them in substantive policy discussions. This pattern gave her a good sense of the world of the careerists, and when the government shutdown occurred in November 1995, she thought about their struggles. The shutdown occurred when Congress failed to appropriate funds to keep the government running. The Republican majority passed a budget with significant spending cuts thinking that President Clinton could either sign the bill or veto it. Clinton vetoed the measure, resulting in an interruption of nonessential government services. This led to a decision within the HHS to deal with the federal government-wide requirement that paychecks be cut in half because of the shutdown. The HHS found a legal way around the pay cut by postponing payroll deductions until after Christmas.

As she describes the situation, it was actually easier to bring in her own second-tier team to the HHS than it had been at both Wisconsin and Hunter. She has often noted that universities are harder to manage than federal agencies because of the autonomy of the separate academic units and the culture of individual discretion exercised by tenured faculty members. Working with the White House, she had control over hiring, and all of the people who were placed on the short lists for subcabinet jobs were acceptable to her. Thus, she was able to build an implementation team of individuals whom she believed could do a good job and were available. This was a strategy she had used in the past and continued to use in the future. She notes that her team "was made up of individuals who were substantively knowledgeable and were great implementers."

Although Shalala had control over hiring, she did not have complete control over the policy agenda. Rather, that agenda came from the president. Indeed, some of the items on the president's agenda involved approaches she did not embrace. Despite this, there were still opportunities to make an impact on the policy agenda, including the State Children's Health Insurance Programs, privacy regulations, the tobacco campaign, and childhood immunization. In several of these cases, Secretary Shalala was able to use the administrative resources of the department to hold hearings around the country, involve regional HHS officials in the process, and generally make the programs visible to the general public.

Health care policy was a notable exception. Shalala reports that "we even had control over the implementation of welfare reform and through our veto of draft bills." Both the health policy process and the welfare reform effort were areas in which there was conflict between what the career staff advised, what her personal values defended, and what loyalty to the White House demanded.

## LESSONS ABOUT MANAGING A LARGE ORGANIZATION

As President Clinton's second term began, Shalala reflected on her experience in a series of lectures at the annual meetings of the American Political Science Association and the American Society for Public Administration, as well as in a guest editorial in *PAR*. She offered her "Top Ten Lessons for Managing a Large Complex Bureaucracy," couching her advice in the context of various elements of the public administration literature (Shalala 1998). She described her perspective as drawn "from two decades of my experience as a sub-cabinet official in the Carter administration, as a student of government and politics, and as a leader of large public universities" (285).

In her article, she noted that "[i]n complex organizations there will be failures for any number of reasons: poor communication, impractical or unclear goals, lack of public or congressional support, lack of sufficient expertise or resources, too much—or too little—oversight, and too much work. Between these two extremes—that nothing works or that everything can be made to work—lies some basic truths about large, modern organizations" (285).

Shalala's lessons reflect the combined attributes of both the political figure and the careerist:

1. Know the cultures of your organization
2. Find ways to assure that appropriate coordination takes place
3. Don't overlook the needs and abilities of the career public service
4. Choose the best and let them do their jobs
5. Stitch together a loyal team
6. Stand up and fight for the people who work for you
7. Set firm goals and priorities and stick with them
8. Don't forget that politics is always part of policy making
9. Look for allies where you don't expect to find them
10. Be flexible, be realistic, and don't expect to win every time.

## CONCLUSION

Clearly, not everyone can craft a career that resembles Donna Shalala's. Yet the lessons that emerge from her experience are instructive to individuals who are in the early stages of their careers. When one looks at Shalala's career as an entirety, it is clear that she was able to apply experiences and lessons from diverse settings to new positions. Her career has been characterized not only by an in-and-out pattern but also by diversity within each of those settings. This pattern has reinforced her personal strength of being a problem solver.

Several strategies can be gleaned from Shalala's career experience. First, she chose to think of her staff not as two separate groups but as a unified cadre of careerists and political appointees who were loyal to the programs, organization, and leadership. She hired first-rate people who were knowledgeable about both the substance and politics of their assignments.

Second, she employed both formal and informal methods to collect data about what people wanted, both inside the organization and in the broader citizenry, and used that information to devise program goals. Although she didn't always have control over the program agenda, she sought to use those data to work through the implementation of agenda items that were handed to her.

Third, she always attempted to keep the people inside the organization informed about was happening. She had a ground rule that asked others not to surprise her, and she practiced it herself. Fourth, her style of decision making was open, fluid, and flexible to changes both inside the agency and in the external environment. She built and rewarded teams. Fifth, her experience within the university setting gave her a sense of organizations as decentralized entities in which top-down change attempts are often not possible.

Finally, she avoided an approach to leadership that emphasized heroic vision. She comments, "I had to figure out how to do the job and how to build allies. So I don't come in with an agenda. People ask, what is your vision for the place? I say that you don't want to hire anyone who has a vision. You need to work it through by being attentive to the people who are there and figuring out what is the appropriate process you will use. It's not heroic leadership."

## REFERENCES

Heclo, Hugh. 1977. *A Government of Strangers: Executive Politics in Washington.* Washington, DC: Brookings Institution Press.

Ingraham, Patricia Wallace, and Carolyn R. Ban. 1986. Models of Public Management: Are They Useful to Federal Managers in the 1980s? *Public Administration Review* 46 (2): 152–60.

Light, Paul C. 1987. When Worlds Collide: The Political-Career Nexus. In *The In-and-Outers: Presidential Appointees and Transient Government in Washington,* edited by G. Calvin Mackenzie, 156–73. Baltimore: Johns Hopkins University Press.

Michaels, Judith E. 2005. *Becoming an Effective Political Executive: 7 Lessons from Experienced Appointees.* Washington, DC: IBM Center for the Business of Government. www.businessofgovernment.org/pdfs/JudithMichaelsReport.pdf [accessed February 15, 2007].

Riccucci, Norma M. 1995. *Unsung Heroes: Federal Execucrats Making a Difference.* Washington, DC: Georgetown University Press.

Shalala, Donna E. 1998. Are Large Public Organizations Manageable? *Public Administration Review* 58 (4): 284–89.

# 5

# WILLIAM ROBERTSON

## Exemplar of Politics and Public Management Rightly Understood

### TERRY L. COOPER AND THOMAS A. BRYER

In this Administrative Profile, we present William Robertson, director of the Bureau of Street Services in the Los Angeles Department of Public Works, as an exemplar of the practice of public administration. We believe he illustrates the way in which public executives can engage in politics appropriately, or, to paraphrase Alexis de Tocqueville, politics and administration "rightly understood." Political activity by administrators is sometimes viewed as an insurmountable problem: Politics is a necessary evil under the circumstances of modern government—the dark side of administration that always threatens to subvert the professional, technical management of public administration. We intend to legitimize political behavior in public management by showing how Robertson uses it effectively on behalf of the citizenry in a society that aspires to be democratic.

Whether one thinks the politics–administration dichotomy has been well behind us since the last half of the 20th century or that it never was advocated in as simplistic a fashion as textbook treatments sometimes suggest, the fact remains that we still lack a generally accepted normative understanding of how politics *should* be accommodated in administrative practice. If politics with a small "p" cannot be fully separated from public administration—and we believe it cannot and *should not*—then the ways in which it should be employed need to be addressed. We believe that focusing on current, practicing public administrators may be the best way to stimulate a discussion about normative politics for public administration. Examining the work of living exemplars may be the best way to ground such a discussion.

We had an opportunity to examine Robertson's conduct over a period of approximately one year as part of an action research project that brought neighborhood councils in Los Angeles together with city departments to work out written agreements about service delivery in their areas.[1] Robertson participated in all of these sessions with his program managers. Since that time, we interviewed nine key people inside and outside the Los Angeles Department of Public Works,[2] and we also conducted two interviews with Robertson himself. In addition, we had opportunities to observe him in other settings, such as meetings of neighborhood councils[3] and the Congress of Neighborhood Councils,[4] as well as in guest lectures to students in the School of Policy, Planning, and Development at the University of Southern California.

Our conclusion, based on these sources of information, is that Robertson has honed his political skills into an art that holds in dynamic balance both the technical and the political dimensions

From *Public Administration Review,* 67, No. 5 (September/October 2007): 816–823. Copyright © 2007 American Society for Public Administration. Used by permission.

of public administration. His political behavior appears to be rooted externally in a respect for citizens and a serious commitment to their empowerment. Inside his department, Robertson's conduct seems to reflect a respect for his subordinates and a devotion to collaborative effort. We view both dimensions of his work as exemplifying democratic values that provide a normative foundation for the political conduct of public administrators. We shall now move on to tell Robertson's story as it has emerged through our observations and interviews, including selected vignettes to illustrate his patterns of work.

## RISING THROUGH THE RANKS

William Robertson presides over the City of Los Angeles' Bureau of Street Services. The bureau today consists of seven unique divisions that are charged with developing, constructing, and maintaining streets, sidewalks, and trees throughout the city. In total, the city maintains a 6,500-mile street system, with approximately 1,000 miles of failed streets. The total budget for the bureau is roughly $130 million annually, with a total staff of approximately 1,300.

Robertson's story is defined, in part, by his quick advancement through the leadership ranks in military and local government service. His story is further characterized by his independent-mindedness in work performance and career choice, his educational learning objectives without formal university education, and his choices to follow lessons and advice from people around him, including his mother. Throughout his military and professional careers, Robertson has developed and refined his general orientation to working with the public: They shouldn't be told lies, and honesty is the best policy.

Robertson's military service was marked by a rapid rise through the ranks. He enlisted in the Marine Corps; out of the 80 or so who were in each boot camp platoon, two or three were promoted early. After being chosen for advancement, Robertson was selected to lead a larger, more diverse group of men. This was his first experience leading a culturally and racially diverse group of people, as he had grown up and attended school in a predominantly white part of Los Angeles County. From there, Robertson was charged with leading a sniper group and, within two months, had his own squad in Vietnam.

Robertson believes the training and experience he gained in his military service provided a greater education than he could have received in a college classroom. For instance, Robertson reports that he learned a sense of responsibility—primarily to his military colleagues, but also to the organization. This lesson was applied recently during particularly bad winter rainstorms in the City of Los Angeles, a story we will return to later.

After completing his military service, Robertson returned to the United States and took a job as a salesman with a textile company, Milliken and Company, in South Carolina and Georgia. He worked there for three or four years but found that sales was "not my niche. I hated sales and didn't like lying to people." After this period, he returned to his childhood home of Los Angeles and bought a truck. For three or four years, he worked as a truck operator, driving through the 48 states. However, his independent trucking business did not last long; his mother did not like him doing that kind of work. At his mother's prompting, Robertson joined the City of Los Angeles' Bureau of Street Services.

Robertson's service in the bureau, like his service in the military, has been marked by rapid advancement. He first joined the bureau as a heavy-duty truck operator. After working for six months, he was tapped to serve as acting supervisor, a position he held for two years beginning in 1986. After this period, Robertson took the civil service test and placed at the top of the list. He went on to earn a street maintenance certificate at Los Angeles Trade Technical College. As a supervisor, he did not need this certification, but he chose to do so because of his interest in learning. He hoped to spread this interest to other people in the organization, which has been a challenging task. According to Robertson, "eighty-five percent of the workforce comes from the construction trade, and education is not viewed as helpful in their advancement."

This test achievement and certification gave him the knowledge and technical requirements to serve effectively as an emerging leader in the bureau. In combination with his military service, which Robertson has described as his college experience, he began his rapid advancement without formal university education.

Robertson's advancement put him in a variety of positions with different responsibilities, including participation in an effort to reorganize the bureau, which coincided with discussion of the neighborhood council system in 1998. He ultimately rose to become assistant director of the bureau under the directorship of Greg Scott. After Scott's retirement, a new director was named but retired quickly as a result of health concerns, and Robertson was subsequently promoted to director. This last advancement was awarded to Robertson because of his proven ability to get the job done, work with competing interests, and satisfy multiple needs. One informant reported that he had been impressed with Robertson's rise through the ranks and the way he had proven himself along the way. Thus, no national search was conducted for the director's position when Robertson was there with all the necessary skills. In all, Robertson went from heavy-duty truck operator to bureau director in 18 years. According to Robertson, "People wait this long to become supervisor."

Robertson's leadership continues to be recognized today. In 2006, he was elected president of the City of Los Angeles' General Manager's Association. Chosen by peers who head other departments in the city, Robertson hopes to use his two-year term to break down walls between departments and to focus on solving the city's problems collaboratively.

## POLITICS WITH INTEGRITY: THE CIRCLE OF PARTICIPATION

Sherry Arnstein's ladder of participation (1969) depicts the way in which citizen participation was typically framed during the 1960s: as a zero-sum power struggle between government and citizens. Providing more participation was viewed as empowering the people at the expense of administrative and political power. As one moves up the ladder from manipulation at the bottom to citizen control at the top, citizens gain increasing increments of power as government gives it up. From an administrative perspective, the dominance of efficiency and technical skill gives way to citizen discretion.

We suggest revising Arnstein's ladder to more appropriately reflect the movement toward the concepts of collaborative governance and management by turning the vertical ladder into a circle. From the perspective of collaboration, encouraging citizen participation in the public management process is not a zero-sum but a positive-sum game. A public executive such as Robertson can gain power by working with instead of against the citizenry. Through collaboration, citizens can introduce their particular knowledge and skills into the work of managing the delivery of public services. The public executive is in a key position to encourage this kind of collaboration by employing the approaches reflected in the steps of the circle of participation.

By further conceptualizing the ladder as a circle, we can visualize an administrator standing not on a rung of the ladder trying to work with citizens, employees, elected officials, and other stakeholders through a single approach, but rather on a platform at the center of the loop. From here, the administrator can easily combine strategies, such as manipulation and citizen control, and move quickly from one strategy to another depending on the needs of a situation. Figure 5.1 illustrates the circle of participation.

The stories recounted here show how Robertson has employed these approaches to produce technically superior and responsive services for multiple stakeholders. First, we relate stories of Robertson's interactions with citizens, particularly representatives of neighborhood councils in

Figure 5.1   **Combining Strategies in the Circle of Participation**

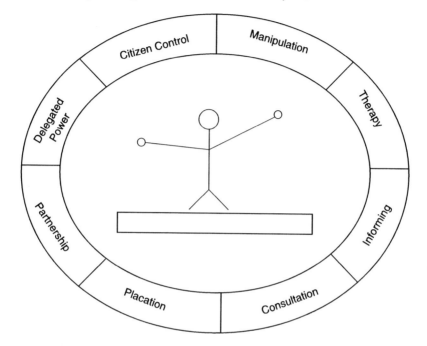

the City of Los Angeles. In these stories, we see how Robertson uses manipulation to convert an angry crowd into one seeking ways to help him acquire new resources for his bureau. We also see how he is able to placate citizens through information sharing and education, as well as how he partners with citizens to develop closer, more trusting relationships. These relationships, once formed, allow him to convince citizens to serve as champions for his bureau with elected officials, which can be seen as a vital resource in bureaucratic governance (Hill 1991).

Next, we relate stories of Robertson's interactions with his subordinates. His actions here reveal the use of partnership formation and delegation of power to obtain desired outcomes for the city. We also see how he manages relationships in times of turmoil and mourning through the use of information sharing and therapy. Following these stories, we offer additional examples of partnering and delegating power, though with a focus on relationships with other city managers outside his bureau.

Operating within the circle of participation, a successful administrator is one who can use each of the strategies identified by Arnstein to meet the conditions and demands presented by a multitude of stakeholders. We show how Robertson successfully operates within this circle through his actions and interactions in the City of Los Angeles' Bureau of Street Services. Based on our interviews and observations, we conclude that Robertson does not treat any single stakeholder group with a single strategy. Rather, across stakeholders, he relies on the entire toolbox of strategies to achieve his desired outcomes of technically superior and responsive service delivery.

## INTERACTIONS WITH CITIZENS

In our interviews with Robertson and others, we solicited stories about him that might reveal his character, motivation, and work style.[5] Three stories provide insights into his work with citizens through the Los Angeles neighborhood council system. Citywide neighborhood councils were incorporated into the city charter approved by voters in June 1999.[6] Many city department heads viewed this new institution for citizen participation with some wariness and skepticism; it was seen, according to one official, as an initiative that asked department officials to do more without additional funding. Robertson, however, enthusiastically embraced the new neighborhood councils from their inception.

One of Robertson's general manager peers in another department told us that Robertson attends more neighborhood council meetings than any other general manager, usually at night and scattered over the 470 square miles of the city. When we asked Robertson about this, he agreed that it may be true. What is his motivation for engaging in this time-consuming and sometimes stressful practice? According to Robertson, it is important for professionals in government to meet citizens on their own ground to show that they care and that they are willing to work with them to solve their problems and respond to their concerns. He wants to move beyond simply telling citizens that he cannot do what they want or that he does not have the money in his budget. Robertson believes that if he shows a genuine interest in finding ways to respond to demands in creative ways, or to offer interim solutions, people will accept that he cannot always do all they may want from his department. They are more likely to trust him if he shows that he takes their requests seriously and tries to respond in some way, however limited that may be.

Robertson maintains that managers need to exercise leadership in working with citizens and explains that one thing he learned in the Marine Corps is that a good leader cannot lead from behind. Leaders must be out on the front lines with the troops. He tries to teach his assistant directors, Ron Olive and Nazario Saueceda, the importance of engaging with citizens in accomplishing the work of the department by insisting that they join him on his visits with the neighborhood councils. Robertson similarly seeks to include lower-level employees in meetings with the public in order to mentor them and "to push our employees to confront their fears of working with the public." They see their boss dealing with citizen hostility and conflict, achieving constructive ends, and building trusting relationships. In this way, he models the conduct of the "citizen administrator" (Cooper 2006) for his subordinates.

### Combining Citizen Control and Manipulation of Citizens

As Robertson engages with the neighborhood councils, he explains that he views honesty as central. He listens patiently to people's demands, complaints, and suggestions. He tells people what he can and cannot do and why. At times, he finds himself challenging citizens on something they may have misrepresented. Sometimes these responses become opportunities to educate citizens about how their government works. For example, when he realized that citizens lacked essential information about how street resurfacing is done, he prepared a presentation titled "Professor Pothole Presents: Everything You Always Wanted to Know about Selecting Streets for Resurfacing in Your Neighborhood Council."

Robertson views this kind of honest exchange and sharing of information as part of the process of empowering citizens. Along with honesty, he uses a lot of humor and self-effacement. He never prepares speeches in advance but rather tries to grapple with whatever is presented to him at a particular time and place. Several of our informants reported they had observed Robertson in these community situations and indicated they had always been deeply impressed by his ability to walk into a room full of angry people and leave them at the end of the meeting thanking him and ready to collaborate.

One informant even reported a standing ovation after one such session, at which, according to Robertson, another public official had earlier been looking for the nearest exit out of fear of the hostile crowd. He accomplished this by being open and honest with the citizens and speaking to them without using technical language. He manipulated them by fueling anger and disappointment about service delivery, but he channeled this anger to create advocates for his bureau with elected officials. This strategy paid dividends, as seen in a second story.

In partnership with former Los Angeles mayor James Hahn, Robertson developed a program that earmarked $100,000 annually for each of the 87 neighborhood councils existing at the time to allocate among the services provided by the Bureau of Street Services. Furthermore, instead of simply announcing this offer, Robertson organized seven meetings in different areas of Los Angeles to meet with neighborhood council leaders to explain how this new program would work and to get their suggestions. Robertson appeared at all of these meetings and stayed until the end, even if it was quite late and even if only a handful of people remained. When asked why he had made this offer, Robertson said it was his way of showing the councils that they are important and have a role to play in shaping service delivery. It was a step toward sharing power, if even in a relatively small way.

### Partnership with Citizens

The third story concerns Robertson's effort to find office space for a neighborhood council that had none. The city provides $50,000 annually to each council for basic expenses, but that does not go very far if a large portion is expended on office rent, so some councils try to obtain donated space. One of our informants was a neighborhood council board member who told us that when Robertson learned that her council had been unsuccessful in finding free space, he took the initiative to locate a room for an office in one of his facilities in that neighborhood council area. When asked why he had gone out of his way to do this, Robertson explained that it was a way of showing respect for the efforts of hundreds of citizens who work all day and then take on responsibilities for their neighborhoods during their free time. He viewed having office space as one of the essential requirements for carrying out their work and contributing to their empowerment.

### Summary of Citizen Interactions

These three stories of Robertson's interactions with citizens reflect his ability to use multiple tools in his efforts to manage relationships with his stakeholders. He uses the art of manipulation to calm a crowd and turn their anger into power based on new information that he provides about the lack of resources or other constraints preventing his bureau from meeting their needs. As he stated in the context of the Collaborative Learning Project (see note 1) and interactions with neighborhood councils, "There is not a lot I can do from this office, but I can help tell other people what to tell other people to tell the mayor." By wooing citizens with office space, information, or increased say in how street funds are allocated in a neighborhood, Robertson creates advocates for his bureau. An outcome of Robertson's activity is increased funds for the Bureau of Street Services through the city's participatory budget process. Increased funds, in turn, help give citizens what they want and expect.

## INTERACTIONS WITH SUBORDINATES

We have already described how Robertson mentors his subordinates in his interactions with members of the public. That anecdote illustrated how he pushes his employees to embrace the conflict that is inherent in the political process; in doing so, he leads by example and develops relationships with his subordinates using the same tools in the circle of participation.

Two stories reveal how Robertson engages with his subordinates using a variety of tools, such as therapy, partnership, and delegated power. The first entails his leadership during a set of resource-intensive, catastrophic, and deadly storms during the 2005 winter season; the second entails his public response to the deaths of two Bureau of Street Services employees who were murdered at a bureau yard.

### Combining Partnership and Delegated Power with Subordinates

In the winter of 2005, Los Angeles was hit by a series of heavy rainstorms that flooded streets, deteriorated infrastructure, caused devastating mudslides, and opened sinkholes on public road-ways. Driving north–south just west of downtown Los Angeles required drivers to navigate a rushing body of water at the convergence of hillsides that are part of the urban landscape. Bureau employees worked in 12-hour shifts to respond to storm-related incidents.

Throughout this winter season, Robertson worked without a day off and on the street with his crew. One informant described seeing Robertson at this time "drenched in water." He worked alongside his employees in the rain, mud, and cold. His motivation to be out front in the storms— rather than in a central office—was based on his desire to lead by example.

Robertson's Marine Corps training taught him that good leaders cannot lead from the back; they need to be out in front with the troops. By doing so, Robertson seeks to accomplish two things: (1) to develop future leaders for the bureau and (2) to make more informed decisions about what the bureau needs to do on the ground. In developing future leaders, Robertson, again recalling his Marine Corps experience, knows that if he falls, the organization needs to continue functioning smoothly and without interruption. "If I die tomorrow," Robertson reflects, "Nazario will step into my office, and nobody would know I was there."

The second goal of being out in front with the troops is to acquire the most up-to-date information that is observed firsthand rather than information that is filtered through a reporting mechanism. Information acquired firsthand is grounded in the real experiences of his crew, which include observations of the challenges of accomplishing certain tasks.

In putting himself in front of his troops, Robertson has grown to know his employees by name, and they know him in the same way. One informant reported that Robertson expects integrity from all bureau employees, and he seeks to deliver the same. As such, a partnership develops between superior and subordinate that builds trust, ensures open communication, and facilitates mutual respect up and down the hierarchy. Given this orientation toward working with his subordinates, Robertson was naturally devastated when two employees were murdered in February 2005 at one of his yards.

### Therapy and Information Sharing in the Face of Tragedy

On Thursday, February 24, 2005, a city maintenance worker fatally shot two employees at a city maintenance yard. One employee was the worker's supervisor; he was the target of the attack, which followed a dispute regarding work performance. The other employee was a fellow street worker, who likely was in the wrong place at the wrong time. A third employee found the bodies in the early evening of that same day.

The incident occurred in the middle of the winter storms that had Robertson and all of his em-ployees working long days without much rest. The call came with the news while Robertson was en route from one worksite to another. He quickly changed direction and went to the scene of the murders. Privately, Robertson reflected on how he had other people to lean on. He experienced a sense of guilt, asking, "What could I have done differently to save these lives?" Publicly, Robertson stressed to bureau employees that the most important assets for the bureau are "the people who work for us." He emphasized that the bureau is a "family," a fact that he felt he was able to talk about more openly than other agency directors because he had come up through the ranks.

The murders came quickly on the heels of another tragic incident in which a street worker fell into a sinkhole during the storms and died. His response to this incident was to get out in front of any rumors that might circulate about the death of the employee with a full report about what had occurred. He gave all employees—at all levels of the organization—the freedom to seek counseling, take time off, or take any other action necessary to heal. Coming from a street worker's background, Robertson actively discouraged field crews from refusing counseling for fear of being labeled a "sissy."

### Summary of Interactions with Subordinates

Overall, in his interactions with subordinates, Robertson seeks to lead by example and to develop strong, mutually supportive relationships across all levels of the organization. These relationships are defined by partnerships in which Robertson actively consults with his subordinates, empathizes with them to give opportunities for reflection and healing, and informs them of bureau policies without concern for rank. He empathizes with employees as someone who came up through the ranks and offers them opportunities to make their own decisions for their own health and for the mission of the bureau. Without this mutual respect, Robertson believes that employees would have no incentive to follow his leadership, thus limiting his ability to communicate to citizens that he is doing everything he can given current resources to meet their expectations. We see similar cultivation of relationships across agencies as well.

## INTERACTIONS WITH OTHER MANAGERS

Crises such as storms highlight the exemplary traits of leaders that might be overlooked in otherwise normal settings. The stories reported here with respect to subordinate interactions are set within the context of a crisis situation, but Robertson's behaviors and actions are not restricted to crises. The importance of relationship management for Robertson can also be seen in his interactions with his general manager peers. Here again, we see behavior oriented toward partnership. In this example, Robertson and his bureau were delegated some new responsibilities. It was hoped that the acceptance of such new responsibility would allow the favor to be returned at some future point if needed.

### Partnering and Delegating Power across Government Agencies

One example is the case of dealing with a service problem that Robertson's bureau could handle functionally but that was under the jurisdiction of another department. The same rains that had allowed Robertson's leadership qualities to shine in 2005 also allowed city trees to grow at a faster rate than normal. Specifically, older or heritage trees grew faster than was typical, and Department of Recreation and Parks employees had to work fast to cut the limbs; however, some trees were chopped in the wrong way. As they grew, the limbs were weaker and threatened to fall, causing possible injury to person and property. Given this situation, a request was made of Robertson by the general manager of the Department of Recreation and Parks to provide workers from his bureau to help trim the trees appropriately. Without hesitation, Robertson agreed.

Robertson reported the situation as involving a choice. On one hand, he and the general manager could wait for the city council to authorize funds to perform the tree maintenance. Alternatively, he could move forward without authorization. He chose the latter option and adopted a perspective that he feels all city managers should adopt—a citywide perspective that is not bound by departmental lines of jurisdiction. If the two managers had waited for city council authorization, damage could have been done to person or property from the falling limbs. By adopting a citywide perspective and accepting responsibility for the quality of life of all aspects of the city, Robertson demonstrated a manner of working collaboratively and across boundaries.

## USING MULTIPLE STRATEGIES TO ACHIEVE TECHNICAL EFFICIENCY

In addition to successfully managing relationships with a diverse set of stakeholders, Robertson promotes technical efficiency. He uses the relationships he has developed among elected officials and citizens to acquire new resources in order to improve service delivery. For instance, one technology that Robertson has successfully promoted is known as Cold In-Place Recycling, which is estimated to be 25 percent to 35 percent more effective than conventional technologies. With this technology, road surfaces are reconstructed at a single time with a single piece of equipment, which, Robertson notes, is much less invasive in neighborhoods.

Another example is the design-build process, in which bureau engineers work in conjunction with other workers to design and build a street project, without depending on the longer design period required by the Bureau of Engineering. By integrating both steps, problems that emerge during the project building process can be addressed on the spot by designers.

Despite earning victories with elected officials to acquire new technologies and attempt new processes, Robertson recognizes that politics can interfere with technical efficiency. For instance, he describes how the paving and maintenance of streets in the city's neighborhoods cannot be completely efficient when decisions about which streets get paved are made by each of the 15 city council members rather than by human experts or computer modeling. A more efficient method would employ a grid system in which streets in a well-defined grid are identified for maintenance each fiscal year using an objective calculation system that considers road condition, road use, and other such factors. Politics can rectify inefficiencies, however, and Robertson urges neighborhood council leaders to select contiguous streets for maintenance using their $100,000 allocation. In this way, he educates neighborhood council leaders, acts honestly, and manipulates them to achieve the technical goals he sets for himself and his bureau.

## LESSONS LEARNED

What emerged from our interviews with Robertson and others who have worked with him as neighborhood council board members, elected officials, general manager peers, and subordinates is an image of a professional manager in the best sense who understands the politics of administering a very large city agency that touches the lives of citizens daily. He never sacrifices technical expertise for the sake of pacifying irate citizens or politicians, and he pays attention to the ways in which his power and knowledge can be put into the service of the people of Los Angeles. He understands that technical prowess alone will not serve the ends of democratic governance, and so he sees the necessity of building trust and collaboration with those he serves.

Robertson values partnership and knows that sharing information in a nonpatronizing manner plays a large part in achieving that goal. He exercises control as the director of the Los Angeles Bureau of Street Services but believes that control must be tempered. It must be based on professional advice and information but also must provide options and information to support citizen discretion. Consultation with citizens as partners is important for the long-range good of the department and the people of Los Angeles.

Robertson's political side can also be seen in the way he handles rules. In one interview, he opined that although rules are important, there are too many of them. He maintains that an administrator in his position must have the flexibility to get to the point of a policy in any particular situation. He insists that he never violates city policy, but he bends the rules if necessary to get to the goal of the policy. He suggests that he "can go political behind the scenes" if necessary but only to benefit the community. He is adamant about not doing so just to make elected officials look good, nor to enrich his bureau's coffers while ignoring the real needs of neighborhoods.

What about the legitimate uses of manipulation for the sake of citizen empowerment? Can such a perspective be acceptable in democratic public administration? Robertson explains that the manipulation of citizens is more legitimate when it is used to open minds. He may massage the emotions of an angry crowd in a community meeting to get them to put aside tunnel vision, prepare them to receive new information, or arrive at a fresher point of view. Robertson may woo citizens to get them to abandon a preconceived notion of the government as the enemy in order to create a more collaborative relationship. Robertson admits to engaging in this kind of manipulation as a legitimate part of the politics of administration. Is it? We think so, as long as it can stand the test of publicity. Full transparency about the motivations for his actions must accompany his decisions and behaviors, and we find this to be the case with Robertson. To conclude, we offer the following lessons for public administrators based on William Robertson's example:

1. Exemplary administrators pursue the interests of their agency, as well as the people whom the agency serves, by cultivating relationships with different classes of stakeholders, including citizens, elected officials, and administrator colleagues.
2. Successful administrators are able to use multiple political tools in the process of cultivating relationships with stakeholders, including the art of manipulation, placation, partnership, and other forms of empowerment.
3. Respected administrators exercise their political skills transparently and without bias.
4. Trusted administrators practice honesty and integrity while expecting the same from those around them.

These are only a few of the lessons that we feel readers can identify in their own reading about Robertson. We hope our observations can be used as a starting point to think more systematically about a normative understanding of administrative politics that is consistent with democratic governance.

## NOTES

1. Collaborative Learning Project is an action research program designed to facilitate collaboration between neighborhood councils and city agencies in Los Angeles. It involved a process called the Learning and Design Forum, which convened participants for three half-day Saturday sessions spaced about one month apart (Kathi and Cooper 2005). Findings from the project suggest it is possible to open or democratize city bureaucracy, but barriers remain, such as the low capacity of neighborhood councils, the culture of agencies, and the influence of elected officials (Cooper and Bryer 2007).

2. These individuals include Ed Ebrahimian, director of the Bureau of Street Lighting, Los Angeles Department of Public Works; Yolanda Fuentes, commissioner of the Board of Public Works; Jacob Motta, constituent services director for Los Angeles mayor Antonio Villaraigosa; Diann Corral, member of the Mid-Town North Hollywood Neighborhood Council; Greig Smith, member of the Los Angeles City Council; Daniel Hackney, former Bureau of Sanitation liaison to neighborhood councils and senior environmental policy analyst with the mayor's office; John Mukri, general manager of the Los Angeles Department of Recreation and Parks; Theresa Tracy, superintendent the Bureau of Street Services; and James Hahn, former mayor of Los Angeles.

3. A citywide system of neighborhood councils was created with the passage of a new charter for the City of Los Angeles in 1999. Today, there are 87 neighborhood councils in the city. Each council defines its own neighborhood borders and elects its own volunteer board. According to the charter, councils act as advisory bodies. Information about the system is available from the Civic Engagement Initiative at the University of Southern California (Cooper and Musso 1999; Musso, Weare, and Cooper 2004; Musso et al. 2004).

4. The city charter requires that a Congress of Neighborhood Councils be convened twice each year. To date, this Congress has served as an opportunity for neighborhood leaders to meet each other, share information, and learn from public administrators.

5. As noted by one of the peer reviewers of this article, one should reveal the flaws and weaknesses of anyone who is presented as an exemplar. Without showing "warts and all," credibility suffers because we are all painfully aware of the lack of human perfection. We very much agree with this point of view and aggressively attempted to draw out this kind of material in our interviews. However, we uncovered little beyond some minor complaints about favoring one part of his department over another. This may be one of the methodological challenges of identifying living administrators as exemplars.

6. See note 3 for a description of the neighborhood council system.

# REFERENCES

Arnstein, Sherry R. 1969. A Ladder of Citizen Participation. *Journal of the American Institute of Planners* 35 (4): 216–24.

Cooper, Terry L. 2006. *The Responsible Administrator: An Approach to Ethics for the Administrative Role.* 5th ed. San Francisco: Jossey-Bass.

Cooper, Terry L., and Thomas A. Bryer. 2007. *Collaboration between Los Angeles City Departments and Neighborhood Councils: Findings and Recommendations from the Collaborative Learning Project.* Los Angeles: Urban Initiative, University of Southern California.

Cooper, Terry L., and Juliet Musso. 1999. The Potential for Neighborhood Council Involvement in American Metropolitan Governance. *International Journal of Organization Theory and Behavior* 1 (2): 199–232.

Hill, Larry B. 1991. Who Governs the American Administrative State? A Bureaucratic-Centered Image of Governance. *Journal of Public Administration Research and Theory* 1 (3): 261–94.

Kathi, Pradeep Chandra, and Terry L. Cooper. 2005. Democratizing the Administrative State—Connecting Neighborhood Councils and City Agencies. *Public Administration Review* 65 (5): 559–67.

Musso, Juliet, Chris Weare, and Terry L. Cooper. 2004. *NPP Diversity Report.* Los Angeles: Neighborhood Participation Project, University of Southern California.

Musso, Juliet, Chris Weare, Kyu-Nahm Jun, and Alicia Kitsuse. 2004. *Representing Diversity in Community Governance: Neighborhood Councils in Los Angeles.* Los Angeles: Urban Initiative, University of Southern California.

# 6

# LILLIAN BORRONE

## Weaving a Web to Revitalize Port Commerce in New York and New Jersey

### Hindy Lauer Schachter

In the mid-1980s, the Port of New York and New Jersey was steadily losing ground to competitors in cargo trade (Lueck 1986). A decade later, the organization crowed that it was the busiest port on the East Coast, by a wide margin (Port Commerce 1998). What caused the comeback? Robert Gleason (2000), secretary-treasurer of the International Longshoremen's Association, attributed the shift to Lillian Borrone's becoming director of the Port Commerce Department in 1988. Her vision and management style propelled newfound cooperation as a route to a successful future.

Among transportation executives, Lillian Borrone stands out as a pioneer who turned around a faltering entity through new ideas, creative marketing, and coalition building. She was able to spearhead the port's recovery while working in a field that even today remains a male-dominated bastion (Bowling et al. 2006). Her story is worth telling as an example of successful public sector leadership by an executive who argued that "the social complexity of our transportation problems requires a more open and social process to produce robust solutions" (Borrone 2005, 16). Her career path also serves as a key information source for learning the strategies women have used to advance in the transportation field (Schachter 2005).

Some feminist scholars have argued that because of female experiences as nurturers, many—although not all—women have a relational rather than an individualistic approach to organizational leadership (e.g., Burnier 2003; Hendricks 1992). Such an approach, which also is practiced by some men, gives organizational participants a sense that decisions should be made through a rich web of relationships rather than by a single executive standing in splendid isolation at the hierarchy's apex. Mary Parker Follett (1924, 1927) articulated an early version of this approach when she posited that change in organizations comes through a genuine interweaving or interpenetrating of understanding among people in groups rather than through a single person's fiat. She noted that this conception makes everyone's work important because the insights of anyone—high or low in society's pecking order—can help weave the guiding will that runs the organization.

Lillian Borrone's approach to management exemplified relationally anchored behavior. In interviews, people who worked with her often commented on her ability to build networks and care about the opinions of multiple stakeholders. This case study suggests some ways that this approach helped her revitalize the port.

## EARLY LIFE AND CAREER

Lillian was born the first child of Santo and Lillian Cerza on August 13, 1945. She spent her child-hood in several New Jersey towns, first in Paterson, and then in Totowa and Pompton Plains. At her birth, her father was a member of the merchant marine; later he came ashore and worked in heating and ventilating. Her mother was a teacher. Both parents were active in community affairs and the local Democratic Party. As a child, Lillian began her public life distributing campaign literature in her neighborhood. Like many women who entered transportation agencies, she did not originally envision such a career. She majored in political science at American University. During her last term in 1968, she took a job with the Council of Governments in Washington, D.C., where she had the good fortune to work under Trudy Muranyi, the only female manager on the organization's technical side. Trudy demanded excellence while serving as a model of how a woman could advance in transportation. Working as a transportation technician, Lillian helped plan roadways for the new metro and instantly fell in love with the field.

When Lillian realized she could not advance in the organization without a natural science degree, she moved to the U.S. Department of Transportation's urban mass transportation unit. Her job in the technical assistance group was to help local governments make decisions about bankrupt transit systems. Traveling around the country, Lillian got to know key people in urban transit. One of her strengths throughout her career was that she was able to piece together a network of contacts that her subsequent colleagues considered unparalleled. Later, when she became a high-level manager, she was able to call on these contacts to help solve problems.

In 1970, Lillian married Michael Liburdi, an operating engineer, and moved back to New Jersey. From 1970 to 1978, she worked for the Port Authority of New York and New Jersey, a bistate organization that provided opportunities to administer multiple transportation modes: aviation, rail and water. She began to stake out what management theorists call a protean career (e.g., Hall 1996), moving in and out of different jobs to acquire specific abilities. Although an early supervisor told her that facilities management was no place for a woman, she had the courage to disregard his advice. She left a position as rail programs coordinator to take rotating assignments managing the George Washington Bridge and Journal Square bus stations, and thus she became the first woman to administer Port Authority facilities. This experience gave her line credentials, an important prerequisite for moving into the executive ranks. She participated in professional associations, chairing committees for the American Public Transit Association and increasing her network of colleagues. She got technical credentials by earning a civil engineering master's degree from Manhattan College. This degree increased her credibility with transportation administrators.

From 1978 to 1981, she returned to the Department of Transportation, where she worked as an associate and then deputy administrator of the Urban Mass Transportation Administration. In 1982, she returned to the Port Authority when Peter Goldmark, the executive director, asked her to analyze the role of aviation in a newly deregulated environment. After working for two years as the aviation department's assistant director, she became director of the Port Authority's management and budget department.

## PORT COMMERCE

On June 20, 1988, Lillian became director of Port Commerce, which owns and operates maritime properties, including Port Newark and the Elizabeth-Port Authority Marine Terminal in New Jersey, as well as the Howland Hook Marine and the Brooklyn Piers/Red Hook Container Terminals in New York. Her new position gave her direct line authority over one of the Northeast's most extensive trade and transportation networks. She became the first woman to head a Port Authority line division and the first woman to head any of the world's major ports.

Lillian was now responsible for the harbor-wide channel, terminal, and transportation infrastructure master planning needed to support all the Port Authority's maritime facilities. The responsibility thrust her into a politically dynamic environment. As part of a bistate agency, Port Commerce must be sensitive to many stakeholders, including the governors of New York and New Jersey, each of whom appoints half of the Port Authority's board of commissioners; federal agencies such as the U.S. Coast Guard, Army Corps of Engineers, and Environmental Protection Agency; New York and New Jersey state agencies; terminal host cities; maritime unions, shippers and environmental groups with their conflicting agendas; and the private companies that lease terminal space and to which the authority subcontracts operations, such as Express Rail.

By 1988, global trade had created a flow of goods from country to country that required aquatic transport. The Port Authority of New York and New Jersey was a gateway in the supply chain of international trade, but a number of problems hindered its ability to play a dominant role. Ship size was growing, and increasingly larger megaships needed deeper channels than the port could supply without constant dredging of its berths. There was concern about the port's ability to use the most efficient intermodal transportation; at transfer points, merchandise shifted to land transport by truck rather than rail, even though rail transport had higher container-handling capacity and was environmentally preferable. The port centered on European and Latin American cargo and had no viable plan for capturing the increasingly important Asian traffic.

Lillian Borrone (2005) once said that she never ran away from a problem of any sort. During her tenure, she faced these problems and successfully addressed each dilemma. The port dredged relevant channels from 35 feet to 45 feet to allow passage of megaships, pioneered an intermodal rail facility at its Elizabeth, New Jersey, marine terminal, and increased the number of imports from Asia. Cargo volume increased by more than 50 percent, sustaining New York and New Jersey's position as the premier East Coast port.

Lillian's ability to turn things around stemmed from her skill in weaving a web of relationships to deal with people both inside and outside her agency. She was able to motivate the people who worked for her to develop excellent ideas, and she was able to get major external stakeholders to put aside their differences and cooperate for the good of the port. She was fluent both at conceiving and implementing innovation. Keohane (2005) argues that it is rare to find a leader who has a rhetorical gift and the ability to be a good listener; Lillian possessed this rare combination. The following three subsections show how she used her skills to handle a trio of contentious issues.

## DREDGING

The dredging issue represented a complex problem. As the harbor's natural depth at Port Newark/ Elizabeth was approximately 19 feet—too shallow for large cargo vessels—maintenance dredging of berths was an operational necessity even in the 1970s and 1980s. With a U.S. Army Corps of Engineers permit, the port continually dredged selected berths and disposed of the material at the Mud Dump, a federally regulated ocean site off the coast of Sandy Hook, New Jersey. As ships became ever larger, they needed deeper water for their hulls.

Concerns developed when tests done as part of the 1990 permit renewal process discovered trace amounts of dioxin and other contaminants in dredged sediments. At the time, no federal standard existed to assess their food chain impacts, but concern grew that toxic substances could accumulate in fish if the port placed the material in the ocean. Some environmental groups opposed any further activity until more was known about the consequences.

No conceivable solution to this issue maximized all positive values. At one level, the issue pitted the port's ocean commerce and its impact on the region's economic vitality against the possible environmental problems caused by dredging. The International Longshoreman's Association, shippers, and many local political leaders supported the port's need to dredge as an economic necessity. They saw the movement of goods and thousands of jobs at stake.

But failure to dredge also promised to bring its own negative environmental consequences. Aquatic shipment is the most environmentally benign transportation mode. If the Port of New York and New Jersey could not accommodate goods for Mid-Atlantic consumers and industries, these goods would enter at another port, perhaps Baltimore or Halifax, Nova Scotia. Trucks would then take the goods to the Mid-Atlantic region, thus generating air pollution and highway congestion in an area that already suffered from clogged roads (Wakeman and Costanzo 2004).

Tom Wakeman (2005), a dredging expert at Port Commerce, says that Lillian's framework for engaging the problem hinged on trying to do what was right for the environment and the port. She worked with scientists from the U.S. Army Corps of Engineers, New Jersey's Environmental Protection Agency, New York's Environmental Conservation Agency, and a number of academic centers—such as Rutgers University's Institute of Marine and Coastal Science—to learn how to stop pollutants from getting into the estuary, model the consequences of the dioxin already in place, and develop a range of acceptable dredged material disposal options. She initiated an assessment study that found that capping disposed material with clean sand reduced ocean disposal risks. She spoke with community groups and local political leaders about the issue, with an emphasis on coming together and "Weaving Environmental and Economic Needs into a Responsible Solution" (Liburdi 1994, 13). Her mantra was that all concerned parties had to come to the table to find answers that worked.

In 1993, the Corps of Engineers issued a permit to allow dredging and ocean disposal with capping of contaminated material. The port completed a round of dredging in September 1993, but the need for additional work was constant throughout the decade as the size of cargo ships continued to grow. Throughout the period, Lillian interacted with Corps of Engineers administrators and federal legislators. She tended to have good rapport with both these stakeholders because she based her ideas on voluminous study and showed energy and enthusiasm in presenting those ideas.

Unlike proponents of reinventing government, she did not see legislators as inhibiting managers from getting the job done or standing in the way of administration by experts. Instead, she saw the legislators as a gateway to public support, saying at one point, "We need a new unity between our transportation experts and our political and social leaders, who are skilled at reaching out for general public support and understanding" (Borrone 2005, 15). In addition, she noted that agencies need clarification through legislation of their roles and responsibilities (Liburdi 1994).

An important point that she tried to make in her presentations was that the port needed to know the rules of the game—to have some idea what amount of dredging would and would not be allowed in the coming years. Her efforts paid off when the port received a blueprint in 1996, the Corps of Engineers Dredged Material Management Plan, that identified permitted volumes of dredged materials until 2040.

The key issue now became where to place the dredged sediments. The port benefited from the simultaneous growth of a movement to slow suburban sprawl by reclaiming urban brownfields, vacant real property whose redevelopment is complicated by the presence of contaminants. Capped dredged material bound with dry concrete provided an environmentally sound, economically supportable way of reclaiming land for urban communities. When OENJ, a developer, approached Port Commerce with a proposal to use dredged material as structural fill, Lillian worked with local officials to craft win-win agreements that allowed the port to dispose of the sediments while furthering the economic revitalization of waterfront jurisdictions. Probably the most successful of the ensuing agreements was the use of dredged material to construct the 1.3 million-square-foot Jersey Garden Mall in Elizabeth, New Jersey—transforming a city dump into a revenue-producing property. Elizabeth's mayor, Christian Bollwage (2006), noted that in discussions of the project, Lillian always saw both sides of any issue and worked to find agreement and get the job done.

## INTERMODAL TRANSPORTATION

A port is a temporary platform for moving goods from ships to landside transport. Growth in intermodal cargo handling was essential for Port Commerce to have global gateway connectivity. Lillian took the position that improved rail transport was vital to moving international cargo once it left the harbor. The land transport system had to maintain pace with aquatic improvements, even though the area's policies to encourage global trade had outpaced policies regarding freight transportation supply (Borrone 2005).

When the 8-acre Express Rail terminal opened at Maher Terminals in 1991, the port acquired an in-house facility for moving containers from ship to train. Lillian quickly made the innovation popular by giving rebates to shippers who used rail rather than trucks to transport goods at least 260 miles within the United States or Canada. This Container Incentive Program worked. Express Rail progressed from handling 20,000 to 30,000 containers a year in the early 1990s to handling more than 200,000 containers a year today—about 15 percent of traffic (Maher 2005). In 1995, Port Commerce completed an expanded Express Rail site, four times as large as the original offering (Menon 1997).

## A NEW ROUTE

After World War II, the Port Authority of New York and New Jersey was North America's dominant port. It lost this status in the 1980s as commerce soared with Asia, principally Japan. Asian shippers sent merchandise to West Coast ports; trains then took the goods to East Coast locations.

In the mid-1980s, Frank Caggiano, a Port Commerce staff member, concluded that the center of Asian manufacturing would soon shift from Japan to China, India, and Southeast Asia's less expensive labor markets. He saw that it might be less costly for businesses in these areas to ship East Coast–destined merchandise through the Suez Canal in an all-water service going directly to the Middle Atlantic states.

In 1988, when Lillian became head of Port Commerce, she seized on the idea's potential even though it would require a major swing in logistical practice. She hired the consulting firms of Paul F. Richardson and Fredrick R. Harris to study whether production was shifting to Southeast Asia and asked the firms to compare cost factors between the traditional West Coast and Suez routes.

Two years later, the consultants reported that enough production existed in Southeast Asia to support an all-water service; cost advantages could exist for shippers at certain points. The problem then became how to convince the first shipping line to break with precedent and try the novel route. Lillian took on marketing the innovation, a task at which she excelled. She traveled to Asia and met with shippers and tried to get at least one to take ownership of the idea. A year after she began her campaign, Singapore's Neptune Orient Line inaugurated the first Suez service. By the late 1990s, seven lines were using it. The port entered into an unprecedented marketing alliance with the Egyptian Suez Canal Authority to publicize the route. Change came, at least in part, because Lillian was able to adapt her thinking to new realities on the ground and convince other players to accept a similar shift in thinking. A port public relations manager said that Lillian "was the best public relations person the port ever had" (Rosciszewski 2005).

## STAFF PARTICIPATION

Follett's (1924, 1927) web metaphor suggests that good ideas percolate from many points in an organization, not merely from the top of the hierarchy; departments that encourage staff participation are often likely to spawn a greater number of innovative ideas than units in which the manager makes all decisions unilaterally. People who worked for Lillian at Port Commerce cite her respect for staff as a spur to their creativity. Victoria Kelly (2005), a junior employee in the 1980s, remembers Lillian conducting meetings in an egalitarian fashion, not as if she alone had the correct answers. In that atmosphere, Kelly always felt that there was no limit on what she could accomplish. Tom Wakeman (2005) joked that she gave people enough rope to hang themselves—or succeed. Her executive secretary, Jacqueline Grossgold (2005), said that she treated people at all levels of the hierarchy with the same respect, that "She took time to make you feel important." Dorothy Rosciszewski (2005) explained that Lillian listened to people; she was open to suggestions from her staff, which made her crew more creative. She let staff members participate in outside committees, whereas many other executives at her level always represented the port on those committees themselves. (At the same time, Lillian maintained a visible presence in professional organizations. She served as chair of the American Association of Port Authorities and of the Transportation Research Board's executive committee—the first woman to hold those posts.)

People remember Lillian as hard driving and perfectionist, setting high standards for herself and other people. This dual approach—respect and high expectations—led staff to develop many good ideas and share them with her, as in the Suez Canal route.

## GENDER AND WORK LIFE

As one of the first female transportation executives, Lillian had a remarkable opportunity to mentor women—an opportunity she fervently embraced. Victoria Kelly (2005) remembers Lillian pushing her to try her hand in a host of new areas, such as lease negotiation and facility management. Lillian then structured the experiences so that Kelly had support while learning. Having thoroughly mastered the field, Kelly became a Port Authority executive in her own right; she is now director of the tunnels, bridges, and terminals department.

Kate Ascher (2005), another Port Commerce employee, says that Lillian attracted capable women and supported them. She gave them informal coaching, helped them understand their own strengths and weaknesses, and offered them contacts for career discussions. The U.S. Department of Transportation's Christina Casgar (2005) says that Lillian "plowed back generously." Of course, Lillian also mentored male employees. Frank Caggiano (2006) recalls Lillian's steering him to broaden his résumé and include operations experience.

In her first stint at the Port Authority in 1978, Lillian helped create Women's Equity, an internal group to help prepare women for senior management positions. Initially, the creation of the group produced shock at the agency. In time, Women's Equity acquired enough legitimacy that senior male managers joined and gave their support.

In the late 1970s, Lillian helped create Women's Transportation Seminar, an international organization to advance female transportation careers through networking and skill acquisition. Over the next 30 years, she gave many presentations to the organization. In 2005, she facilitated a seminar for the New York chapter on the value of volunteering and networking, two areas she has always seen as crucial to career development.

Hale (1999) argues that it is important to understand how gender affects perception in concrete work situations. Because transportation is still male dominated, women leaders are often evaluated through gender stereotypes. Several people noted to me that Port Commerce stakeholders sometimes underestimated Lillian before they met her. When Lillian became port executive, one union leader asked a port employee, "Who is this girl and what can she know?" After he dealt with Lillian, he came to respect her understanding. Several people told me that Lillian was known as the "Queen of the Port"—a phrase that acknowledges her status and power but also focuses on her gender. (It is doubtful that earlier incumbents of her position were known as Port Kings.)

In the early phase of her career, Lillian suffered from discrimination, which was then prevalent in the field. Traveling in the Midwest for the Department of Transportation, she often faced mayors or council members who were shocked that a woman represented a federal agency on transit matters. Once she was excluded from an informal get-together held at a venue that did not admit women. Later, her organization apologized and she worked with the civil rights office to publicize that federal administrators should not do business in male-only clubs.

In her first stint at the Port Authority, she received a salary lower than that paid to male administrators at her level. When she returned to the Port Authority in 1982, she insisted on receiving equal pay. She took a playing field that was far from level and helped to straighten it out.

Gender-based perceptions also influenced the intersection of her career and personal life. Throughout most of the 20th century, virtually the only women able to make successful careers were women who did not marry. By the time Lillian entered the workforce, societal sanction against careers for married women had atrophied, but issues concerning how wives allocated their time still resonated for some people. Indeed, even today, women tend to work fewer hours at paid employment and more hours at home than men do (Buelens and Van den Broeck 2007).

Lillian's husband was supportive of her career in its early phases. Difficulties arose in the early 1980s, when she was in Washington, D.C., during her second stint at the Department of Transportation, and he wanted to return to New Jersey. She accepted his request and they returned to the Mid-Atlantic area, but later he saw her Port Commerce promotion as taking too much of her time, a complaint that a wife would be much less likely to make to her husband given society's different social expectations. The couple separated in 1988; Lillian married Edward Borrone in 1995.

Some port employees suggested that Lillian's gender facilitated behavior that was beneficial to the organization. These administrators saw her humane leadership style and interest in promoting positive feminine behavior traits that contrasted with the "lone wolf" management style more common among transportation men. Thus, these practitioners agreed with feminist scholars, who argue that the reality of women's lives leads many women to have a relational orientation to management.

## AN ACTIVE RETIREMENT

Lillian Borrone's retirement from the Port Authority in December 2000 did not end her public service career. In July 2001, President George W. Bush appointed her to the Commission on Ocean Policy, a body giving Congress recommendations on ocean use and sustainability. After the 9/11 attacks on the World Trade Center, Donald DiFrancesco, acting New Jersey governor, asked her to coordinate the Office of Recovery and Victim Assistance, a task she undertook from September 17 to December 31, 2001. In 2004, she became an inaugural member of the federal Homeland Security Science and Technology Advisory Committee. She currently chairs the Eno Transportation Foundation.[1]

While Lillian has provided excellent service in all these positions, her major legacy is fostering the transformation of New York and New Jersey's port into an exemplary international commerce platform. Her relational skills are widely credited as part of the ability set that helped her get this job done. A study of her accomplishments, therefore, adds some evidence to debates about how a manager's relations to affiliation and achievement interact in the workplace.

Some organizational behavior literature posits an either/or relationship between a manager's need to achieve and to relate well with other stakeholders. One textbook even says that organizations should be leery of hiring too many people with a high need for affiliation because such people are more concerned with getting along with others than performing tasks (George and Jones 2008). The advice seems to suggest that executives should hire men and women who do not particularly care about other people.

Lillian's career, on the other hand, suggests that weaving strong relational networks is a prerequisite to superior task performance in at least some situations. In interview after interview, respondents reported that she was very goal oriented and also very concerned with integrating the views of many people. She understood the importance of creating and building a team. Her success may embolden other administrators—male and female—to question whether the relationship between a concern for affiliation and performance is "either/or," or rather, as Lillian Borrone's career seems to imply, "both or neither."

## NOTE

1. Established in 1921, the Eno Transportation Foundation, named for William Phelps Eno, is a nonprofit organization dedicated to improving ground, air, and water transportation.

## REFERENCES

Ascher, Kate. 2005. Personal communication, September 26.
Bollwage, Christian. 2006. Personal communication, January 5.
Borrone, Lillian. 2005. Sparking the Globalized Trade and Transportation Connection: Supplying Freight System Responses to Global Trade Demands. Thomas B. Deen Distinguished Lecture, Transportation Research Board, January 10.
Bowling, Cynthia J., Christine A. Kelleher, Jennifer Jones, and Deil S. Wright. 2006. Cracked Ceilings, Firmer Floors, and Weakening Walls: Trends and Patterns in Gender Representation among Executives Leading American State Agencies, 1970–2000. *Public Administration Review* 66(6): 823–36.
Buelens, Marc, and Herman Van den Broeck. 2007. An Analysis of Differences in Work Motivation between Public and Private Sector Organizations. *Public Administration Review* 67(1): 65–74.
Burnier, DeLysa. 2003. Finding a Voice: Gender and Subjectivity in Public Administration Research and Writing. *Administrative Theory and Praxis* 25 (1): 37–60.
Caggiano, Frank. 2006. Personal communication, January 17.
Casgar, Christina. 2005. Personal communication, December 15.
Follett, Mary Parker. 1924. *Creative Experience*. New York: Longmans, Green.
———. 1927. The Meaning of Responsibility in Business Management. In *Business Management as a Profession,* edited by Henry C. Metcalf, 318–38. New York: A.W. Shaw.
George, Jennifer M., and Gareth R. Jones. 2008. *Understanding and Managing Organizational Behavior*. 5th ed. Upper Saddle River, NJ: Pearson Prentice Hall.
Gleason, Robert. 2000. Remarks delivered at Port Industry Day, Jersey City, NJ, October 5. http://ilaunion.org/speeches_portindustryday.asp [accessed September 12, 2005].
Grossgold, Jacqueline. 2005. Personal communication, November 9.
Hale, Mary. 1999. He Says, She Says: Gender and Worklife. *Public Administration Review* 59 (5): 410–24.
Hall, Douglas. 1996. Protean Careers of the 21st Century. *Academy of Management Executive* 10 (4): 8–16.
Hendricks, J.J. 1992. Women-Centered Reality and Rational Legalism. *Administration & Society* 23 (4): 455–70.
Kelly, Victoria. 2005. Personal communication, September 14.
Keohane, Nannerl. 2005. On Leadership. *Perspectives on Politics* 3 (4): 705–22.

Liburdi, Lillian. 1994. Regulated's Perspective—The Port Authority of New York and New Jersey. Paper presented at the Annual Meeting of the Transportation Research Board, January 11, Washington, DC. http://ntl.bts.gov/DOCS/DUP.html [accessed November 8, 2007].

Lueck, Thomas. 1986. New York Port Changes with Shifting Economy. *New York Times*, June 1.

Maher, M. Brian. 2005. Personal communication, November 10.

Menon, Chris. 1997. Smooth Operation at Express Rail. *Containerisation International* 30(2): 55, 57.

Port Commerce, Port Authority of New York/New Jersey. 1998. Port of NY/NJ Improvements Meant Banner Year in 1997. News release, March 27. http://www.panynj-gov/pr/98-40.html [accessed November 8, 2007].

Rosciszewski, Dorothy. 2005. Personal communication, September 29.

Schachter, Hindy Lauer. 2005. Successful Transportation Women in a Time of Downsizing. *Public Administration Quarterly* 28(4): 460–81.

Wakeman, Thomas. 2005. Personal communication, September 28.

Wakeman, Thomas, and Thomas Costanzo. 2004. International Trade and Port Infrastructure Development. Unpublished paper, Port Authority of New York and New Jersey Waterways Development.

# 7

# LEADERSHIP AND CHANGE AT NASA

## Sean O'Keefe as Administrator

### W. HENRY LAMBRIGHT

Sean O'Keefe was administrator of the National Aeronautics and Space Administration (NASA) from December 2001 to February 2005, a little more than three years.[1] During that time, however, he achieved what Doig and Hargrove (1987) set as a key requirement for effective entrepreneurial leadership—the establishment of a new mission for his agency. His prime legacy to NASA was the presidential decision that the agency return to the moon and then eventually go to Mars. Called the Vision for Space Exploration, the decision was broader than the Moon-Mars initiative and entailed an ongoing quest to explore space through robotic and human flight. Moon-Mars was the focus, particularly the moon, but the key word in the decision was "exploration."

Getting NASA's manned space program out of Earth's orbit and back to the moon and its original exploration mission had been a goal of space enthusiasts since the end of the Apollo era. That O'Keefe steered this ambition into decision, and did so in so brief a tenure, was not only notable but also an unexpected accomplishment.

O'Keefe did not come to NASA as a space enthusiast. He was a generalist administrator whose expertise was financial management. He was sent to NASA primarily to mitigate the International Space Station's $4.8 billion overrun problem. He specifically rejected destination-driven goals (i.e., Moon-Mars) in favor of science-driven objectives in his first year (O'Keefe 2002).

Yet, in late 2003 and throughout 2004, he promoted the Vision for Space Exploration and thus the Moon-Mars goal, and he reorganized and reprioritized NASA to implement the new mission. What caused this change? And why did he also, at the same time, make a decision to terminate the immensely popular Hubble Space Telescope? Wasn't Hubble NASA's prime example of a science-driven mission? Wasn't it involved in exploration of the space frontier, albeit through non-manned means?

Behind the decisions to launch a new mission and to end an old one—two huge technological choices—was the *Columbia* space shuttle disaster of February 2003. That accident, which took seven astronauts' lives and resulted in a major investigation, seared O'Keefe to the core. Yet he dealt with the crisis and its aftermath with a rare blend of strength and compassion. *Columbia* hurt, but it also opened a window of opportunity for change. O'Keefe skillfully guided a presidential decision process to determine NASA's post-*Columbia* future. Not so skillfully, he dealt with Hubble.

From *Public Administration Review*, 68, No. 2 (March/April 2008): 230–240. Copyright © 2008 American Society for Public Administration. Used by permission.

In his first year, O'Keefe was widely seen as an incremental manager, competent but not a bold innovator. His critics called him a "bean counter," and he did not reject that characterization. In his third year, he led NASA in what was potentially transformative change. He was praised by space enthusiasts for the Moon-Mars decision and condemned by many of the same people for trying to kill Hubble. In between his first and third years, the *Columbia* disaster struck. That event defined O'Keefe's time at NASA and his approach to subsequent decisions.

## APPROACH

Our focus is on the NASA administrator in relation to policy innovation. Policy innovation can be conceived as moving through six stages: (1) agenda setting, (2) adoption, (3) early implementation, (4) execution, (5) evaluation and modification, and (6) later implementation to completion. Termination of the change process can occur at any point (deLeon 1999).

The model suggests incremental change. However, innovation in policy can be abrupt and discontinuous rather than gradual and evolutionary. Events can disrupt or, as some scholars say, "punctuate" a particular "equilibrium" of interests that control a policy. New actors can come into the fray. An occasion for discontinuous change opens. If there is an able policy entrepreneur present to take advantage of the fluid situation, he or she can redirect and enlarge policy in a substantial way (True, Jones, and Baumgartner 1999). Transformational change becomes possible.

Many administrators seek to introduce policy change and move it forward. Whether they are effective depends on many factors, only some of which they can control. Change, especially major change, requires the use of executive power. Leaders can use power deftly or clumsily. They can avoid or invite struggle. Influencing policy change requires skill in the right context of organization and times. It necessitates having allies with political clout. It also requires an element of luck (Doig and Hargrove 1987). Top administrators make controversial decisions and engage in contests with other political forces. As O'Keefe's experience shows, they win some and lose others.

## BACKGROUND AND STYLE

O'Keefe was 45 years old at the time of his appointment to NASA. Born in Monterey, California, he was the son of a naval officer who was also a nuclear submariner under the legendary Hyman Rickover. He received his bachelor's degree from Loyola University in New Orleans and then attended the Maxwell School of Syracuse University, where he earned a master of public administration degree in 1978. Awarded a Presidential Management Internship, he began his Washington career as a budget analyst for the U.S. Department of Defense. During the 1980s, he served on the staff of the Senate Appropriations Committee. There, he got to know a number of influential lawmakers, including Dick Cheney, Republican congressman from Wyoming. When George H.W. Bush became president in 1989, he appointed Cheney his secretary of defense. Cheney selected O'Keefe to serve as comptroller and chief financial officer of the Defense Department. When the U.S. Navy suffered a sexual harassment scandal (Tailhook) in 1992, Cheney sent O'Keefe to the navy as its secretary to fix the mess (Vistica 1995).

O'Keefe left Washington when the Bill Clinton administration took office in 1993. He worked first for Pennsylvania State University and then moved to an endowed chair at the Maxwell School, running the school's National Security Program. When George W. Bush became president in 2001, with Cheney as his vice president, O'Keefe returned to Washington as deputy director of the Office of Management and Budget (OMB). There, he addressed a $4.8 billion overrun on the International Space Station that the Bush administration had inherited from its predecessor. He negotiated a series of cuts and delays in various hardware components, along with an independent review of NASA's space station financial woes. In line with the independent panel's finding, he identified an explicit phase of construction during which NASA would restore its financial credibility (NASA 2001). This was called "U.S. Core Complete." It would be the period of approximately three years between the existing configuration (essentially a U.S.–Russian station "core") and later assembly, when other international partner modules would be linked. The United States would be launching certain components during U.S. Core Complete that would make subsequent international partner assembly possible. It was a time when NASA could get its financial house in order and get the station back on track. If NASA could not deal with its money and scheduling problems, the implicit threat was that the space station program would be halted in its smaller-scale form.

When NASA administrator Dan Goldin left the agency in November 2001, President Bush, on Cheney's recommendation, named O'Keefe to replace him. It was a surprise choice but generally well received by NASA watchers. O'Keefe had helped put NASA on "probation" to fix the station's overrun, and now he would be the "probation officer," supervising the reforms. No expert on space policy, O'Keefe was viewed askance by some scientists and engineers inside and outside the agency who wanted someone more technically astute and who visibly shared their enthusiasm for space. But all agreed that he brought something that NASA desperately needed: strong links to the Bush administration (Sietzen and Cowing 2004, 52).

What O'Keefe also provided was a well-honed management style. Intelligent, hardworking, steady, and nonideological, O'Keefe had developed experience as a generalist vis-à-vis specialists (i.e., the military) in the Defense Department. With his budgetary background, he cast a skeptical eye on technical proposals from program officials in the Department of Defense. Like the military services, NASA had historically emphasized technical excellence and subordinated cost considerations in promoting technical programs, particularly in human spaceflight. But O'Keefe believed that costs counted equally, and NASA needed to balance costs with the rewards of technology. Also, he urged NASA professionals to justify their programs in terms of broader benefits than that NASA should go into space "because it's there," or "manifest destiny," or "it's in our DNA." His predecessor, Goldin, had felt those values in his soul and expressed them, but not O'Keefe (Lambright 2007). He wanted more tangible rationales.

O'Keefe emphasized process in decision making. He especially linked policy and budget. The annual budget process created deadlines and pushed managers to consider programs, priorities, options, costs, and justifications. More than a budgeteer, O'Keefe thought beyond policy decisions to consider how to get them sold to political masters and then executed. O'Keefe believed that "management" was a legitimate field and that he could manage NASA even though he was not a longtime spaceman. A fast learner, he listened to and questioned subordinates. He brought a team-player approach to administrative leadership rather than coming across as a one-man show.

He preferred to work behind the scenes and was comfortable with politics inside the beltway. He knew Congress well and could deal one on one in private with lawmakers. He had former mentors and supporters in Congress, but there were also lawmakers (and media people) who chafed at his rhetorical style. He could speak in long, complex sentences that seemed to critics a form of "bureaucratese" intended to obscure rather than answer questions directly.

Like any leader, O'Keefe had his strengths and weaknesses, his supporters and detractors. To admirers, he was determined; to critics, he was stubborn. But few questioned his genuine devotion to public service. He took the practice (and theory) of public administration seriously. He wanted to do well at NASA. Many Washington insiders believed that if he succeeded at NASA, he might become defense secretary if President Bush won a second term and Donald Rumsfeld did not stay on at the Pentagon.

## SETTING AN AGENDA

O'Keefe arrived at NASA at the beginning of January 2002. He encountered a myriad of briefings at NASA's headquarters and in its various field centers. He soon began to mold his executive team. He chose Fred Gregory, then NASA associate administrator for space flight, for the deputy administrator slot. Gregory was a former U.S. Air Force flier and NASA astronaut. He chose Bill Readdy, who had worked as deputy to Gregory and who at one time had been a naval aviator and NASA astronaut, to take Gregory's position. He brought over from the OMB key officials with whom he had worked, notably Steve Isakowitz, the OMB's top budget examiner for NASA. He appointed Isakowitz NASA comptroller. He also made Paul Pastorek, a lawyer and man he had known since college, NASA's general counsel. Pastorek would be his closest confidante.

Some observers worried that O'Keefe, being nontechnical, needed to have more high-powered, highly credentialed scientists and engineers in his inner circle. Others pointed out that he relied on associate administrators at the program level for technical expertise, as well as the chief scientist position. He valued loyalty along with competence, but it was more a personal than a partisan form of loyalty.

O'Keefe initially focused on change in the human space flight program. He pulled power up to headquarters from Johnson Space Center in Houston. He put his appointees in key posts at Johnson Space Center, which was most responsible for the shuttle and International Space Station. He personally negotiated with international partners (Europe, Japan, Canada, and Russia) in the space station program. He directly dealt with influential lawmakers. He sought to recast the manned space program financially while rebuilding the space station's credibility.

Consolidating his power and speaking of "one NASA" as a rhetorical strategy to overcome field center feudalism, he increasingly gave thought to communicating a broad "vision" for the agency and its many constituencies. He believed that NASA needed a common vision to help pull its disparate components closer together. The vision would be also a statement of his own agenda for NASA. After three months in office, he felt ready to convey his philosophy. On April 12, he went to his alma mater, the Maxwell School of Syracuse University, and delivered a highly publicized and anticipated address on the direction in which he wished to take the agency (O'Keefe 2002). Saying that NASA's role was "to improve life here, to extend life to there, and to find life beyond," he declared that NASA "must be driven by the science, not by destination." This was, he emphasized, "the big change" he intended to make. He rejected calls from space enthusiasts that NASA seek a bold mission back to the moon and on to Mars. "We will go," he avowed, "where the science dictates that we go, not because it's close or popular."

If becoming "science driven" was the first element in his vision, then "technology as enabler" was the second. He wanted to take NASA back to its roots as a research and development agency and to develop technology that would allow NASA to advance, step by step, "to great achievements." In a special initiative, he called for going beyond solar and chemical propulsion to a high-priority nuclear propulsion program that would enable deeper and longer robotic spaceflight missions with much greater science payoffs. Nuclear propulsion had been downplayed under O'Keefe's predecessor. O'Keefe, familiar with nuclear propelled submarines from his navy days (and father), had no such reticence.

There was much more in his speech, including the revival of the educator in space program, his plan to launch a teacher into space, and a general emphasis on NASA's educational and inspirational role. But the most critical policy change, as he acknowledged, was the explicit call for NASA to be science driven rather than destination driven. Space enthusiasts who heard or read the address were extremely unhappy. Tom DeLay, a Republican from Texas, the influential majority leader in the House, and a strident space advocate, sharply criticized O'Keefe's speech and called his vision "tepid, anemic" (Weiner 2002; Morring 2002a, 24). Other legislators, aware of the budget realities in a post-9/11 world, praised O'Keefe's cautious and, in their view, realistic approach.

## PURSUING ADOPTION

In the months that followed, O'Keefe could see the costs of the space station becoming increasingly "manageable." He concluded that it would be possible to go beyond U.S. Core Complete to add international partner modules for a finished space station. In line with his policy of emphasizing science requirements, he had an advisory panel of leading researchers study station utilization issues. The panel advised him that good science required fully completing the station so that it would go from its present complement of three astronauts to at least six. With a larger and fully functional station, more astronauts could be aboard doing science rather than mere maintenance (Morring 2002b).

The big problem with finishing and using the International Space Station was the space shuttle. It was getting old and was limited in the number of flights it could provide. Under O'Keefe's policy, technology was to enable science. Hence, in November, he revealed a new technology development program for adoption. Called the Integrated Space Transportation Plan, his program had three aspects. First, beginning in the current year, NASA would launch a major effort to upgrade the shuttle to make it viable until 2020. Second, beginning in the next year, NASA would initiate a major development project, the Orbital Space Plane (OSP). This would be an "interim" transportation system. Its purpose was to supplement, and thus help preserve, the shuttle. It could take astronauts to and from the International Space Station and serve as a possible rescue vehicle. It would use expendable rockets and thus not be a true shuttle replacement. That would come much later and constitute the third aspect of the Integrated Space Transportation Plan (CAIB 2003, 116).

The centerpiece for policy adoption was the OSP. O'Keefe and his associates expected to outline the OSP proposal more fully in early February 2003, as part of NASA's presidential budget proposal for the new fiscal year. That immediate future of NASA and its international partners was linked to finishing the space station and putting it to the maximum scientific use. O'Keefe and his associates were optimistic about the era ahead (Pastorek 2003). It was not spectacular, but it was technically and financially feasible, or so it seemed to its architects.

## SUSPENDING POLICY: *COLUMBIA*

On February 1, 2003, just a few days before O'Keefe could officially detail NASA's proposed OSP development program and other plans, disaster struck. As it came into the atmosphere in preparation for landing, the *Columbia* space shuttle disintegrated, killing all seven astronauts aboard. Waiting at Cape Canaveral, O'Keefe was at first in a state of shock. Then, steeling himself, he ordered NASA to put its contingency plan for a shuttle disaster into effect. This was a plan he had seen his first day on the job and never expected to employ (O'Keefe 2004a).

The plan called for appointing an expert board of inquiry. This was done quickly, the first day, with retired Admiral Harold Gehman agreeing to head what became known as the *Columbia* Accident Investigation Board (CAIB). President Bush told O'Keefe, "You're in charge!" (Pastorek 2003). This meant that the president would not appoint an independent body similar to the Rogers Commission that investigated the *Challenger* shuttle disaster in 1986, even though many in the media and Congress called vociferously for such a body. The president's decision notwithstanding,

O'Keefe realized that CAIB's credibility depended on its independence. What O'Keefe wanted was for CAIB to find out what had gone wrong so that NASA could make needed changes and return to flight as rapidly as possible. The space station was still in orbit, and with the shuttle fleet grounded, NASA was dependent on Russia for transportation services. To conserve supplies, the number of astronauts aboard the station was reduced from three to two.

On the day *Columbia* disintegrated, which he called "the worst . . . of my life," O'Keefe made another important decision—that NASA be as open and transparent as possible to the media and public (Sietzen and Cowing 2004, 69; O'Keefe 2004a). This decision meant that as NASA found relevant information for CAIB, including e-mails, this information would be made widely known, even if embarrassing. After the *Challenger* accident, NASA had not appeared to be forthcoming, and its perceived bunker attitude had hurt the agency. Moreover, on the first day, O'Keefe became the human face of NASA to the country, and he would subsequently appear on television often. He came across as compassionate and with heavy heart, but also as a man in control.

As the inquiry began and information became available, debate within NASA over many safety issues prior to the accident was revealed. Many of these issues were disturbing. Along the way, O'Keefe tried to answer media questions about the decision-making process prior to launch. He was supportive of his organization, but he conveyed an overriding desire to get at the facts.

For six months, CAIB labored intensely. O'Keefe and Gehman had a mutually helpful relationship. Whatever Gehman requested in the way of resources, he usually got. Both men were conscious that in order for the agency to have credibility, it needed the appearance and reality of CAIB's autonomy. There was one serious clash along the way, over NASA personnel at Johnson Space Center. Gehman wanted to exclude certain individuals from access to CAIB's operations. O'Keefe, trying to protect his employees, disagreed, saying such explicit exclusion prejudged their complicity in the accident. Gehman held his ground and leaked information to Congress and the media, thereby forcing O'Keefe to acquiesce. For the most part, however, there was a spirit of arm's-length cooperation. As CAIB discovered technical and organizational factors relating to the disaster's cause, it made them known to O'Keefe so that he could get an early start on corrective action (Gehman 2005; Langewiesche 2003, 73).

The CAIB report came out in August 2003. It was hard-hitting and highly critical of NASA. The technical cause was insulating foam from the shuttle's external tank. It had broken off at launch and hit the leading edge of a shuttle wing, causing a rupture. When the shuttle penetrated the atmosphere upon return from its flight, extreme heat entered the vehicle and caused its destruction. Beyond technical factors were organizational causes. NASA did not get photos of the shuttle damage that it might have obtained because of bureaucratic confusion and management errors. There was a pervasive attitude at NASA that the shuttle was "operational" rather than "experimental," and this attitude caused managers to enter into decision making with a "prove it's not safe to launch" rather than "prove it is safe to launch" mentality. O'Keefe himself came in for criticism, CAIB saying that his February 2004 deadline to end U.S. Core Complete had created "schedule pressure" (CAIB 2003, 131). But the underlying causes, CAIB emphasized, were not recent; they went back years and were systemic.

Even before the CAIB report was published, O'Keefe pledged publicly that NASA would abide by CAIB's recommendations "without further argument . . . without further equivocation." He declared, "The effort we need to go through, the high bar we need to set for ourselves ought to be higher than anything anybody else would levy on us." Some of his associates felt that O'Keefe was going too far, too soon and should keep options open on implementing the CAIB report. But O'Keefe was anxious to get started on safety reforms and felt that his and NASA's credibility were at stake (Carreau 2003; O'Keefe 2005).

As the CAIB report became available, O'Keefe moved quickly to put NASA to work on mitigating the foam and other technical problems. He established an independent advisory group to oversee NASA's general compliance with the CAIB report. He hired a consulting firm to work with NASA on "cultural change." He reassigned personnel at Johnson Space Center and elsewhere. He set up an independent technical review entity to better "check and balance" shuttle program office decisions. He arranged for photos to detect damage at the time of launch and banned night launches. In these and other ways, O'Keefe acted swiftly, starting some reforms before the report was out.

The CAIB investigation gave way to a congressional inquiry in September. The major question that Congress asked O'Keefe was "who was to blame." O'Keefe would not name names, saying he would not be party to a "public execution." He had specifically refused an early offer of Readdy, associate administrator of space flight, to resign. He did make several personnel changes, mostly at Johnson Space Center. No one seriously blamed O'Keefe, who was seen as unlucky to have had the event occur on his watch. Gehman backed up O'Keefe, saying the NASA administrator was dealing with the problems CAIB had found, and he reinforced the finding that systemic causes were at fault that went back years, in some cases to the very beginning of the shuttle program (Cabbage and Harwood 2004, 168; Berger 2003; O'Keefe 2004a).

Congress and the media gradually shifted from the debate over the accident to looking ahead. Both wanted to know what NASA would do about another conclusion of CAIB—namely, that NASA was lacking a "compelling mission requiring human presence in space" (CAIB 2003, 209). Without such a mission, it said, NASA would not get the public support and resources it needed to manage its program effectively.

## EVALUATING OPTIONS

Soon after the *Columbia* disaster, various staff in the Executive Office of the President, including individuals connected with the White House Office of Science and Technology Policy, met on an ad hoc basis to discuss the implications of the accident for space policy (Sietzen and Cowing 2004, 115). At the same time, space enthusiasts inside and outside NASA sought to turn the national attention that space was suddenly receiving to positive advantage. A general mood in the country emerged that it did not make sense to risk astronauts' lives simply to go to near-Earth orbit again and again. The International Space Station, whatever its merit, did not seem a goal worthy of sacrificing human lives. Also, the shuttle had now experienced two traumatic accidents. It had to be replaced—sooner, not later. The space enthusiasts wanted what O'Keefe had refused to give them in his 2002 vision speech—they wanted a bold destination, back to the moon and on to Mars!

O'Keefe was hesitant to go along with the enthusiasts. He sensed there was a window of opportunity for large-scale policy change. But he was not at all certain what that policy change should be, especially while CAIB was still meeting and determining causation. His initial stance in the early months after the *Columbia* disaster was to adhere to his pre-*Columbia* policy. This meant an emphasis on the OSP, needed even more now that the shuttle was questionable. Space enthusiasts pointed out that the OSP simply got astronauts up to the space station, and that was an inadequate mission, at least for them.

In the spring, O'Keefe conferred with Cheney, Josh Bolton (White House deputy chief of staff), John Marburger (President Bush's science advisor and director of the Office of Science and Technology Policy), and others about the post-*Columbia* planning process. O'Keefe's strategy was to create a process for national policy decision. The ad hoc group of staff-level people meeting would, in his view, not lead to such a decision, which had to culminate with the president. There were two top-level interagency policy mechanisms available, the National Security Council (NSC) and the Domestic Council. The NSC was far more established and influential. In the summer, he persuaded Stephen Hadley, NSC deputy director, to lead an interagency activity. He also enlisted Margaret Spellings, who led the Domestic Council. He thus designed a hybrid NSC–Domestic Council process. It became known as the Hadley Committee. It was also called the Deputies Committee, in view of the involvement of deputy secretaries of a number of cabinet departments, including the U.S. State Department, as well as senior NASA and White House officials (Sietzen and Cowing 2004; O'Keefe 2004b, 2005). O'Keefe's support from the influential Vice President Cheney helped ensure the attention of the various high-level agency officials.

Throughout the summer and into the fall, as CAIB ended its work and Congress conducted its hearings, the Hadley Committee met periodically behind closed doors and considered virtually every option possible—from shutting down the shuttle program to making a manned voyage to Mars. In August, once CAIB had called for a "compelling vision," expansive options became more legitimate. O'Keefe did not play the "space enthusiast" role. If anything, others urged him to move beyond Earth orbit and his OSP–space station orientation. As discussions continued, the issue came down to finding a goal that was bolder than the space station but also feasible financially and politically. Eventually, the group leaned toward a return to the moon as a new mission. It was a goal that Marburger said had scientific value. Given O'Keefe's desire for a "science-driven" NASA, Marburger's view was important.

Meanwhile, President Bush was briefed on the Hadley Committee process, the options vented, and the direction in which the process seemed headed. Bush made it clear that he wanted something bolder to back. Bush's father had unsuccessfully called for a Moon-Mars goal in 1989, and the son wanted to make a similarly big decision, but one that had a chance to succeed. The key word that Bush liked was not "science" but "exploration" (Sietzen and Cowing 2004, 118).

Whatever reservations O'Keefe might have had about advocating a large new mission, by late October they had given way to his need for the Hadley Committee to produce a consensus decision the president would back. Bush was engaged and awaiting the outcome from the planning process. O'Keefe increasingly exerted leadership in the interagency effort as he strove to link it with the budget process and its timetable. In doing so, he collided with the OMB. Bush might have indicated informally he wanted to make a big space decision, but he was also simultaneously telling the OMB to hold the line on spending that was not related to the Iraq war or security generally.

O'Keefe, therefore, had to do battle with the OMB to get resources for an expanded NASA mission. Moreover, there had to be closure by Thanksgiving or early December to get the results of the planning process incorporated into the upcoming presidential budget. O'Keefe lobbied aggressively for a substantial raise with Mitch Daniels, the director of the OMB, his former boss. He pointed out that bold decisions without resources to back them "will make us [NASA] look ridiculous" (Sietzen and Cowing 2004, 119).

The budget deadline and universal realization that the window for policy innovation was closing forced decisions to come to a head. O'Keefe, the OMB, and others connected with the interagency process concluded that a new "exploration initiative" would be approved and jump-started with additional money the first fiscal year, with more coming for the initiative over the next four years and after. As funds for exploration ramped up, expenditures for the shuttle and space station would go down to make room for the exploration initiative. The new would gradually replace the old.

On December 19, O'Keefe, Cheney, Hadley, Marburger, and others met at the White House with President Bush. "This is more than just the moon, isn't it?" Bush asked. Assured that it was, Bush declared, "Let's do it!" He then told Hadley to schedule a date when he would announce the decision for maximum visibility (Sietzen and Cowing 2004, 152).

## ADOPTING MOON-MARS

On January 14, 2004, President Bush came to NASA's auditorium and announced the agency's new mission: back to the moon, on to Mars, and beyond. His decision was entitled a "Vision for Space Exploration." It was vastly different from the vision proclaimed in early 2002 by O'Keefe. In all, $11 billion would go to the new program in its first five years, starting with an add-on to NASA's budget of $1 billion the first year. Most of the $11 billion would come by reprioritizing within NASA's overall budget (Sietzen and Cowing 2004, 162; Lawler 2004a, 293; Allen and Pianin 2004).

The key financial strategy, as negotiated between O'Keefe and the OMB, was for money for exploration to go up as funding for the shuttle program and the International Space Station went down. The president's decision called for retiring the space shuttle by 2010, with a new spacecraft, called the Crew Exploration Vehicle, taking its place by 2014. This rocket-powered vehicle would not only be able to go to the space station but, more importantly, also to the moon, with the moon voyage set for 2020.

The Moon-Mars program of Bush was a giant leap from the Integrated Space Transportation Plan of O'Keefe. The prime technology development program set in motion—the Crew Exploration Vehicle and associated rocket system—was much more ambitious than the shuttle upgrade–Orbital Space Plane concept of the Integrated Space Transportation Plan. The destination of the moon was similarly a prodigious leap from the OSP's aim, the low-Earth orbit space station. In a multitude of ways, the decision represented not a reorientation of an existing program but the adoption of a new one. O'Keefe could take a large measure of the credit for steering the Moon-Mars decision into being. He had used a coalitional strategy to put NASA's mission into a national policy context. The coalition included the president. Now he needed congressional endorsement.

## TERMINATING HUBBLE

O'Keefe wanted to get off to a fast start in promoting and implementing the new policy. On the day after President Bush spoke, January 15, O'Keefe announced the first steps in implementation. He created a new NASA division, which he called Exploration Systems. O'Keefe selected retired Admiral Craig Steidle, who had guided the Defense Department's huge Joint Strike Fighter program, as the division's chief. O'Keefe said that NASA was pursuing "exploration informed by science" in an address to NASA officials and employees, the words marking his shift from earlier rhetoric, "driven by science." The president was surely in the manifest destiny tradition of exploration, and now he seemed interested in the space program—although the depth of that interest was ambiguous. When President Bush gave his State of the Union address, shortly after his space exploration speech, he failed to mention his Vision for Space Exploration. Cheney, however, was actively aiding O'Keefe with senior lawmakers, lobbying behind the scenes (O'Keefe 2004c).

As O'Keefe began his own process of extending his coalition of support to Congress, the media, scientific community, and general public, he suffered a serious blow. It arose from his decision to terminate the immensely popular Hubble Space Telescope by not sending a future shuttle-based servicing mission to make needed repairs. The same day, January 15, that he announced his reorganization to carry out the Moon-Mars mission, the *Washington Post* published a front-page article on the president's decision. It concluded by noting one of the impacts of the decision, namely, that there would be "no further servicing missions to the Hubble Space Telescope" (Sawyer 2004). The direct linkage of Hubble's termination to Moon-Mars was incorrect as far as O'Keefe was concerned. But that was the "truth" that was conveyed, through an inadvertent leak from a White

House staffer, and publication in the *Post*. It was the perception that Hubble would be sacrificed to get money for Moon-Mars (Sietzen and Cowing 2004, 172).

The reality for O'Keefe was that the link was to *Columbia*, not a budget trade-off for the new mission. O'Keefe had promised publicly and clearly that NASA would adhere to the CAIB report. He had pledged to abide by CAIB "without . . . equivocation." Moreover, he wanted desperately to change NASA's safety culture, from one of "prove to me it's unsafe to launch" to "prove to me it is safe to launch." CAIB had recommended that NASA develop a way to repair shuttle damage in space. While the space station offered a safe haven for astronauts to make repairs, there would be no such haven for Hubble repair, which was in a different orbit from the International Space Station. O'Keefe made a judgment call based on technical information he had gleaned over time about NASA's ability to make repairs in space to the shuttle. It was that the extra servicing of Hubble repair, in the wake of *Columbia*, in the face of the CAIB recommendation, was unacceptable risk. Moreover, how could he talk about changing NASA's safety culture if he appeared to be making a huge exception on Hubble?[2]

He knew the decision would be controversial. He reached it personally and gradually, in conversations with NASA officials, often indirectly, without much open discussion and debate. It came across as a one-man decision—the converse of O'Keefe's more customary management style, which favored processes in which competing views could be aired. Moreover, it reached apparent finality around Thanksgiving, when he sat down with Steve Isakowitz, his comptroller, to make final decisions on NASA's budget for the following year. For Hubble termination, this meant deleting funds for a potential repair mission, the precise timing of which was dependent on the shuttle's return to flight. Because of the uncertainty of the shuttle's return, the decision could have been delayed, more persuasive evidence gathered about risk, and more technical and political people involved in the decision. But O'Keefe's style was to connect policy and budget, and thus he decided sooner rather than later. Why spend money preparing for a flight that would not take place?

When he subsequently made the decision known to his top science officials, it did not come across to them as subject to change but as a decision made, with the administrator concerned mainly about how to present the bad news to those affected. Hubble proponents within NASA were surprised when they heard about the decision. NASA's chief scientist, an avowed "Hubble Hugger," who was also an astronaut and had himself made a servicing mission to the telescope, felt that he had been deliberately excluded from decision making and almost resigned (*Science* 2006, 903).

After the *Washington Post* announced the termination to the world, a cacophony of protest sounded. Critics asked, how could O'Keefe talk about Moon-Mars while being so risk averse when it came to Hubble? The former seemed far more hazardous than the latter. The fact that the decision became known the day after Bush's Moon-Mars announcement connected it irrevocably with the president's Vision for Space Exploration. Those who opposed Hubble termination were convinced it was a budget trade-off decision despite O'Keefe's fervent denials. The nucleus of the Hubble proponents consisted of astronomers and institutions whose fates were linked to Hubble's survival. However, support for Hubble extended well beyond them. It was a public icon.

The die was cast. Because of the leak, there had been no time for steps to be taken to prepare the Hubble science community, and its supporters in Congress, the media, or general public, for the stark decision. O'Keefe's intent had been to talk with those scientists inside and outside NASA who were most affected, along with their allies in Congress, before making an official announcement some time hence. Absent such activity, the decision came across as arbitrary and capricious. The political backlash was immediate, loud, and harshly personal. O'Keefe was put on the defensive, and Hubble became a severe distraction from his main priority, which was to build support for Moon-Mars, including support from the scientific community.

As soon as he saw the story in the *Post*, O'Keefe called and sought to placate Senator Barbara Mikulski (DMD), the ranking Democrat on the Senate appropriations subcommittee controlling NASA's budget, in whose constituency were the principal scientific institutions working on Hubble (NASA's Goddard Space Flight Center and the Johns Hopkins University–based Hubble Space Telescope Science Institute). She demanded that O'Keefe get a "second opinion." O'Keefe agreed and asked Gehman to provide his perspective. Because O'Keefe was basing his decision largely on CAIB's recommendations, he had reason to believe that Gehman would side with him in shifting the balance in shuttle decision making from "prove to me it's not safe" to "prove to me it is safe" (O'Keefe 2004d; Sietzen and Cowing 2004, 172–75).

But Gehman did not support O'Keefe. Instead he undercut him, writing on March 10 that "only a deep and rich study of the entire gain/risk equation can answer the question of whether the extension of the life of the wonderful Hubble Telescope is worth the risks involved, and that is beyond the scope of this letter." Senator Mikulski pounced on Gehman's suggestion, calling on O'Keefe to ask the National Academy of Sciences (NAS) to conduct an in-depth study. O'Keefe felt that he faced a Hobson's choice on Hubble. He had to decide, and he saw no good options (O'Keefe 2004d; Sietzen and Cowing 2004, 175).

Then, a group of NASA officials came to O'Keefe to tell him it might be possible to service Hubble robotically. This possibility appealed to O'Keefe. It avoided putting shuttle-based astronauts at risk, and it aided Moon-Mars, as it would advance robotic technologies. It would also get O'Keefe off the hook from the barrage of criticism he was receiving. If there was one space technology with a large, supportive constituency, it was Hubble. Advocates called it "the people's telescope," to project its broad public appeal. O'Keefe found himself having to defend his decision on the *60 Minutes* television program. He had virtually no vocal allies outside NASA.

O'Keefe told Mikulski that he would ask NAS to do the study she wanted, but also to weigh the robotic option he hoped to use. On June 1, he went to a meeting of the American Astronomical Society in Denver to offer an olive branch of peace. He reiterated his position as opposing a shuttle mission to Hubble because of safety. Then, he announced he would let a contract to industry to explore the option of a robotic rescue effort. This gesture won him strong applause from his audience and lowered the scientific, congressional, and media heat on O'Keefe. It also allowed him to devote his attention more fully to selling Moon-Mars and to regaining the momentum he had lost as a result of the Hubble controversy (O'Keefe 2004d, 2004e; Sietzen and Cowing 2004, 256–57).

## GETTING CONGRESS ABOARD MOON-MARS

On November 2, the American people reelected George W. Bush to the White House and enlarged the Republican majority in Congress. These and other political developments helped ensure the near-term continuity of the Moon-Mars exploration mission. Moreover, redistricting in Texas put the Johnson Space Center directly under the jurisdiction of Tom DeLay. The powerful majority leader personally held up a vote in the House on an omnibus budget bill to make sure NASA got virtually all the $16.2 billion appropriation it had requested. Senator Ted Stevens (R-AK), a onetime O'Keefe mentor and current backer and chair of the Senate Appropriations Committee, worked in tandem with DeLay not only to get a substantial "start-up" raise for NASA but also authority for O'Keefe to reprogram funds within NASA's budget as necessary to launch the Moon-Mars program.

O'Keefe took the congressional appropriations action as an endorsement of Bush's decision. Others noted that although Congress had funded one year of Moon-Mars, it had yet to fully debate, consider, and legislatively authorize the new mission. O'Keefe had a different view. He had a go-ahead from the president *and* Congress. He declared to his agency, "We have a mandate, we have the president's direction. We have the resources." It was now up to NASA, he said, to deliver (Berger 2004, 10).

## LEAVING NASA

O'Keefe seemed visibly tired. He had never really overcome the sense of loss he had suffered with *Columbia*. He had gone to funeral after funeral, and even kept up contact with the families of the deceased astronauts. He had soldiered on to sell Moon-Mars, but he had not gotten much public support from the president subsequent to the January 2004 speech. The Hubble decision had brought him under "withering" attack. He had a family to support and children to educate. If he had harbored ambitions of becoming secretary of defense, those ambitions were suspended when Donald Rumsfeld decided to remain at the Pentagon.

On December 13, O'Keefe wrote to President Bush that he was resigning, effective in February 2005. He was leaving to become chancellor of Louisiana State University. He could exit knowing that NASA was going to get another Moon-Mars raise in the president's upcoming budget, to $16.45 billion. It was $500 million short of what Bush had promised earlier, but it was a raise greater than most other nonsecurity agencies got (Berger 2005, 4).

However, the shuttle was months away from a return to flight, the International Space Station assembly remained on hold, and many of O'Keefe's financial reforms had a long way to go. Shortly after announcing his impending departure, he heard the National Academy of Sciences report that the robotic mission to service Hubble could not be ready technically in time to save the telescope. Instead, it urged him to reinstate the shuttle mission (Lawler 2004b, 2018). O'Keefe left NASA adamantly refusing to do that. If Hubble were to be saved by a shuttle mission, the decision to send a shuttle would have to come from his successor.

## CONCLUSION

Sean O'Keefe put his stamp significantly on NASA, even though his tenure was only a little over three years. He came in primarily to fix the cost overrun afflicting the International Space Station. He left having steered into being the Moon-Mars program, thereby changing NASA's course. The incremental, linear model of policy innovation noted earlier did not hold. That for transformative change applied to this process. The "punctuation point" in O'Keefe's tenure was the *Columbia* disaster. It defined his three years in the starkest way possible, changing discontinuously not only O'Keefe's space policy agenda but also that of NASA and the United States. As O'Keefe put it as he left, "I had to play a different hand than I thought I would be playing. What I was dealt was not what I had expected" (O'Keefe 2005).

The brevity of O'Keefe's tour had its costs. He probably left too soon, before he could consolidate many of his initiatives from space nuclear propulsion to financial reform. He did not get the resources for the Vision for Space Exploration he would have liked. The budget projections for subsequent years that he left for his successor proved inadequate, especially for the space shuttle. He made progress on space station financial management, only to have *Columbia* set that project back. He obviously stumbled on the Hubble termination decision.

The Hubble case shows that top administrators engage in many battles over change-oriented policies. Some they win, some they lose. It may be easier to start major programs than to end them. O'Keefe lost the Hubble encounter, and his successor reversed his decision. But on the most significant challenges on his watch—*Columbia* crisis management and Moon-Mars—he did well.

He got NASA through the *Columbia* disaster and its investigatory aftermath relatively intact. He made organizational changes to enhance shuttle safety. He used *Columbia* to get a presidential decision to return to the moon and eventually go on to Mars.

It is doubtful that a NASA administrator lacking O'Keefe's skills and contacts with the Bush White House could have gotten this presidential decision. The Moon-Mars mission was not the policy O'Keefe had originally intended when he came to the agency, or even later, but it was the policy he left as his prime imprint. *Columbia* made it possible, and others were significantly involved, but he deserves credit for converting *Columbia* into a change in course for his agency that has potential historic significance.

The Moon-Mars decision, like Hubble, has broad lessons for administrative leadership that go beyond O'Keefe's experience. Among these is the criticality of powerful political allies for transformative and controversial decisions. O'Keefe did not have the allies he needed for Hubble, but he did in the case of the Moon-Mars program. Adopting Moon-Mars required Cheney and Bush in the White House and DeLay and Stevens in Congress.

Another lesson is that windows of opportunity for major policy change open rarely and briefly. *Columbia* in 2003. President Bush announced his Moon-Mars decision and Congress appropriated start-up funds for the decision in 2004. The nation turned its attention to the Iraq war and Katrina's devastation of New Orleans in 2005. Big decisions and new missions need coalitions, catalysts, and timely advocacy by an advocate with influence. O'Keefe, as NASA administrator, was an effective policy entrepreneur behind the Moon-Mars mission when NASA needed him to lead, and that milestone decision marks his most important legacy. If the decision is sustained in the years to come, O'Keefe will be viewed as the administrator who initiated the epic transition of NASA's human space flight program from low-Earth orbit back to the space frontier.

## NOTES

1. The author thanks the IBM Center for the Business of Government for providing research support in preparing an earlier study of O'Keefe's NASA experience, *Executive Response to Changing Fortune* (2005). This article builds on the IBM study and subsequent research.

2. The section on Hubble draws on research that the author and Steve Dick, NASA historian, have under way on the Hubble Space Telescope.

## REFERENCES

Allen, Mike, and Eric Pianin. 2004. Bush Outlines Space Agenda. *Washington Post,* January 15.

Berger, Brian, 2003. Congress Begins Hearings on *Columbia,* NASA's Future. *Space News,* September 3.

———. 2004. Congress Grants $16.2 Billion Budget for NASA. *Space News,* November 29.

———. 2005. NASA Budget Request Falls Short of Expectation. *Space News,* February 7.

Cabbage, Michael, and William Harwood. 2004. *Comm Check: The Final Flight of Shuttle Columbia.* New York: Free Press.

Carreau, Mark. 2003. NASA Chief Vows to Implement New Standards for Shuttle Safety. *Houston Chronicle,* June 27.

*Columbia* Accident Investigation Board (CAIB). 2003. *Report.* Vol. 1. Washington DC: National Aeronautics and Space Administration. http://caib.nasa.gov/news/report/volume1/default.html [accessed November 13, 2007].

deLeon, Peter. 1999. The Stages Approach to the Policy Process: What Has It Done? Where Is It Going? In *Theories of the Policy Process,* edited by Paul A. Sabatier, 19–34. Boulder, CO: Westview Press.

Doig, Jameson W., and Erwin C. Hargrove, eds. 1987. *Leadership and Innovation: A Biographical Perspective on Entrepreneurs in Government.* Baltimore: Johns Hopkins University Press.

Gehman, Harold. 2005. Interview with the author, March 15.

Lambright, W. Henry. *Executive Response to Changing Fortune: Sean O'Keefe as NASA Administrator.* Washington, DC: IBM Center for the Business of Government. http://www.businessofgovernment.org/pdfs/LambrightReport4.pdf [accessed November 14, 2007].

———. 2007. Leading Change at NASA: The Case of Dan Goldin. *Space Policy* 23 (1): 33–43.

Langewiesche, William, 2003. *Columbia's* Last Flight. *Atlantic Monthly,* November. http://www.theatlantic.com/doc/200311/langewiesche [accessed November 13, 2007].

Lawler, Andrew, 2004a. President Bush Reaches for the Moon. *Science,* January 16, 293.

———. 2004b. O'Keefe to Go, but Hubble Remains Battleground. *Science,* September 17, 2018–19.

Morring, Frank, Jr. 2002a. O'Keefe Vision Gets Tepid Hill Response. *Aviation Week and Space Technology,* April 22.

———. 2002b. O'Keefe: Science Goals Setting ISS Capability. *Aviation Week and Space Technology,* July 15.

National Aeronautics and Space Administration (NASA). 2001. Report by the International Space Station (ISS) Management and Cost Evaluation (IMCE) Task Force to the NASA Advisory Council. http://history.nasa.gov/youngrep.pdf [accessed November 13, 2007].

O'Keefe, Sean. 2002. Pioneering the Future. Address delivered at Syracuse University, Syracuse, NY, April 12.

———. 2004a. Interview with the author and Howard McCurdy, March 29.

———. 2004b. Address to the National Security Program, Maxwell School, Syracuse University, Syracuse, NY, April 23.

———. 2004c. Address to NASA employees, January 15.

———. 2004d. Interview with the author, June 1.

———. 2004e. Address delivered at the Annual Meeting of the American Astronomical Society, June 1.

———. 2005. Interview with the author, January 24.

Pastorek, Paul. 2003. Interview with the author, November 20.

Sawyer, Kathy. 2004. Vision of Liftoff Grounded in Political Reality. *Washington Post,* January 15.

*Science.* 2006. Back in Orbit. November 10, 903.

Sietzen, Frank, Jr., and Keith L. Cowing. 2004. *New Moon Rising: The Making of America's New Space Vision and the Remaking of NASA.* Burlington, Ontario: Apogee Books.

True, James L., Bryan D. Jones, and Frank R. Baumgartner. 1999. Punctuated-Equilibrium Theory: Explaining Stability and Change in American Policymaking. In *Theories of the Policy Process,* edited by Paul Sabatier, 97–116. Boulder, CO: Westview Press.

Vistica, Gregory L. 1995. *Fall from Glory: The Men Who Sank the U.S. Navy.* New York: Simon & Schuster.

Weiner, Mark. 2002. NASA to Send Teacher into Space. *Syracuse Post Standard,* April 13.

# 8

# GEORGE TENET AND THE
# LAST GREAT DAYS OF THE CIA

RICHARD D. WHITE, JR.

The dreary little restaurant located in the Virginia suburb just across the Potomac River from the nation's capital is worth mentioning only for its beer-soaked chili dogs and for its waitresses who never give checks to the customers. After diners finish their lunch, they walk up to the cash register, tell the owner what they ate, and pay their bill. This unusual honor system seems odd in today's untrusting world, but there is a good reason. Many of the customers work nearby at the Central Intelligence Agency (CIA) headquarters, and they cannot tell a lie. The CIA ensures honesty by requiring its employees to take unannounced polygraph tests to see whether they have recently committed a crime. To the CIA faithful, even shirking a lunch bill would be a crime, and trying to lie about the misdeed would make the polygraph needle go haywire. The super-secret environment, in which the truth is sacrosanct and Big Brother is always looking over one's shoulder, creates an organizational culture that few outsiders can comprehend, and it was into this clandestine world that George Tenet immersed himself when he became the director of central intelligence (DCI) in 1997.

As DCI, Tenet understood that managing a large and complex government bureaucracy would be difficult enough, but managing one that operates under a shroud of secrecy would challenge even the most talented and energetic leader. To complicate his task, the CIA at the time was really two separate agencies, each with its own operating procedures and organizational personality. As the spy side of the agency, the Directorate of Operations managed covert operations and the collection of human intelligence. Its officers were a hard-nosed lot, and many were ex-military who worked undercover around the world collecting intelligence. The larger, less secretive Directorate of Intelligence was the analytic side that refined raw intelligence from many sources and produced the nation's two most important finished intelligence products, the President's Daily Brief and the National Intelligence Estimate. Staffed with academics and pipe-smoking PhDs, the Directorate of Intelligence resembled a college campus, and it was not unusual for an analyst to spend 30 years studying the political situation of one particular country.

One of the bigger challenges of any DCI was to ensure that the Directorate of Operations and the Directorate of Intelligence communicated with each other. Besides managing the CIA, the DCI served as the president's principal intelligence advisor, as well as the head of the entire intelligence community, composed of 15 agencies including the National Security Agency, the Defense Intelligence Agency, and a couple of others so secret that their existence was classified.

From *Public Administration Review,* 68, No. 3 (May/June 2008): 420–427. Copyright © 2008 American Society for Public Administration. Used by permission.

Coordinating the nation's intelligence apparatus was like herding cats—blindfolded! Tenet knew his responsibility was huge. "A strong case can be made that the three roles in which I served were too much for any one person," he later wrote. "Perhaps so" (Tenet 2007, 501). But he was impressed with the CIA's "streak of eccentric genius," as he put it, welcomed the challenge and the excitement of the job, and charged ahead (Coll 2004, 359). He had no idea at the time, however, that he would play a major role, for better or worse, in the abolition of the DCI and the demise of the CIA as the world's most powerful and prestigious intelligence agency.

## BLUNT, STRAIGHTFORWARD, AND TOTALLY LOYAL

George Tenet grew up in a two-story row house on Marathon Parkway in Little Neck, Queens. His father and mother had emigrated from Greece during the Great Depression and later opened the Twentieth Century Diner around the corner from their home. They worked 16-hour days at the diner, where she was the baker and he was the chef, while George and his brother bused tables (Tenet 2007, xx). As a kid, George loved sports, playing stick ball in the street and guard on the St. Nicholas Greek Orthodox Church basketball team. He was a loud, sloppy, and boisterous kid, unlike his studious twin brother Bill, who became a cardiologist (Coll 2004, 355). Tenet attended Georgetown University, where he received a bachelor's degree in foreign affairs in 1976, and, two years later, earned a master's degree from Columbia.

After moving to Washington, D.C., Tenet spent four years as a lobbyist. In 1982, he took his first job on Capitol Hill as a legislative assistant for Senator John Heinz, a Pennsylvania Republican. In the summer of 1985, he began working for the Senate Select Committee on Intelligence (SSCI), where he monitored Cold War arms control negotiations and earned a reputation as an "effective and efficient staffer who served his bosses well" (Isikoff and Corn 2006, 30). When Oklahoma senator David Boren took over the SSCI, he found Tenet to be "very blunt, straightforward, and totally loyal." Impressed, Boren appointed him staff director, one of the most prized and influential positions on the Hill. As director of the SSCI's 40 professionals, Tenet's duties included keeping track of the CIA's budget and operations. He was tough on the agency, tightening oversight over covert operations and cutting its funding (Coll 2004, 357).

Senate staffers remember Tenet as a gregarious, comical, and profane colleague but nevertheless a straight arrow, a high-strung workaholic, and a sports fanatic with season tickets to Georgetown basketball games. The cigar-smoking Tenet was a natural coalition builder, a rare commodity on the Hill, but, according to a Senate staffer, he was prone to oversimplifying difficult issues. At the SSCI, he rarely discussed politics and was so religiously nonpartisan that his closest friends did not know his political affiliation (a registered Democrat). Bulky and a little overweight from junk food, he "could have been a longshoreman," a staffer remarked (Coll 2004, 254, 354–58; Isikoff and Corn 2006, 30; Woodward 2002, 2; Woodward 2004, 117).

Soon after the presidential election of 1992, Tenet joined Bill Clinton's transition team as director for intelligence issues, a position that really served as an audition for the new administration. Tenet impressed the Clintonites, who appointed him senior director for intelligence at the National Security Council. He worked so hard in 1993 and 1994 that he had a heart attack, causing him to stop lighting the ever-present cigar stuck in his mouth but never forcing him to slow down. In 1995, he moved to the CIA to become deputy to DCI John Deutch, primarily because his popularity on both sides of the Senate aisle made him easy to confirm. While deputy, Tenet did not waste time. He spent the next two years meeting the CIA's people, learning its dark tradecraft, and absorbing the agency's problems "the way a Geiger counter absorbs radiation signals" (Coll 2004, 354–55, 359).

When Deutch quit after only 19 months, President Clinton nominated his national security advisor, Tony Lake, as DCI, but Senate Republicans blocked Lake as being too liberal. That left Tenet, who got the job almost by default. He possessed two qualities that appealed strongly to the White House: He was well liked, and, again, he could be easily confirmed by Congress.

Before arriving at the CIA, Tenet had never run for political office, managed a large organization, worked as an intelligence officer, shaped American foreign policy, earned academic credentials by authoring a scholarly publication, or served in the military (Coll 2004, 353–54). But it was not unusual for an outsider like Tenet to head the agency. Only four previous heads—Allen Dulles, Richard Helms, William Colby, and Robert Gates—had been professional intelligence officers, while seven had been civilians with political connections but little intelligence background, and six had been military officers. To rank-and-file CIA employees, the back-slapping Tenet would be a breath of fresh air after the abrasive Deutch. Old hands, in fact, still remembered the notorious days of Stansfield Turner, President Jimmy Carter's DCI who had mistrusted clandestine operations and decimated the agency by firing hundreds of operatives, and the opposite extreme, William Casey, President Ronald Reagan's hawkish DCI who had used covert operations to meddle in the internal affairs of foreign governments. By comparison, Tenet was an acceptable, low-risk choice whose two years as deputy gave him some measure of credibility.

## AN AGENCY IN DISARRAY

On July 11, 1997, 44-year-old George Tenet was sworn in as the eighteenth director of central intelligence. President Clinton did not attend the ceremony but sent Vice President Al Gore (Coll 2004, 353). Officially Tenet was a cabinet member, but he remained outside the president's inner circle. According to Tim Weiner, "Clinton did not find the time to understand what the CIA was, how it worked, or where it fit in with the rest of government" (2007, 447). Clinton did not require the DCI to be present for the daily intelligence briefing, often preferring to read intelligence documents on his own. Tenet was not surprised to have little personal contact with the president. Clinton's first DCI, James Woolsey, had served from 1993 to 1995 and, according to one journalist, had never met one on one with Clinton. "Remember the guy who in 1994 crashed his plane onto the White House lawn?" Woolsey sarcastically told an *Insight* reporter. "That was me trying to get an appointment to see President Clinton."

The CIA was in disarray when Tenet took over. The agency had suffered inconsistent leadership since the fall of the Soviet Union, and he was the fifth DCI in seven years. Morale sagged badly. Since 1991, the agency had lost more than 3,000 of its best people—more than 20 percent of its workforce—including many of its more experienced case officers (Weiner 2007, 470). Some had left from budget cuts, others from disgust. Recruiting was at a standstill. Indeed, when Tenet arrived, the Federal Bureau of Investigation had more agents in New York City than the CIA had clandestine officers around the world (Tenet 2007, 14). The agency budget was a mess, and there was no central accounting of funds spent. At the same time, the CIA had lost the technological edge that had enabled it to compete and triumph during the Cold War. The agency had not kept abreast of breakthroughs in private industry in communications technology, satellite surveillance, and supercomputing (Tenet 2007, 21). Though required to coordinate the intelligence community, the DCI had little real authority over other agencies and controlled less than 20 percent of overall intelligence spending (Kean and Hamilton 2006, 197). "The fact is that by the mid- to late-1990s American intelligence was in Chapter 11," Tenet wrote, "and neither Congress nor the executive branch did much about it" (2007, 108).

When Tenet became DCI, he did not have a grand, compelling strategy concerning world affairs, nor did he seek one. Instead, he focused on the CIA's internal, institutional needs. His top priorities were a more clearly defined mission, improved morale, better execution of intelligence collection and analysis, more recruits, better training, and a substantial increase in funding. He sounded like a football coach when he told his staff that "this is all about focusing on basics" (Coll 2004, 355).

Tenet immediately started rebuilding. Turning to private industry, he appointed a chief financial officer to straighten out the agency's spending and a chief information officer to upgrade its computing capacity. He called talented veterans back from retirement, including Jack Downing, a Harvard-educated ex-Marine who had served as station chief in Moscow and Beijing, to reenergize the clandestine service (Weiner 2007, 67, 471). He also sought more funding. He sent two personal letters to President Clinton, one in November 1998 and another a year later, seeking an additional $2 billion over five years. His requests annoyed the White House, and he got only a small increase (Tenet 2007, 107). Late in 1999, Tenet went through back channels to Republican Congressmen Newt Gingrich and Porter Goss, who controlled the agency budget in the House of Representatives, and secured an "emergency" $2 billion supplemental appropriation, the agency's biggest increase in 15 years (Weiner 2007, 468; Tenet 2007, 21). At the same time, Tenet attempted to revamp the agency's personnel structure by implementing a pay-for-performance incentive system, but Congress refused to authorize it (Tenet 2007, 25).

Tenet's energy and hands-on leadership paid off. Morale seemed to improve overnight as word spread quickly around Langley about the new DCI's "management by walking around" style. He became a familiar sight strolling headquarters corridors, chomping on his unlit cigar, throwing his arms around people, or plopping down at cafeteria tables (Coll 2004, 360). Over the agency's history, few DCIs had been true people persons and fewer had made themselves readily accessible to the rank and file. Now, most employees addressed the new DCI simply as "George."

## DIPLOMAT RATHER THAN SPYMASTER

"At CIA we don't make policy; we implement it," George Tenet said on numerous occasions (2007, 55). He saw the agency's role as that of an honest broker that avoided direct involvement in foreign policy making. His role as DCI became more politically complicated, however, in the fall of 1998, when President Clinton hosted peace talks between the Palestinians and the Israelis. During the Wye Oak negotiations, Tenet served as the go-between for Yasser Arafat and Israeli prime minister Binyamin Netanyahu. "We were the one entity both sides could trust," Tenet explained (2007, 64). This new role was more diplomat than chief spymaster, which made many insiders "distinctly uncomfortable" (Posner 1998; Tenet 2007, 74). Late in the negotiations, Netanyahu demanded that the United States release convicted spy Jonathan Pollard. At first Clinton was inclined to grant the Israeli request, but Tenet told the president that he could not remain DCI if Pollard were released. After Tenet threatened to resign and Speaker of the House Newt Gingrich objected to the release, Clinton backed down (Risen 2006, 8).

Sometime in 1998, the Clinton administration became aware of the threat that Osama bin Laden posed and planned to capture him. At the time, Bin Laden was seeking chemical and biological weapons and sending his operatives into at least 60 countries (Tenet 2007, 109, 130). In December 1998, Tenet warned top intelligence officials of the al-Qaeda threat. "We are at war," he wrote. "I want no resources or people spared in this effort, either inside CIA or the Community." According to the 9/11 Commission report (2004, 357), however, the memorandum did little to mobilize the intelligence community. Meanwhile, despite Tenet's efforts to rebuild his agency, the CIA continued to experience major intelligence failures. On May 11, 1998, India began its nuclear testing program, to the surprise of the U.S. intelligence community. "We didn't have a clue,"

Tenet confessed to Senator Richard Shelby after the test became public (Bamford 2005, 129). A year later, warplanes relied on faulty intelligence and mistakenly bombed the Chinese embassy in Belgrade. Like a loyal soldier, Tenet again shouldered the blame. Soon after, a *Washington Post* reporter wrote ominously that "politicization of intelligence estimates continues to flourish under Tenet's leadership . . . We all have reason for grave concern" (Eddington 1999).

## A MEMBER OF THE INNER CIRCLE

When George W. Bush won the presidency, George Tenet expected to be replaced as soon as the Republicans took off. In early 2001, however, Senator David Boren called Bush and urged him to keep Tenet as a gesture of bipartisanship. The senator suggested that Bush ask his father, himself a former DCI, about Tenet. President George H.W. Bush had been impressed by Tenet, who had shepherded Robert Gates through the Senate confirmation process in 1991 and later led the effort to rename CIA headquarters for the elder Bush (Woodward 2002, 2). Tenet stayed.

On paper, Tenet was no longer a cabinet member, but, despite being a Clinton holdover, he soon became a trusted insider of the Bush national security team. According to Tenet, the Bush administration had a more traditional, and "perhaps more appropriate," view regarding the CIA's involvement (2007, 80). Unlike Clinton, Bush was fascinated by the CIA and insisted that Tenet personally brief him each morning at eight o'clock (Woodward 2004, 68). As Tenet became more deeply involved in providing daily intelligence to the president and attending White House policy meetings, he no longer was able to focus on rebuilding the agency. There were just not enough hours in his day.

"I like the president, plain and simple," Tenet wrote (2007, 480). Bush and Tenet bonded so well that one White House official remarked that they "were like fraternity brothers," and the two men defended each other on every occasion. Some CIA officers complained that the DCI was too close to the president, still acting like a congressional staffer overly concerned with pleasing his boss (Isikoff and Corn 2006, 31, 268). In his morning briefings to Bush, Tenet sometimes took along a field officer, still needing a shave and a shower, who had just flown in from some hot spot on the far side of the world. "I wanted to take the person closest to the action, the one with hands-on experience, to tell the Commander in Chief what was really happening" (Tenet 2007, 183).

## GEORGE TENET GOES TO WAR

On September 11, 2001, George Tenet sat under an ornate Louis XVI chandelier having breakfast with Senator Boren at the St. Regis Hotel at 16th and K streets. Tenet never finished his breakfast. His security detail whisked him away when news reached them that an airliner had crashed into the World Trade Center (Bamford 2005, 18). The DCI knew immediately that the attacks were the work of al-Qaeda. Two months before, he had raced to the White House to brief Condoleezza Rice on his fears of an imminent terrorist attack based on intelligence that "literally made my hair stand on end" (Goldberg 2007). A week after the attack, Tenet wrote to top intelligence officials that "there can be no bureaucratic impediments to success. All the rules have changed. There must be an absolute and full sharing of information, ideas, and capabilities. We do not have time to hold meetings to fix problems—fix them—quickly and smartly" (2007, 169). In a perverse way, 9/11 made Tenet's job easier. It gave him clarity, allowing him to know exactly what his priority was, that he had the full support of his president, and that he would have a blank check for more people, more funding, and expanded covert authority to do his job. A week after the attack, Bush signed a secret order giving the CIA more than $800 million (Suskind 2006, 20).

Tenet and the CIA focused on wiping out al-Qaeda in Afghanistan, a country where the agency had a long history of involvement, especially during the Russian occupation. For a change, the CIA was ahead of the Defense Department in the planning and execution of a paramilitary assault to dislodge al-Qaeda from its sanctuaries in the rugged country. On November 14, 2001, the Northern Alliance, along with CIA operatives and U.S. Special Forces, rolled into Kabul. The takedown of Afghanistan was the CIA's—and George Tenet's—finest hour.

## "SLAM DUNK" AND WEAPONS OF MASS DESTRUCTION

On August 26, 2002, Vice President Richard Cheney announced to the Veterans of Foreign Wars convention in Nashville, Tennessee, that "there is no doubt that Saddam Hussein now has weapons of mass destruction . . . many of us are convinced that he will acquire nuclear weapons fairly soon." Cheney's remarks troubled Tenet, who wrote that the speech "went well beyond what our analysis could support." Tenet believed that policy makers have a right to their own opinions, but not their own set of facts. "I had an obligation to do a better job of making sure they knew where we differed and why," he later confessed. "I should have told the Vice President privately that, in my view, his VFW speech had gone too far . . . I should not have let silence imply agreement" (Tenet 2007, 315–17; Drogin 2007, 107).

Cheney's speech marked the beginning of a huge dispute over the presence of Iraqi weapons of mass destruction, as well as possible collusion between Saddam Hussein and al-Qaeda terrorists. By this time, the Bush administration was determined to change the regime in Iraq, and for good reason. Saddam was a brutal tyrant who threatened his neighbors, sought to annex Kuwait into Iraq, shot missiles into Israel, and tortured his own people. He had used chemical weapons in the past and, in the late 1980s, had made progress toward acquiring nuclear weapons (Pfiffner 2007b, 2). According to some insiders, Bush had made up his mind to go to war with Iraq in the summer of 2002, but Tenet defended the president (Pfiffner 2007b, 3). "To me, the president still appeared less inclined to go to war than many of his senior aides," he wrote (Tenet 2007, 319). But Tenet also revealed that the administration had decided earlier to go to war when he told Kurdish leaders in March there would be a military attack on Iraq (Woodward 2004, 115–16).

Meanwhile, Tenet tried to keep a low profile and stay out of the public limelight, but as a member of the president's small war cabinet, he found himself increasingly involved in the policy debate. He did not object when both the Office of the Vice President and the Defense Department formed their own ad hoc intelligence units that pressured the intelligence community when intelligence products did not fit their political expectations and stovepiped raw, unverified intelligence straight to the White House (Pfiffner 2007b, 1).

When the SSCI became aware of the Iraqi intelligence dispute between the Office of the Vice President, Defense Department, and the intelligence community on whether Iraq possessed weapons of mass destruction, it ordered the CIA to complete a crash National Intelligence Estimate (Tenet 2007, 321–22). The new estimate concluded that "Baghdad has chemical and biological weapons . . . and could make a nuclear weapon within several months," but Tenet later admitted the estimate was "flawed" and contained little hard evidence (Weiner 2007, 487). As the inconsistent intelligence fueled more controversy, the DCI attempted to quell a press leak that the CIA's internal analysis conflicted with that of the White House. Supposed to stay above the partisan fray, Tenet found himself in the odd position of downplaying the conclusions of his own analysts at the CIA (Gordon and Trainor 2006, 129). Meanwhile, a senior CIA official threatened to resign after the National Security Council pressured her to confirm that Saddam had collaborated with al-Qaeda. She refused to rewrite her report, and Tenet defended her with a tirade of f-words aimed at White House staffers (Pfiffner 2007a, 14; Suskind 2006, 191).

In October, Tenet removed material from a presidential speech claiming that Iraq had tried to buy 500 tons of uranium oxide from Niger. Analysts at the CIA concluded that the information had originated from an unreliable source and forged documents (Remnick 2003). Two months later, however, Tenet supposedly assured the president in the Oval Office that the evidence for Saddam possessing weapons of mass destruction amounted to a "slam dunk," although he provided no new intelligence (Tenet 2007, 359). On January 28, 2003, President Bush delivered his State of the Union address and announced that "the British government has learned that Saddam Hussein recently sought significant quantities of uranium from Africa" (Tenet 2007, 449). This was the same bogus intelligence the CIA had found to be unsupported and flawed. But even if Tenet had objected to the use of the questionable intelligence, would the decision to invade Iraq have been different? Probably not, for by this time the Bush administration was committed to ousting Saddam, with or without hard evidence of weapons of mass destruction. Whatever Tenet did at this late date may not have had much impact on a decision already made.

A few days later, Secretary of State Colin Powell traveled to New York to address the United Nations. Tenet spent a week with Powell trying to agree on which intelligence could be used in the speech. "After all the back-and-forth, we believed we had produced a solid product," Tenet wrote (2007, 374), but he later contradicted himself by admitting that Powell's speech contained some of the flawed analysis from the National Intelligence Estimate. Powell made a powerful and persuasive delivery to the United Nations and helped galvanize support for the invasion of Iraq. In an unusual public appearance for the DCI, Tenet accompanied Powell and, according to a former CIA analyst, sat behind the secretary of state during the speech "like a potted plant" (McGovern 2006). When journalists later revealed that the intelligence in the speech was doubtful, Powell's reputation suffered permanent damage, as did the credibility and usefulness of Tenet and the CIA (Risen 2006, 151). "If we are not believed," former DCI Richard Helms once said, "we have no purpose" (Weiner 2007, 488).

## HARD QUESTIONS NEVER ASKED

Some CIA officers felt that George Tenet could not carry out his role as DCI objectively because he was too close to George W. Bush. But Tenet really had no choice. If the president wanted him in his inner circle, then he must follow orders and join. Tenet's choice, however, was to decide what his role was to be once he joined that inner circle. He claimed that his task was clear. "I mean, you know, you don't cross that policy line," he told the New Yorker. "You're supposed to provide objective assessments and analysis" (Goldberg 2007). But during the Iraq War buildup, he no longer served primarily as an honest broker of hard intelligence but instead allowed himself to be swept up in the politics of the day. According to one CIA official, he helped the administration use intelligence "not to inform decision making, but to justify a decision already made" (Pfiffner 2007a, 14).

Tenet's performance should not be surprising, for he had a bad habit of too often telling people what they wanted to hear, not what they needed to hear (Risen 2006, 12). He tried to please all parties instead of stepping back and letting the analysis speak for itself. At a time when he needed to stick to the facts, Tenet continued to act primarily as a consensus builder. Chester Barnard once wrote, "It seems to me inevitable that the struggle to maintain cooperation among men should as surely destroy some men morally as battle destroys some physically" (1938, 278), and indeed, Tenet may have placed himself in such a dilemma. He worried about political consequences rather than speaking truth to power and asking the hard questions that needed answers. He should have been asking whether the intelligence used in the National Intelligence Estimate was accurate, appropriate, and analyzed according to prevailing standards. Was the evidence believable, coming from diverse sources, and tested for credibility? Were the arguments persuasive and balanced rather than one sided? (Wildavsky 1979). Never asked, the hard questions were never answered.

Tenet was too good a guy to lie intentionally, but unfortunately, his loyalty to the president and his inner circle was greater than his loyalty to his agency's analysis and, ultimately, his loyalty to the truth and his responsibility to have that truth heard. Tenet would later blame the intelligence community for failing to do its job: "Why so many opportunities to sound the alarm were missed is a mystery to me," he wrote (2007, 380). But as DCI, it was Tenet's role to sound the alarm. "It's not enough to ring the bell," Richard Helms used to say. "You've got to make sure the other guy hears it" (Weiner 2007, 479).

## THE DEPARTURE OF GEORGE TENET

In March 2003, American forces invaded Iraq, fought their way into Baghdad, and nine months later captured Saddam Hussein. Soon after occupying Baghdad, U.S. civil administrator Paul Bremer ordered that the new Iraqi government remove all Ba'ath Party members from office, as well as disband the Iraqi army. Tenet and the CIA strongly opposed these actions, arguing that the Ba'athists were the only experienced civil servants in Iraq and were needed to rebuild and run the country. The agency also argued that disbanding the army would drive thousands of Iraqis into the ranks of the insurgents. Unfortunately, the CIA's credibility had been seriously weakened, and some high-level officials, particularly Vice President Cheney and Defense Secretary Donald Rumsfeld, believed the agency was too cautious and not aggressive enough for the war on terror (Pfiffner 2007a, 15). Bremer, supported by the vice president and Defense Department, ignored the CIA's objections (Tenet 2007, 428).

After U.S. inspectors found the existence of weapons of mass destruction to be "more chimerical than chemical," increasing public skepticism arose regarding the intelligence used to justify the invasion (Remnick 2003). In June 2004, after Tenet admitted the intelligence flaws in the president's State of the Union speech, Senator Richard Shelby called for the DCI's resignation (Tenet 2007, 449). Tenet knew that his days were numbered when Condoleezza Rice told the press that if the DCI "had said, 'take this out of the speech,' it would have been gone, without question." When reporters started asking him whether the president still had confidence in him, he knew that he was "in a world of trouble" (Tenet 2007, 464).

On July 11, 2004, with the political firestorm over weapons of mass destruction still building, Tenet resigned as director of central intelligence. Five months later, he stood in the East Room of the White House, where President Bush, still loyal to his former DCI, praised the CIA and awarded Tenet the Presidential Medal of Freedom.

## THE DEMISE OF THE CIA

Eleven days after George Tenet resigned, the 9/11 Commission issued its report and, as expected, soundly criticized the CIA for committing "a major intelligence failure" of a magnitude that "we simply cannot afford." The report blamed Tenet for not developing a strategy for a war against Islamist terrorists prior to 9/11. Calling the intelligence community a disorganized "confederacy," the report recommended the most ambitious intelligence reorganization since the CIA was created in 1947. Responding to both the report and a hot debate during the 2004 presidential campaign, President Bush signed legislation in April 2005 that created the Office of the Director of National Intelligence (DNI). The new position would report directly to the president and would take over the role, previously played by the now-defunct DCI, of coordinating the separate intelligence agencies. In effect, the CIA director no longer would produce the President's Daily Brief, oversee the production of the National Intelligence Estimate, or personally brief the president. Instead, the new DNI would build up his own bureaucracy of more than 1,500 personnel, many siphoned from the CIA, and take control of interagency bodies such as the National Counterterrorism Center (Pfiffner 2007a, 15).

Tenet, having taken a faculty position at Georgetown, opposed the creation of the DNI and the demotion of the CIA director post. Labeling the legislation an "effort destined to provide only a false sense of progress and security," he argued that the new intelligence design created an "over-centralized, multilayered structure that, at least where terrorism is concerned, lacked the speed and agility to meet the challenges we face." Tenet also wrote that the new DNI "may be too distant from the people he is supposed to lead and may be divorced from the risk taking and running operations" (Tenet 2007, 490, 501–4).

The larger, more enduring impact of the intelligence reorganization will unfold in future years. But for better or for worse, Tenet ushered in the end of the CIA era and, in many respects, was the last influential DCI to manage the agency at the height of its power and prestige—an agency that began as the Office of Strategic Services during World War II, helped win the Cold War and dismantle the Soviet Union, and more recently has faced the modern, unconventional challenges of international terrorism, rogue nation-states, nuclear proliferation, narcotics trafficking, and other emerging threats. For more than 50 years, Washington insiders referred to the CIA cryptically as "the Agency," but under the new DNI framework, the CIA has become merely another bureaucracy whose director no longer holds sway over the rest of the intelligence community.

Tenet must share both praise and blame for the demise of the DCI and the weakening of the CIA. The reorganization may have happened without him, as the catastrophic magnitude of 9/11 demanded change, whether needed or not. But he did prove that the huge job of the DCI was too difficult for one man—at least for him. Tenet is fundamentally a decent man, but his legacy will not be that of a man who displayed moral courage when the country needed him to do so. At times he showed a burst of fortitude, as when he stood up to President Clinton and insisted the president not release Jonathan Pollard, and later, in March 2003, when he told President Bush that he opposed a speech to be given by Vice President Cheney that linked Iraq and al-Qaeda (Tenet 2007, 341). But too often, Tenet did not object to the misuse of intelligence for political purposes, nor did he have the courage to quit when it was misused. One high-ranking CIA analyst compared— perhaps too harshly—Tenet's role in the Iraq controversy to Watergate, when Attorney General Elliott Richardson and his deputy William Ruckelshaus both quit rather than follow the orders of President Richard Nixon to fire the special prosecutor. "You don't see that kind of courage anymore," the analyst remarked, referring to Tenet (McGovern 2006).

As the debate over the Iraq War drags on, the muddled legacy left by Tenet revolves primarily around his "slam dunk" remark in the Oval Office, the uranium oxide in the president's State of the Union speech, and even the seven-figure advance he received for his recent book, in which he tries to distance himself from the failures of the intelligence community. His blaming of others has been disingenuous. "Quite simply," he wrote, "the NSC did not do its job. . . . Those in charge of U.S. policy operated within a closed loop. Bad news was ignored. Our own reporting—reporting that eventually would prove spot-on in its predictions of what came to pass on the ground—was dismissed" (2007, 447). But Tenet, too, was in the closed loop and deserves a large part of the blame that he casts on others. He may have admitted his true, less stalwart legacy when he confessed weakly that "perhaps I should have pounded the table harder" (2007, 493–94).

## ACKNOWLEDGMENTS

The author is grateful to James Pfiffner and Hal Rainey for their helpful comments. Any conclusions, of course, are solely those of the author.

## REFERENCES

Bamford, James. 2005. *A Pretext for War: 9/11, Iraq, and the Abuse of America's Intelligence Agencies.* New York: Anchor Books.

Barnard, Chester I. 1938. *The Functions of the Executive.* Cambridge, MA: Harvard University Press.

Cheney, Richard. 2002. Remarks by the Vice President to the Veterans of Foreign Wars 103rd National Convention, August 26, Nashville, TN. http://www.whitehouse.gov/news/releases/2002/08/20020826.html [accessed January 20, 2008].

Coll, Steve. 2004. *Ghost Wars: The Secret History of the CIA, Afghanistan, and bin Laden, from the Soviet Invasion to September 10, 2001.* New York: Penguin.

Drogin, Bob. 2007. *Curveball: Spies, Lies, and the Con Man Who Caused a War.* New York: Random House.

Eddington, Patrick G. 1999. George Tenet's CIA Record. *Washington Post,* August 27.

Goldberg, Jeffrey. 2007. Woodward vs. Tenet: The New Intelligence War. *New Yorker,* May 21.

Gordon, Michael R., and Bernard E. Trainor. 2006. *Cobra II: The Inside Story of the Invasion and Occupation of Iraq.* New York: Pantheon.

Isikoff, Michael, and David Corn. 2006. *Hubris: The Inside Story of Spin, Scandal, and the Selling of the Iraq War.* New York: Three Rivers Press

Kay, David. 2006. Interview, *Frontline,* PBS, June 20.

Kean, Thomas H., and Lee H. Hamilton. 2006. *Without Precedent: The Inside Story of the 9/11 Commission.* New York: Vintage Books.

McGovern, Raymond. 2006. Interview, *Frontline,* PBS, June 20.

9/11 Commission. 2004. *The 9/11 Commission Report: Final Report of the National Commission on Terrorist Attacks upon the United States.* New York: W.W. Norton.

Pfiffner , James P. 2007a. The First MBA President: George W. Bush as Public Administrator. *Public Administration Review* 67 (1): 6–20.

———. 2007b. Intelligence and Decision Making before the War with Iraq. In *The Polarized Presidency of George W. Bush,* edited by George C. Edwards and Desmond King, 213–42. New York: Oxford University Press.

Posner, Steve. 1998. The Spy at Wye. *Washington Post,* October 27.

Remnick, David. 2003. Faith-Based Intelligence. *New Yorker,* July 28.

Risen, James. 2006. *State of War: The Secret History of the CIA and the Bush Administration.* New York: Free Press.

Suskind, Ron. 2006. *The One Percent Doctrine: Deep Inside America's Pursuit of Its Enemies since 9/11.* New York: Simon & Schuster.

Tenet, George. 2007. *At the Center of the Storm: My Years at the CIA.* New York: HarperCollins.

Weiner, Tim. 2007. *Legacy of Ashes: The History of the CIA.* New York: Doubleday.

Wildavsky, Aaron. 1979. *Speaking Truth to Power: The Art and Craft of Policy Analysis.* Boston: Little, Brown.

Woodward, Bob. 2002. *Bush at War.* New York: Simon & Schuster.

———. 2004. *Plan of Attack.* New York: Simon & Schuster.

# 9

# COLLEEN JOLLIE, STATE TRIBAL LIAISON

## A Story of Transformational Change

### CHERYL SIMRELL KING AND MEGAN BEEBY

The history of relationships between Washington State government and the American Indian tribes within the state borders is fraught with problems, not unlike the history of relationships between tribes and other governmental units across the United States (Aufrecht 1999; Aufrecht and Case 2005; Mays and Taggart 2005; Oritz 2002). Yet while there is much work still to be done, the state of Washington and the tribes of Washington have come a long way toward crafting working relationships founded on strong principles of respect and recognition of the sovereign rights of tribes. These relationships were not formed necessarily out of harmony. They come as a result of tribes and individual Indians being willing to do the hard work of compelling the state to act effectively, reasonably, and responsibly. Some of this work is done through collaboration. Some of this work is done through dissension.

One person involved in both collaboration and dissension is Colleen Jollie, the state tribal liaison at the Washington State Department of Transportation (WSDOT). Jollie, a descendent of the Turtle Mountain Chippewa tribe, is a self-confessed Coyote-type character. In many Native American myths and stories across tribes and nations, the Coyote is seen as a transformer or a changer. The Coyote, in some traditions, is a "trickster," using one's wiles to disrupt, refuse, and dismantle ways that are not working in order to creatively, and sometimes chaotically, build new ways. Tricksters use their skills to subvert colonial worlds. As such, tricksters draw attention to transgressions in order to transform and enlighten (Conroy and Davis 2002).

Patterson (2001) sees the trickster as the personification of the "anti-administrator" (Farmer 1995, 2001). As Patterson states, when the trickster

> is on the scene, prevailing rules are thwarted, uncertainties are incarnated, imagination is embraced, conflicts are sidestepped, and paradoxes are transformed. Neither saints nor devils, neither good citizens nor psychopaths, tricksters disturb categories and modes of thinking and get folks "unstuck" from usual routines. Although others audition, tricksters star in anti-administrative roles . . . trickster figures often embody the idea that we can develop alternative constructs, rather than choose merely among existing ones. (2001, 531, 536)

From *Public Administration Review,* 68, No. 6 (November/December 2008): 1142–1150. Copyright © 2008 American Society for Public Administration. Used by permission.

At the outset of Colleen's work at the WSDOT, her mission was to create a culture of cooperation. Here, Colleen would harness transformational energy to encourage cooperation where differences prevailed. To foster change in her organization, Colleen established a Coyote Award for people who go the extra mile to make changes and improve relations between the agency and the tribes.

It is probably important to note that Colleen, like Coyote the trickster, frequently finds herself in troubling situations. The language on the brochure announcing the WSDOT's Coyote Award says it best:

> In many Native American traditions the Coyote is known as the Changer, or the Trickster, who transforms our world. By whatever means—going over, under, around or through, but mostly by thoughtful effort, Coyote finds a way to create change.

Like the Coyote, Colleen has been a changer in the agency and has transformed operations and functions in many ways, but mostly through systematic, thoughtful effort. In her work, she practices a type of "critical management theory" that seeks to transform people and places by exploring and bringing to light unexamined assumptions and practices. Critical management practices also work to link power and resources to people and communities that are marginalized (King and Zanetti 2005). In her work, Colleen focuses not just on projects but also on people, believing that transformation in organizations and society will only occur when people and the life conditions of marginalized people and communities are transformed. As the Coyote knows and as Colleen's story illustrates, transformative work and the work of the anti-administrator are neither easy nor popular. Nonetheless, they are crucial.

## THE CONTEXT

Washington, like other states west of the Rocky Mountains, has a comparably high number of tribal governments within its state borders. An American Indian tribe is an indigenous group of people with a shared culture, history, and government. Nationally, there are approximately 561 federally recognized tribes; 29 of these tribes are located in Washington State (37 tribes operate as governmental entities within the state, irrespective of federal recognition). Federal recognition means that the tribe has a distinct and continuing political relationship with the federal government through a treaty, executive order, or legislation. The U.S. Constitution, nation-to-nation treaties, federal statutes, case law, executive orders, and other administrative policies protect this government-to-government relationship.

The preponderance of federally recognized tribes in the Western United States is partly the result of original settlement patterns, historical forced removal and migration patterns, and the lack of lands for tribes to migrate into as nonnative white settlements continued to expand toward the westernmost edge of the continent. Of course, the land mass of the Western states is larger than in the Eastern United States, which also explains the higher rate of "nations within" the Western United States (Deloria and Lytle 1998). The number of tribes in a state makes a difference in how governments interact with the various tribes. So, too, does the body of federal policy on self-determination. For example, the Indian Self-Determination Act of 1975 required state and local governments to interact with American Indian tribes within a government-to-government relationship. In other areas of the country, the existence of fewer tribes tends to result in less political power and less pressure to change intergovernmental relations. Governing agencies, then, may be able to skate around government-to-government relationships. This is not the case in the state of Washington.

Gambling compacts and revenues from gaming bring many states to the table with tribal governments, and this is certainly true for the state of Washington and Washington-based tribes. Tribes in Washington have always been at the forefront of the movement to protect and assert Indian tribal sovereignty. In addition, tribes and the state come together in Washington because of a particular and significant legal matter rising from the 1974 district court decision in *United States v. Washington* (384 F.Supp. 312 [W.D. Wash.]), better known as the "Boldt decision."

Briefly, the controversial and precedence-setting Boldt decision affirmed the "reserved" or treaty-based rights of Washington State tribes to fish and to fisheries. This landmark decision recognized, indeed affirmed, the fishing rights reserved by tribes through various treaties signed with the U.S. government (e.g., the historic 1854 Treaty of Medicine Creek). What makes this decision particularly significant, not to mention controversial, is the contemporary affirmation of treaty rights that had eroded or were not recognized over time. In other words, in 1974, the court decreed that tribes' rights reserved in the 1850s could no longer be ignored or denied, setting a legal precedent that has had resounding significance for Washington State–based tribes and for intergovernmental relations in Washington State.

The other significant element of this decision as it relates to intergovernmental relations is the way in which Judge Boldt interpreted the "in common with" clause from the original treaty language. Expressed in the Medicine Creek Treaty, that clause stated that "[t]he right of taking fish, at all usual and accustomed grounds and stations, is further secured to said Indians *in common* with all citizens of the Territory."[1] The language had historically been interpreted by the government as limiting the fishing rights of American Indian tribes. The Boldt decision, however, interpreted that clause quite differently. Judge Boldt held that the tribes and the state of Washington are *equal partners* in the harvest and management of the fisheries' resources, beginning a practice of *comanagement* that has since influenced tribal and state relationships.

Following Boldt, and the changing practices between tribes and the state, the parties entered into the Centennial Accord in 1989. The Centennial Accord is based on the principles of mutual and respective sovereignty in order "to better achieve mutual goals through an improved relationship between their sovereign governments . . . [and] to provide a framework for government-to-government relationships and implementation procedures."[2] In 1999, the tribes and the state signed the New Millennium Agreement, strengthening and affirming the Centennial Accord and institutionalizing the government-to-government relationships established in the first accord.[3] It is within this particular context that Colleen Jollie does her work as the state tribal liaison for the Washington State Department of Transportation.

## CREATING THE WSDOT'S STATE TRIBAL LIAISON

Prior to becoming state tribal liaison for the WSDOT in 2001, Colleen worked for the state's Governor's Office of Indian Affairs (GOIA). The GOIA serves as a statewide liaison between state and tribal governments; the office affirms "the government-to-government relationship and principles identified in the Centennial Accord to promote and enhance tribal self-sufficiency and [it] serves to assist the state in developing policies consistent with those principles."[4] It is while working at the GOIA that Colleen first met the newly appointed secretary of transportation, Doug MacDonald, early in his tenure with the organization.[5] Soon after their meeting, Secretary MacDonald created the state tribal liaison as an executive-level position. The liaison would report directly to the chief of staff. Secretary MacDonald, relying on his previous experience working with tribes in the Boston area, convinced Colleen of his transformational vision for the WSDOT. Recognizing Colleen's Coyote nature (MacDonald has a bit of Coyote himself), he recruited her to be the first tribal liaison for the WSDOT.

Creating "firsts" is what Colleen does, exhibiting the creative energy of the Coyote. Prior to her work with the WSDOT, Colleen convinced The Evergreen State College to build a first-of-its-kind Native American-style longhouse on the college campus; 10 years hence, other universities in Washington are doing the same. She also created a native art nonprofit organization called the Northwest Native American Basketweavers Association[6] and a nonprofit philanthropic organization called the Potlatch Fund.[7]

A number of Washington State agencies have tribal liaison positions; some of these positions are staffed by American Indians, others are staffed by non-Indians acting in the role of "messengers," bringing the state's interests to the tribes and working, in a unilateral direction, to build relationships with tribes. Early in his tenure at the WSDOT, MacDonald surmised that the intentions of the Centennial Accord and Millennium Agreement were not going to be realized with the organizational structure he had inherited. At the time, the WSDOT had a non-Indian in a part-time, below mid-level management liaison position. This position was located in the agency's planning department. MacDonald knew that in order to realize the intentions of government-to-government relationships, and following on the practices of social service agencies, the liaison position should be filled by an Indian who acts as facilitator, developing relationships and working with both the tribes and the state government to build capacities. MacDonald also knew this position must be part of the agency's Government Relations Department, as tribes are governments with whom the WSDOT must interact in the same way the agency interacts with federal, local, and regional governments. Finally, the position had to be located at the executive level for it to be an effective position and for the tribal liaison to be effective on the job.

Colleen's father is Turtle Mountain Chippewa (Belcourt, North Dakota), and her mother is the daughter of pioneer immigrants from Ireland and France. Colleen believes that her mixed heritage uniquely qualifies her for the liaison position because she literally stands between and within both Indian and non-Indian worlds. While growing up, Colleen lived on and off reservations and in rural and urban areas; another Coyote trait, as told in some stories, is Coyote walks between two worlds—the world of the humans and the world of the stars. In addition, Colleen throughout experienced poverty and the effects of classism, racism, and sexism. Thus, she knew she would need to make her way without much outside support and that she needed to find her inner strength buried deeply beneath layers of oppression. She did this work at The Evergreen State College, both in the undergraduate Native American program and in the master of public administration program (she received her master's degree before Evergreen began offering a concentration in tribal governance). She started working for the state of Washington because she needed a good job that would allow her to provide for her daughter; moreover, she didn't want to leave Olympia. As Olympia is a "company town" for state government, she chose to educate and prepare herself to work for the state. It was, in effect, a decision born not of idealism but of pragmatism and the need to make a living. Ultimately, it proved fortuitous for the state and for Washington State tribes.

## THE ESSENTIAL WORK

Shortly after beginning her work as tribal liaison, Colleen realized that achieving results would require not simply working with tribal planners and public works directors; she also needed to work with tribal human resource managers, cultural resource and economic development managers, tribal councils, transportation planners, natural resource managers, and fisheries managers.

Colleen quickly came to understand that there were two distinct types of relations with tribes and the WSDOT: consulting with tribes on WSDOT projects that affect tribal rights and resources—such as impacts on cultural resources—and facilitating tribes' access to resources in order to develop their own transportation projects and infrastructure. As she was not an expert in transportation, Colleen had much work to do in order to understand the world of transportation and each of the different departments within the WSDOT. Every department, from planning to design to construction to maintenance, works with tribes in one capacity or another, and Colleen had to learn as much as she could about all of the ways in which the agency interacts with tribes.

The WSDOT project teams know that successful tribal consultation can play a key part in delivering projects on time and within budget, a top organizational goal for the agency. As a tribal liaison and a key support person on projects, Colleen is asked to serve in many capacities, including facilitator, interpreter, and sometimes even as "psychic"—that is, she is often asked to predict what tribes want and what their response will be. Equally important, Colleen helps tribes understand the transportation project development process so that they know when to engage. She travels across the state to assist on projects and work with tribes through the consultation process. Through these experiences, she has identified many policy and procedural gaps in tribal consultation and has worked with tribes and agency staff to address these.

One of Colleen's initial goals as tribal liaison was to raise awareness within the state's Indian Country about critical transportation issues. When she began her work, transportation was not a big issue in Indian Country. Roads were historically handled by the Bureau of Indian Affairs (BIA), the federal agency with which tribes historically have had a trust relationship. At that time, Indian Country was thinking about economic development and meeting the resource needs of their people; roads and traffic safety often were not a top tribal priority. Perhaps the most salient transportation issue for tribes is traffic safety. For example, in 2003, there were 20 traffic fatalities on the Colville Reservation, a large reserve located in central Washington. Colleen discovered that across the nation and in Washington State, traffic fatalities in Indian Country are two to five times higher than they are in non-Indian communities. In Indian Country, the roads are frequently bad, cars are often in disrepair, and tribes, as sovereign governments, do not necessarily enact and enforce traffic safety laws, such as seatbelt or motorcycle helmet laws.[8]

Given the resource constraints and historical cultural and economic degradation experienced in Indian County, one has to bring a very different set of expectations to work in this region, particularly if the work is highly technical. When it comes to roads in Indian Country, there is a great deal of contradiction and confusion—roads are interjurisdictional, and they can be owned and managed by the tribe (or by the BIA on their behalf), the state, the county, or the city. Simply identifying which segments of roads were owned by which government turned out to be a daunting task. There is often a great deal of conflict about who is in control of the roads.

In Indian Country, information is often gathered narratively and relationally. One is not privy to stories unless one is trusted and seen as an ally, no matter whether one is Indian or non-Indian. Colleen found out about the tragic death rates on tribal lands through stories told around a table of people gathered for another purpose, as a board member of the Potlatch Fund, which promotes philanthropy in Indian Country. She was privy to this story because she is a trusted ally in Indian County and because of the way in which she defines her work as "service." She was shocked to learn that individuals and officials of Colville thought the high death rates on their tribal roads were normal.

One of the most important elements of Colleen's job is to work with tribes and individuals to raise awareness of the lack of normalcy of conditions in Indian Country and to connect tribes to information and resources they can use to improve these conditions. As such, she works closely with tribes to raise awareness and match tribal needs with existing resources. The other important part of Colleen's job is to work with WSDOT personnel to raise cultural awareness and sensitivity among non-Indian employees of the agency. The year she started working with the agency, only 20 employees in the agency had gone through GOIA's one-day training, which covers the tribal historical perspective, legal issues, tribal sovereignty, and tribal government, all intended to lead to a deeper understanding of tribes, their people, and their unique culture, as well as an enhanced awareness of the importance of multiculturalism. Colleen is proud to say that, to date, more than 800 agency employees have been trained, most of them through in-agency training that adapts GOIA's program for employees working in transportation.

Colleen believes that most people who have completed the training—from frontline technicians to traffic engineers and managers—have a deeper understanding of cultural issues and approach their work with tribes from a more considered perspective. She also believes they are creating a culture of caring in an agency that is often stereotyped as being narrow, rigid, and focused only on the rationality or reason behind the engineered solutions (e.g., Does it "pencil out?"). To find cultural competency and caring in a social service agency is expected; to find it in an agency such as the WSDOT is exceptional, and it has proved essential to Colleen's efforts to realize the goals of the Centennial Accord and New Millennium Agreement. It certainly points to Colleen's and her staff's creative, transformational natures. As Colleen maintains, it is not enough to simply transform organizational practices; people have to be changed, shifted, or transformed.

## TRANSFORMING PEOPLE AND PRACTICES

The goals of the Centennial Accord can be achieved through increasing cultural competency and working directly with tribes, and through comanagement processes aimed at identifying problems and crafting solutions in order to shift or change the ways in which individuals in the agency approach Indians and Indian policy. The goals can also be met by increasing the number of Indians employed by and with the WSDOT. Colleen's job includes working to increase both the number of Indians employed by WSDOT and the number of Indian organizations awarded WSDOT contracts. When Colleen started working with the agency, there were 80 American Indians working for the agency. Currently, the agency employs 124 American Indians. Since 2001, four new tribal liaison positions have been created. WSDOT job announcements are disseminated to tribal agencies and are heavily promoted in Indian Country. This effort has resulted in employment figures that are on par with the targeted goals of the agency. Colleen says, "I come from the perspective of going the extra mile, working a little bit harder to get things and ourselves out there where we need to be, at the tables in council meetings and meeting with tribal professionals. It's an affirmative action. This is part of my civic activism."

One of the challenges of Colleen's job is that she is required to be neutral, showing partiality to neither tribal nor agency perspectives in her work. Because she sees her work as an extension of herself and as a calling to assist her people—a practice of civic activism—neutrality is hard to achieve. Therefore, her transformational Coyote management style is sometimes at odds with the dominant management style of the organization. Working with Secretary MacDonald validated and enforced her style and perspective. What she particularly appreciated about working with MacDonald is that he relied on his emotions to inform his decisions. He realized the importance of how and what Colleen practices: One needs to be moved in one's work by what is right and wrong and by what is just. When justice is not served or when justice is in question, it creates an emotional situation. Working with governments and with people who have suffered social injustices for centuries and who, for the most part, are culturally communal and relational requires cooperative and collaborative management and decision-making approaches that seek to work across significant differences. Colleen has found herself in situations in the agency in which she has been discounted by fellow executives for what they deem nonprofessional practices, stemming from her cooperative and collaborative practices, which, ironically, sometimes include dissension to bring social injustices to the executive table to be righted. Colleen's vision is very clear: She is in this position to serve her people, and she will do so in a way that honors and respects Indian Country. Yet at the same time, she cannot do so in a way that destabilizes essential relationships that are needed to ensure her ends. Thus, she must be moderate both in Indian Country, where she may be mistrusted because she represents the state, and in the agency, where she may be mistrusted because she is different from others. Like the Coyote, because of the shape-shifting she must practice, she may not be trusted anywhere. The paths to trust or mistrust, within the agency and with tribes, are not always clear, as the following stories illustrate.

## TRUST OR MISTRUST? TWO STORIES

The path of one of Colleen's first major projects with the WSDOT was relatively straightforward—assisting with traffic safety on the Colville Reservation. Her job was, simply put, to bring people together to change the fatality statistics on Colville's roads. She made connections with federal organizations (e.g., the BIA and DOT) and tribal councils, planning departments, and law enforcement teams, all of which eventually joined together in a newly created Tribal Traffic Safety Task Force, staffed by the Washington State Traffic Safety Commission. She went to the Colville Reservation and other tribal communities to listen to stories. She connected the tribe with university-based resources for training in data collection and helped develop monitoring capacities within the Tribe. With the task force, she encouraged the passage of tribal safety laws, and she encouraged the Colville Tribe to develop enforcement plans and procedures. She was always present, showing up on the reservation where the problems lay. She did not attempt to solve this problem from the safety and security of her office or her cubicle. As Colleen says, "You've got to be present to win. [In Indian Country it is expected], whether you are Indian or not, that you show up."

In Colville, seatbelt compliance increased from 36 percent to 86 percent in one year's time. Colleen says, "I feel really grateful, really blessed to be in this position where I can get the information, share it with people who care and we can make a difference." And seatbelt compliance is making a difference in traffic fatalities on the reservation. A while back, several teenagers were involved in a rollover accident on a Colville road, and all were wearing seatbelts. They walked away from the accident; they would have been another statistic had they not been wearing seatbelts. In the Colville community, as in other Indian communities, these are not just statistics but people who are known to everyone in the communities. It is not possible to look at Indian Country data as objective measures of something that doesn't personally touch the data collector or analyst. One has to do both—see the statistics as people and have the capacity and resources to see the statistics as information that can help access resources to solve problems. One has to be a Coyote, addressing the problem by any means, going under, over, through, or around, but mostly by thoughtful effort.

The Colville story has a happy ending. Fatalities have been reduced, and Colleen is working with other tribes in the state on traffic safety. Other tribes want to establish traffic safety task forces and, with the Washington State Traffic Commission, federal grants are being written to access federal transportation resources to staff their work. The Colville tribe's authority to manage traffic and roads has increased significantly; other tribes see this and are encouraged to work with the WSDOT in similar ways.

The second story has a less clear path and a less happy ending. It is a story that speaks to the possibilities and limitations of government-to-government relationships in managing and implementing large, cross-jurisdictional projects. Readers are encouraged to read the full report, which can be accessed from the WSDOT library,[9] or the *Seattle Times*'s special report.[10]

In the summer of 2003, the WSDOT began work in Port Angeles, Washington, on a dry dock or "graving dock" in preparation for a massive project to fix and modernize the Hood Canal Bridge. Soon after construction began, workers began uncovering artifacts and bone fragments. Further excavation by archeologists and members of the Lower Elwah Klallam Tribe revealed remnants of Tse-whit-zen, the largest Indian village ever discovered in Washington. So many graves were found that the WSDOT eventually walked away from the site in December 2004 after spending $60 million and unearthing the remains of more than 300 Lower Elwah Klallam ancestors.

The *Seattle Times* called the Port Angeles graving dock project "the costliest mistake ever."[11] The presence of the ancient Klallam village had been known to historians and tribal members, and there was a high probability that the WSDOT would unearth something related to the ancient village in their work. The WSDOT did do an archaeological survey before beginning the project, but this review was limited. Prior to construction, the government-to-government consultation that occurred between Lower Elwah Klallam Tribe and the WSDOT amounted to correspondence in letters, and it did not reveal that the project was likely to unearth a village and gravesites.

When WSDOT leaders first visited the graving dock site in Port Angeles, what they saw was a seemingly appropriate site, and local and tribal leaders were pleased that money and jobs were coming to an economically stagnant area. As Secretary MacDonald said, "the collective amnesia is so profound that no one [including the Tribe] ever even asked the question" of whether or not this was a sacred site. The project was necessary, and the town was more than pleased to experience the economic dividends of the work. The Tribe, in turn, had been consulted in accordance with the established government-to-government relationships and agreed with the WSDOT's assessment, although the tribe warned the agency of the proximity to known historical Klallam village sites. The Lower Elwah Klallam Tribe is not as economically prosperous as other tribes in the state, and it did not have cultural resource professionals on tribal government staff. In addition, neither the Tribe nor the WSDOT consulted with elders. Consulting with elders is not a parameter of by-the-book government-to-government relationships, but, as this situation revealed, it is an essential element of intergovernmental relations between tribes and other governments.

After the initial discovery, the Lower Elwha Klallam Tribe and state and federal agencies worked together for more than a year in an attempt to complete the project. Colleen attempted to facilitate the dialogue between the tribes and agencies to bring the two points of view toward resolution. "Which side do you work for, the state or the tribes?" was a question asked by both the agencies and tribes, and often in confrontational tones. Her response was always "both." Because she walked both sides and encountered the effects of doing so in both worlds, her experiences on this project were the most challenging of her personal and professional life.

The graving dock project had not been on her radar screen when it began; she was called in after the first artifacts and bone fragments were excavated. She went to visit the site and partici-pate in a meeting with the Tribe; she then reported her findings to MacDonald, who immediately picked up the phone and temporarily stopped work on the project. Doing this threw everyone into a panic—no one stops a project of this magnitude. The surveying work with the tribe met or exceeded legal requirements. The agency did what it needed to do, according to law. Laws in place are in favor of getting projects done, not in favor of shutting projects down because a few bones have been discovered. As it turns out, unearthing native graves is a regular occurrence in most major construction projects in Washington State. But tribes have no legal jurisdiction on nonreservation land. Yet MacDonald and Colleen followed their intuition and sense that there was something seriously wrong on that site; both could feel it, though neither could name it. But they knew something was there.

MacDonald was subsequently advised to do the legal minimum and get on with the project, or all hell would break loose. As Colleen says, "All hell broke loose anyway but imagine," she says, "what would have happened if they had unearthed the hundreds of human remains with a backhoe. They didn't tear into those burial sites with massive earth movers, they did it with paintbrushes and trowels. This made all the difference."

The relationship between the Tribe and the agency was one of mutual respect and understanding. The Tribe and the agency were partners in this work; they were "walking together." As the agency was responsible for disturbing the remains of the ancestors, the Tribe asked the WSDOT to sponsor a burning ceremony, an ancient ritual to feed and shelter the ancestors. Colleen says, "The disturbance to their ancestors was not going to be healed with a check or a donation of a site to rebury the ancestors; it needed much more than that." Agency personnel took lead roles in preparing the ceremony and were invited to attend the ceremony. Non-Indians rarely, if ever, are included in ceremonies such as these. The inclusion of the agency in the healing ritual and the work stoppage is what Colleen calls "a miracle of public administration," and, no doubt, a result of the transformational nature of both Colleen and MacDonald.

Over and over again in trying to bring resolution to this situation, the agency did the right things, as did the Tribe. Yet in the end, the historical injustices played out in tribal communities across the nation factored into the relational equation, irrespective of the good intentions of the Tribe, the agency, and Colleen's work. You can do everything "right" yet, in the end, it may be impossible to get beyond historical relationships.

The graving dock project was as painful as projects get, yet possibilities were presented to work toward healing and reconciliation. Small steps forward were taken. These small steps may be the most important tribal liaison work done by the WSDOT. Much was learned through this sad and difficult process. These lessons have been translated into other projects at the WSDOT. Government-to-government relationships, particularly with indigenous nations, mean more than just consultation and comanagement. They mean working together to honor the historical and spiritual legacies of our cultures and doing so with honor and dignity as we negotiate and work through deeply difficult situations.

The graving dock story has an unusual ending, as most projects go. The project work was stopped. The future of the site was negotiated between the Tribe and the agency and was eventually settled in court. The WSDOT cleared the site of the sheet piling and concrete pads, and the site was given to the Tribe. The Tribe will rebury the remains of their ancestors and construct a modest curation or interpretation center on the site. With the construction of pontoons, the Hood Canal Bridge repair work was relocated to the Seattle area.

Significant tax dollars were spent on this project, and Washington citizens are holding the WSDOT and the governor accountable for this expenditure. Responses to citizen outcries that are framed by of what is "right" and what is "just" don't always fall on friendly ears. This is particularly true at a time when citizens demand fiscal accountability from their governments and see themselves as individualistic owners or shareholders of governments rather than as citizens working with their governments toward some positive public good. For some in Washington State, the dollars "wasted" on this project exacerbated raw nerves related to the Boldt decision and the effects of that decision on non-Indian fisheries; this, in turn, has fed racist views toward American Indians. As the WSDOT states on its Website,

Whether denominated as the Hood Canal Graving Dock misadventure or the Tse-whit-zen Village re-discovery, the substantial delay and added cost to the bridge rehabilitation project is only a small part of what the events at Port Angeles now represent. Now this experience is marked as a major moment in cultural discovery that, though burdened with pain of many kinds, contributed much more than a trove of archaeological artifacts to our search for meaning in our past and our present.[12]

To further complicate relations between the tribes and the WSDOT, in 2007, the so-called culvert case received a summary judgment in favor of the tribes (20 tribes joined the case). The culvert case, *United States v. Washington* (U.S. Dist. LEXIS 61850 [W.D. Wash.]) is also referred to as "Boldt II," as the judgment relies on the precedence of the Boldt case, in which the tribes received rights reserved by original treaties. As a result of the judgment in the culvert case, the WSDOT must accelerate its schedule to repair or replace hundreds of culverts that block fish passage in western Washington. The WSDOT agrees that the repairs and replacements are needed, but legal action requiring them to do so strains relationships and budgets. We carry our past with us into the present day, and both are at the table in government-to government relationships with the tribes.

## CONCLUSION: WHAT'S NEXT?

Like the Coyote and other tricksters, Colleen's work with the WSDOT is paradoxical. Sometimes the work, although complicated, yields positive results, as seen in her work with the Colville Tribe and her work on educating and training agency personnel. Sometimes the work is fraught with difficulties, involves legal action, and yields mixed results, as in the graving dock project. The difficult projects serve as bridges between the tribes and the state and create opportunities for healing historical wounds. Not everyone, however, is pleased with the results, and two steps forward are sometimes followed by three steps backward.

The work of a transformational public administrator is difficult. The transformation of people and organizations is not easy and requires personal and professional sacrifices that go beyond what is typically involved in public service work (King and Zanetti 2005). As Colleen says, "The first wave of transformation was the easiest. When you get down to the deeper layers—the layers where people are resistant to change because it's the way things have always been done, the typical response of people is to resist change." Practicing cooperative and collaboration among and between entities that have a long history of animosity and have relied on solutions crafted through litigation instead of collaboration can create significant roadblocks for the transformational public administrator in troubling situations. Walking the line between the state and tribes can lead, as indicated earlier, to neither the state nor the tribes having trust in the person doing the walking. Tribes may think the person working for the agency has "sold out," whereas agency employees may not trust anyone who cannot, and will not, be neutral. Colleen put both of these trust relationships to the test in her work, particularly in the work on the graving dock project. It's not a matter of whether Colleen has failed personally or if collaborative management and transformational administrative practices are impossible. As Oritz states,

> This unique relationship [no clear boundaries on sovereignty and the need for intergovernmental cooperation] requires dealing with tribes on an administrative policy level that must encompass the past, present and future. It requires careful consideration of cultural, historic and socioeconomic aspects of Indian tribes, which are almost always intertwined. (2002, 487)

Doing work that encompasses the past, present, and future for both non-Indian and Indian governmental entities is often difficult and will not always yield success. Yet as Colleen has demonstrated, perseverance is key to increasing the probability of success in collaboration and cooperation across significant differences.

Colleen is beginning to ask herself whether her ability to engender change both within state agencies and within tribes is limited and whether it is time to move onto other work. She wonders whether, like Coyote in some stories, she has done all she can here and whether it is time to move on. But she knows that transformation is complete only when one's efforts become institutionalized, when there is no need for liaisons because all agency employees work as liaisons as a regular part of their daily activities. This is her goal. She knows that sometimes it is important to "cut your losses"—that it is both the most humane and appropriate business decision to walk away from projects. Given the great challenges she continues to face, it will, according to Colleen, "take a tremendous amount of political will to stay the course of maintaining great tribal relations." If maintaining and strengthening viable government-to-government relations continues to be the goal, then agencies and tribes have to stay the course in these sometimes difficult, troubling times.

No matter what Colleen does next, there is no doubt that she, and the team with which she works, has significantly contributed to how one agency, and perhaps an entire state, realizes the intricacies and intentions of government-to-government relations as charged by the Centennial Accord and the New Millennium Agreement. Colleen's work indicates the possibility for all of us, governments and individuals, to work toward a radically different way of considering and working with our tribal nations.

## NOTES

1. See the Boldt decision at http://en.wikipedia.org/ wiki/Boldt_Decision [accessed July 28, 2008].

2. See http://www.goia.wa.gov/Government-to-Government/CentennialAgreement.html [accessed July 28, 2008].

3. See http://www.goia.wa.gov/Government-to-Government/millenniumAgreement.html [accessed July 28, 2008].

4. See http://www.goia.wa.gov/AboutUs/AboutUs.htm [accessed July 28, 2008].

5. For a profile of Secretary MacDonald, see King and Zanetti (2005).

6. See http://www.nnaba.org/ [accessed July 28, 2008].

7. See http://www.potlatchfund.org/ [accessed July 28, 2008].

8. Because tribal lands are sovereign nation lands, federal and state laws do not automatically apply on tribal lands. For more information on tribes as "nations within" a nation (making the U.S. territory international within our borders), see Deloria and Lytle (1998).

9. See http://www.wsdot.wa.gov/Accountability/HCBGravingDock/default.htm [accessed July 28, 2008].

10. See http://seattletimes.nwsource.com/news/local/klallam/ [accessed July 28, 2008].

11. See http://seattletimes.nwsource.com/html/localnews/klallamday3.html [accessed July 28, 2008].

12. See http://www.wsdot.wa.gov/accountability/hcbgravingdock/ [accessed July 28, 2008].

## REFERENCES

Aufrecht, Steven E. 1999. Missing: Native American Governance in American Public Administration Literature. *American Review of Public Administration* 29 (4): 370–91.

Aufrecht, Steven E., and David S. Case. 2005. Indians 78, Washington State 0: Stories about Indians and the Law. *Public Administration Review* 65 (4): 450–72.

Conroy, James C., and Robert A. Davis. 2002. Transgression, Transformation and Enlightenment: the Trickster as Poet and Teacher. *Educational Philosophy and Theory* 34 (3): 255–72.

Deloria, Vine, and Cliff M. Lytle. 1998. *The Nations Within: The Past and Future of American Indian Sovereignty*. Austin: University of Texas Press.

Farmer, David. 1995. *The Language of Public Administration: Bureaucracy, Modernity and Postmodernity*. Tuscaloosa: University of Alabama Press.

———. 2001. Mapping Anti-Administration: Introduction to the Symposium. *Administrative Theory and Praxis* 23 (4): 475–92.

King, Cheryl Simrell, and Lisa A. Zanetti. 2005. *Transformational Public Service: Portraits of Theory in Practice*. Armonk, NY: M.E. Sharpe.

Mays, G. Larry, and William A. Taggart. 2005. Intergovernmental Relations and Native American Gaming: A Case Study on the Emergence of a New Intergovernmental Relations Participant. *American Review of Public Administration* 35 (1): 74–93.

Oritz, James. 2002. Tribal Governance and Public Administration. *Administration & Society* 34 (5): 459–81.

Patterson, Patricia M. 2001. Imagining Anti-Administration's Anti-Hero (Antagonist? Protagonist? Agonist?). *Administrative Theory and Praxis* 23 (4): 529–40.

# 10

# BEING THERE MATTERS—REDEFINING THE MODEL PUBLIC SERVANT

## Viola O. Baskerville in Profile

### JANET R. HUTCHINSON AND DEIRDRE M. CONDIT

Civic trailblazing comes more easily to some than to others. While many struggle to break new ground, making their way through the public underbrush, others seem to cut inviting paths to new visions of what is possible in the civic realm. Viola Baskerville is one such natural civic trailblazer. The swath she has cut in Virginia politics and government for women of all colors and ethnicities has been remarkably wide and generous, and she seems to have accomplished it all with extraordinary grace and élan.

Viola Osborne Baskerville was born in Richmond, Virginia, on October 29, 1951. She was educated in the segregated Virginia public school system until the eighth grade, graduated from the College of William & Mary in 1973—where she was one of six African Americans in her class—won a Fulbright scholarship in German literature that same year, and earned a law degree from the University of Iowa's College of Law in 1979. She is married to her life partner, Dr. Archer Baskerville, and is the mother of two grown sons.

Baskerville, a Virginia native who traces her maternal family's roots in the state to 1790, began her public career in 1994 when she was elected to the Richmond City Council. Prior to that, she had worked for many years as a civic volunteer while raising her children. In 1997, she was elected to the Virginia House of Delegates, where she served four terms before resigning in 2005 to run for lieutenant governor in the Democratic Party primary. Following her primary loss to fellow Democrat and former U.S. congresswoman Leslie Byrne, Baskerville was appointed to run the transition team of the newly elected governor, Democrat Tim Kaine. In recognition of her success co-chairing the transition, the governor tapped her to serve as the state's secretary of administration, the position she currently holds. In announcing her appointment, Kaine, a former colleague on the Richmond City Council, noted that Baskerville "impressed me as one of the hardest working members of the City Council when we served together in Richmond. She has continued to show that work ethic and that commitment to making government work more efficiently and serve its citizens as a member of the House" (*Washington Post* 2005).

In her role as secretary of administration, Baskerville oversees nine state agencies, including the Virginia State Board of Elections, Department of General Services, Department of Human

From *Public Administration Review*, 69, No. 1 (January/February 2009): 29–38. Copyright © 2009 American Society for Public Administration. Used by permission.

Resources Management, and Department of Minority Business Enterprise. While the governor's cabinet reflects some diversity, with four of the 14 positions held by people of color, and four of the posts held by women, as the sole African American woman in the cabinet, Baskerville's intersectionality distinguishes her among her colleagues (Crenshaw 1998).

Our profile of Baskerville is part of a two-year-long research project examining women in elective office in Virginia. During the first project year, a series of unstructured, in-depth interviews was conducted with Secretary Baskerville to elicit an understanding of her background, her history, her philosophy and motivation to engage in public service, and her perceptions of herself as a woman and African American policy maker in Virginia.

The highest offices of public service in the United States continue to exclude women, in general, and African American women, in particular. Some have expressed skepticism that the absence of historically marginalized populations "makes a difference" to our democracy; research indicates that they do. Researchers writing on representative bureaucracy point to the relationship between having a government that "looks like America" and the ability to fully represent the interests of a diverse electorate (Naff 2001; Selden 1997). Different life experiences afford different abilities, perspectives, and leadership styles. Moreover, according to a research report of the Institute for Women's Policy Research, women's representation in elective office has a measurable effect on policy making and outcomes: "[W]omen's presence in legislatures and other state-level elected offices is closely associated with better policy for women" (Caiazza 2002, 4). An earlier study on women in Congress, conducted on behalf of the Institute for Women's Policy Research by Swers and Caiazza (2000), also found that women members of Congress sponsored legislation relevant to women's unique experiences and shared concerns much more frequently than did men. Elected women and minorities also tend to bring with them other women and minorities, thereby opening up government positions that were previously inaccessible (Riccucci and Saidel 2001). This profile, which examines the personal history and public life of Viola Baskerville, offers an intriguing vision of how one African American woman trailblazer is redefining the model of the public servant in Virginia.

## RECOGNIZING WOMEN'S ABSENCE IN THE PUBLIC LANDSCAPE

To be a woman in either high elective or administrative office in the United States epitomizes the trailblazing life. Only a handful of American women have been elected to state and national legislative office. For example, between the founding of the republic and April 2008, only 2 percent, or 240, of the 11,582 members of the U.S. Congress have been women, and only 32 of those women have been women of color. Carol Moseley Braun is the only African American woman ever to have been elected to the U.S. Senate (CAWP 2007a). According to a 1994 estimate from the U.S. Department of State, at the current rate, women will not gain proportional representation in Congress until the year 2333. While women have a greater presence in state legislatures, their relative numbers remain low there as well. As of April 2008, only 23.7 percent or 1,746 of 7,382 state legislators in the United States were women, and of those, a mere 329 or 4.5 percent were women of color (CAWP 2008). The 1994 State Department project for gender parity in America's state legislatures predicts that women could reach 50 percent of all legislative seats as early as 2038.

Women fare only slightly better in public administrative posts. As of 2007, a total of 33 women have served in federal cabinet-level positions (CAWP 2007b), and data from the previous year found that women occupied only 27 percent of the elite ranks of the federal Senior Executive Service (Dolan, Deckman, and Swers 2007). At the state level, research conducted in 2001 found that 30 percent of all state executive department heads were women (CWG 2001), and research by

Riccucci and Saidel (1997) found that white women held only 22.1 percent, and persons of color only 13.4 percent, of gubernatorial posts around the country. There is little evidence that women have made significant gains as appointed policy makers over a decade later.

The history and status of elected and public administrative women in the Commonwealth of Virginia lags even more markedly behind the nation. By April 2008, Virginia ranked forty-second among the states in the number of women elected to the legislative body; only 16.4 percent, or 23 of 140, of the state House seats were held by women. Between 1791 (the earliest date of our research database) to 2006, only 62 of the 6,830 people who have served in the Virginia House of Delegates have been women. (The Virginia House of Burgesses was initiated in 1619 but became the House of Delegates in 1791.)

Since the commonwealth's founding, no woman has ever served as Virginia's governor or lieutenant governor. In 1993, the only Virginia woman to have ever secured a major party nomination to run for the top executive spot was defeated in the general election when Democrat Mary Sue Terry lost to Republican George Allen. Terry was the first and only woman to date to run for and win as attorney general. Until Viola Baskerville competed with former Congresswoman Leslie Byrne, the only Virginia woman Democrat ever elected to the U.S. Congress, Virginia's candidates for lieutenant governor had all been men. Women are equally absent from the administrative posts in Virginia's government. The historical paucity of women public administrators in Virginia appears to confirm the findings of Riccucci and Saidel (1997), just as they mirror the data on elected women's historical underrepresentation at the national level.

When Viola Baskerville was elected to the Virginia House of Delegates in 1998, only 15 percent of the members were women. Baskerville's election made a total of three seats that were occupied by African American women. As of January 2008, five African American women serve together in the House of Delegates, marking an all-time high in representation by women of color.

## EXPLAINING WOMEN'S ABSENCE

A robust literature has considered women's absence from the public landscape. Ample evidence demonstrates that when women run, they are as likely as their male counterparts to win (Darcy, Welch, and Clark 1994; Dolan, Deckman, and Swers 2007). The explanation for their absence lies elsewhere. Researchers point to the fact that Americans' devotion to incumbents results in their reelection over 90 percent of the time, which then locks out all newcomers to the public landscape. Thus, increasing the number of women in public office first requires that the seats of entrenched incumbents be vacated (Seltzer, Newman, and Leighton 1997).

Other literature indicates that the pool of eligible women candidates is smaller when compared to that of men (Fox and Lawless 2004). This is so because "too few women occupy high-level positions in the professions that serve as pipelines to careers in politics" (Fox and Lawless 264–65, citing Darcy, Welch, and Clark 1994). However, more recent research by the same authors points to the "candidate emergence phase" as a significant source of the underrepresentation of women in public office. They found that parties and party elites are less likely to select, recruit, or encourage women than they are men. Moreover, women are more likely than men to rely on their own internal perceptions about what it means to be "qualified." As a result, they are less likely than men to perceive themselves as qualified. The upshot is that, overall, women are less likely to self-select and thus self-promote themselves toward seeking public office (Fox and Lawless 2004, 275).

The size of women's eligibility pool is also affected by the differing family constraints typically experienced by women. Many women who wait until their children are grown to seek office confine themselves to local offices such as school boards and county councils. The result is a "substantial winnowing process" of potential women candidates, thus shrinking the pool of those women who will eventually seek public life (Fox and Lawless 2004, 275).

For African American women, who have grown up surrounded by both racism and sexism, the issue is surely compounded. Our interviews with African American women reveal a determination and drive to succeed and to make a difference that equals, if not surpasses, that of their white women colleagues. At least anecdotally, this suggests that African American women in our study might be less inclined to see themselves as unqualified when compared to their white women colleagues. Our interviews with both African American and white Virginia delegates demonstrate that a common thread among them is a moral certitude and strong sense of self-confidence that, we suspect, is the result of strong family support and the unwavering encouragement to succeed passed on by one or both parents. Experience with adversity may also play a role.

When asked why she thinks so few women run for political office, Baskerville speaks about her own experiences. She married very young and had her first child at 24, while a law student. It was not until her two children were in school and her family had moved back to Richmond that she became involved in civic and professional organizations and with political campaigns. As her network in the community expanded, she was encouraged to run for Richmond City Council. Three years later, when the 71st State Legislative District incumbent, Jean Cunningham, announced her retirement, Baskerville ran for, and easily won, Cunningham's seat. As noted earlier, researchers Fox and Lawless (2004) support the view that it is at the emergence stage of political candidacy that women lag men; the eligibility pool differs by gender, with men receiving encouragement to enter the field. If, as was Baskerville's experience, women are encouraged to enter the race, they are equally likely to win it. Baskerville also notes that women may be less inclined to play the games that men play, referring to political gamesmanship: "[Y]ou have to play your own game and be comfortable with it and stick to it. But you've got to be wise to the other game, too."

## ON BECOMING "QUALIFIED"

Viola Baskerville's Virginia roots go deep. She describes memories of her childhood growing up in Woodville, a predominantly African American working-class neighborhood in Richmond, Virginia:

> I'm a native Richmonder born at Saint Philips Hospital (a racially segregated hospital that later became the Medical College of Virginia) in October, 1951, one of a set of twins, born prematurely. I was 4 lbs. 12 oz. My sister weighed 3 lbs. 15 oz. I wasn't expected to survive. But I did. I have an older sister and younger brother. We were baby boomers, post-WWII babies. My dad was a carpenter and my mom was a nurse's aid. My dad didn't finish the eighth grade, and my mom, the youngest of twelve children, was the first to go to college when she entered Virginia Union University in 1939. Her father was a laborer born December 25, 1872. His father was born in 1848, and his father was born in 1814, and *his* father born in 1790. So I can trace my family on my mother's side to 1790 when my great, great, great grandfather Robbin Braxton was born on a plantation in Hanover County. He was either a slave of Carter Braxton or was owned by one of Carter Braxton's relatives. Braxton was one of the signers of the Declaration of Independence and a member of the Virginia General Assembly.

Her pride in her family, especially her mother and grandmother, is palpable. She tells of the bit of land that her grandparents owned, which was then given to her own parents on their wedding day, and she speaks fondly of a photograph of her parents working side by side to build their home with their own hands. She proudly notes, "My mother could wield a hammer just as well as my dad; she could cook, hoe a garden." Baskerville underscores the historical view that the strength of African American women grew out of a necessity to command a living and to maintain family ties in the face of uncertainty. This uncertainty emanates from a lack of assurance that their male partners will always be there for reasons that suggest institutionalized racism. To paraphrase Baskerville, this tradition of survivorship creates strong black women with an equally strong sense of motherhood and sacrifice for their children. In her own case, civic participation was emphasized by Baskerville's mother, who remembered the poll taxes created to prevent African Americans from voting. Her mother wished her happiness on her eighteenth birthday and then told her to register to vote. She did, and she has voted at every opportunity since.

Civic interest ran strong in the Osborne family. Baskerville recalls that her illiterate maternal grandfather had an avid interest in community and civic affairs. He was proud of who he was and proud of his heritage. He was also a continuing influence on the Osborne children as their frequent caretaker while their parents worked. The family shared a fundamental resourcefulness. Although poor, there was always food on the table. The family gardened, canned fruits and vegetables, and brought wild game from their relatives in the country. Baskerville emphasizes the importance to the family that they not take anything from the government.

The family, like so many others in their circumstances, saved enough money for a set of encyclopedias, the *World Book Encyclopedia*. "Like almost every other African American family we knew, we had a picture of Jesus, Martin Luther King and John F. Kennedy hanging somewhere in our house, and a set of encyclopedias." They read the encyclopedias from cover to cover, and took piano and band lessons. Baskerville played the viola and the clarinet and sang in the church choir. The family went to Mount Olivet Baptist Church, which Baskerville's grandparents had founded in the late 1800s in Richmond. The church still exists today.

The Osborne girls' strong work ethic toward their schooling, instilled by their parents, resulted in a prestigious scholarship for Baskerville from the A Better Chance (ABC) Program of Boston, Massachusetts. The program was designed to give promising urban minority children the rare opportunity to expand their horizons by attending a scholastic summer camp held at Mount Holyoke College. Baskerville was thirteen at the time. At the end of the six-week program, she was offered a scholarship to attend a member school for her high school education. She attended Northfield School (now Northfield Mount Hermon), a preparatory school in East Northfield, Massachusetts, on a full, four-year scholarship.

After graduating from Northfield, Baskerville entered the College of William & Mary, also on a full four-year scholarship. She placed into a third-year German literature class in her freshman year. Although academically successful, she was one of only six African Americans in her class in a student body of 4,000, and she was unhappy in what was, at the time, an indifferent and insensitive environment. Nevertheless, to honor her parents' sacrifices and to demonstrate the tenacity that her parents had taught her, she remained there until graduation. With the support and encouragement of her German literature professor, she applied for and won a Fulbright scholarship to study in Germany. With her degree in German literature, Baskerville spent a year in Bonn studying post–World War II German women writers.

Upon her return from Germany, she married her fiancé, who had graduated from the Medical College of Virginia in 1973. While he was training at the Mayo Clinic, Baskerville applied to and was accepted on a full scholarship to the University of Iowa's College of Law. She attended law school while raising their first child; after completing law school, the family moved to California, where their second son was born. Once Archer Baskerville completed his training at the University of Loma Linda Medical School, the Baskervilles returned to Richmond. While a homemaker, Baskerville became active in the neighborhood civic association and joined the hospital auxiliary, a local chapter of One Hundred Black Women, and the local chapter of the NAACP, developing the networks that eventually propelled her into public office.

## A PUBLIC LIFE THAT MAKES A DIFFERENCE

Baskerville began her political career when she was elected to the Richmond City Council in 1994. She chose to run for political office after being encouraged to do so by a network of friends and neighbors who were impressed by her civic leadership in the community. Baskerville's story confirms our research, which suggests that encouragement from women peers is the single most common reason for women's entry into politics. This finding is supported by Githens's (2003) work on women's "recruitment" into elective office.

Baskerville was also motivated to run by a desire to bring a sense of dignity and leadership to the often rancorous city council deliberations, a motivation common to many women in public leadership roles (Fine 2007). Her ambition was to change the image of council deliberations in the eyes of Richmond's citizens, who, she felt, were disenchanted, even disgusted, with their government. She was elected to the position of vice mayor by her council peers, who were clearly influenced by her leadership, her dignified demeanor, and her ability to get warring factions to negotiate.

Later, as a member of the House of Delegates, Baskerville saw herself as a loner seeking to remain aloof from the "horse trading" that is the common quid pro quo among legislators. It was her belief that the bills she sponsored should stand on their own merits, and that her colleagues should vote for them because they were worthwhile, not because they sought her vote on their own legislation. Fine (2007) notes that women leaders tend to define themselves by such ethical norms. As a first-term legislator, Baskerville was strongly warned by senior members against taking an unpopular stand or speaking out on the floor; however, she did both—successfully. Less than 30 days into her first term, she chose to speak out on a last-minute Richmond city charter amendment that was supported by influential senior delegates but opposed by her constituents. Remarkably, she was able to persuade a small majority of delegates to remove the offending language, a unique success for a first-term woman legislator, according to researchers (Bratton and Haynie 1999; Kathlene 2001; Rosenthal 2000).

Engineering legislation through to a successful vote is not for the faint of heart. If you are not a horse trader, then votes are earned through the sponsor's ability to convince colleagues that the legislation is good for, or at least not harmful to, their constituents and to their party. Baskerville became known for "doing her homework" for each piece of legislation, which at times entailed consulting with constituents, reading detailed reports, and, as she says, "Googling." Rosenthal (1998a) suggests that women legislators are more inclined to research issues than their male counterparts. Baskerville believes that good research is a manifestation of the democratic process. Her work ethic helped build her reputation for leadership, integrity, attention to detail, and commitment to the legislative process.

Her committee work often focused on families and children; she served on the Health, Welfare and Institutions Committee and on the Commerce and Labor Committee, where she championed the development of opportunities for women and minority business owners. Her work on the Joint Subcommittee on Lead Poisoning and the Committee Studying Access and Diversity in Higher Education reflected her central concern with children, their economic empowerment, and the ways in which issues of race and gender affect them. She was one of only three African American women serving in the House at the time of her election. She also served as secretary of the Virginia Legislative Black Caucus from 2000 until leaving the House of Delegates in 2005.

As an unabashed liberal in a conservative House, an independent woman in an overwhelmingly male delegation, and an African American in a largely white House, her record of accomplishments is indeed exemplary. Policy sea changes require, at a minimum, both inaugurating new ideas and marshalling them into legislative reality. The first requires a kind of singular courage—the willingness to break new ground and go it alone, if necessary. The second requires garnering numbers of supporters. Baskerville succeeded admirably in the first. Her comparative lack of success in the second is attributable in large measure to her status as a minority party member in a predominantly conservative, Republican House of Delegates, dominated by an overwhelming majority of white men.

Research demonstrates that when women make up only a small proportion of an organization, their willingness to engage in "critical acts," such as offering legislation, may actually be constrained (Childs and Krook 2006; Dahlerup 1988; Dahlerup and Freidenvall 2005; Kanter 1997). Baskerville is not much concerned with such legislative setbacks. Rather, she simply transferred her commitment to civil rights, women, children, and small business owners to her work as Virginia's secretary of administration. There are many routes to policy change, and Baskerville has seized every opportunity—and continues to do so—to fulfill her lifelong commitment to economic and social justice.

Baskerville vacated her 71st District legislative seat to seek the Democratic nomination for lieutenant governor in 2005. During the campaign, the *Washington Post* described Baskerville as "by far the best candidate in the Democratic field . . . a principled liberal who does not try to cloak her views . . . and an independent thinker" (Scarborough 2005). Despite such accolades, Baskerville lost a close primary election.

With her history of academic opportunities and accomplishments, Baskerville has actively supported education for all children, but especially those who have lived with discrimination and poverty. On the day after Baskerville lost out on the democratic nomination for lieutenant governor in 2005, she was awarded *Good Housekeeping* magazine's "Women in Government" award. The award recognized her work to repair the harm done by the massive resistance to desegregation that occurred in Virginia during the 1950s and 1960s. Baskerville sponsored legislation (H.B. 846, 2004) to create state-funded scholarships for those whose educations had been disrupted by public school systems that had closed rather than desegregate. According to the press release, the *Good Housekeeping* award is intended to honor "remarkable women who have worked endless hours overcoming huge hurdles to make the world a better place" (Ruff 2005). This award was one among dozens over the years honoring Baskerville for her outstanding public service. As secretary of administration, she has continued to champion children's education by maintaining and directing state funds to public broadcasting entities to implement instructional television programming for K–12 schools, even in tight budget years.

In many ways, Viola Baskerville's life was an apt prelude to her appointment as one of the state's most powerful administrators. The array of offices and responsibilities that come under her auspices is impressive. The secretary of administration has wide reach and authority. The secretary's scope of responsibility involves managing the state's properties and buildings, administering employee policies and benefits, overseeing state procurement, overseeing elections, directing state funds to constitutional officers and public broadcasting entities, overseeing charitable gaming, and the broad and daunting task of protecting Virginians' human rights. In our interviews with her, Baskerville repeatedly emphasized service to the people as her first priority.

Common among the many diverse departments, agencies, and responsibilities housed under the umbrella of the secretary of administration in Virginia is care for the people's investment in themselves, their communities, and their government. Serving as the chief protector of such precious public treasures is a natural role for one who sees herself as a public servant concerned not with her own welfare, but with the welfare of those whom she serves.

As a delegate, and now as secretary, Baskerville has had a particular interest in and passion for enhancing the opportunities for working people, particularly women and minorities. Bills introduced during her career as delegate included measures to assist with procurement opportunities for women and minorities, options for military spouses to collect unemployment compensation when leaving employment because of spousal redeployment, state tax relief aimed at saving rural family farms and family-held businesses, and authorization for a study on the status of women-owned businesses. As secretary of administration, Baskerville supports increasing procurement opportunities for small businesses and for women- and minority-owned businesses. As delegate, her time spent on the Sciences and Technology Committee has continued with her instrumental role in the development of Virginia's eVA program to streamline the state's procurement and purchasing systems by making them available online.

Throughout her career, Baskerville has remained grounded with her local community, with grassroots interests, and with regional and national organizations that reflect her policy concerns and her values. She is a lifetime member of the National Council of Negro Women and the Coalition of 100 Black Women. She also sits on the board of directors of the Virginia Foundation for Women. Her efforts have been recognized with numerous awards and honors. The Planned Parenthood Federation of Virginia awarded her its prestigious Best Choices award in 2002, and she was recognized as the Outstanding Domestic Violence Advocate by the Richmond Domestic Violence Coordinating Committee in 2001. Most recently, in 2006, she was honored for her outstanding commitment to civil rights by Equality Virginia, a grassroots organization dedicated to lobbying against discrimination in all forms. Again in 2008, Equality Virginia gave Baskerville its Public Servant Award. In her acceptance speech, Baskerville responded to a question about the active role of the African American community in the passage of Virginia's regressive "marriage amendment," saying,

> I only wish the same amount of energy could be spent combating poverty, health care disparity, educational disparities, economic disparities, the escalating imprisonment of fathers and sons in the black community, and underage parents with limited or no support systems. These are some of the true stresses in the black family that need to be addressed . . . I stand here as a representative of two minorities, to urge those who look like me to join in this fight by speaking out for human rights and human dignity.

## LESSONS LEARNED

The impact of Viola Baskerville's achievements is not easily quantifiable; however, her record of leadership as an active and involved private citizen, as a member of the Richmond City Council, as a delegate in the Virginia state legislature, and now as a member of the governor's cabinet must, by virtue of her uniqueness, personality, accomplishments, and visibility, offer a role model for all women, and women of color who aspire to positions of leadership.

There appears to be a relationship between similarities with one's constituency and the ability to effect policy making and policy outcomes. The presence of women and minorities in the bureaucracy and in state-level elective offices has a salutary effect on policies that affect both. Furthermore, the presence of women and minorities increases the accessibility to professional positions and to elective office of others who share these attributes. Empirical evidence supporting these assertions has been found in the research of several prominent public administration theorists (Dolan 2002; Keiser et al. 2002; Meier and Bohte 2001; Meier, Wrinkle, and Polinard 1999; Riccucci and Saidel 2001; Selden 1997).

Women are often motivated to enter public service by a desire to positively affect the lives of others. This is a common theme when students are queried about their reasons for entering public administration programs. It is also a common conclusion drawn by researchers in women's leadership studies (Fine 2007, 182). Condit and Hutchinson's ongoing research confirms this. Baskerville exemplifies this ethic of public caring. As we came to know her through our interviews, we concluded that there are several lessons that can be useful for women and minority public administrators.

- *Envision success and dare to fail.* This implies a willingness to take risks in one's professional life. Cantor, Bernay, and Stoess note that "[t]he word risk comes from the Greek 'to sail around a cliff' which implies that we don't know what's around the bend" (1992, 165). Baskerville repeatedly articulated this in our interviews with her. For example, she sponsored controversial legislation on racial reparations that, through her able stewardship, was enacted into law. Her unsuccessful yet groundbreaking run for lieutenant governor exemplifies her mettle. She is not afraid to take on challenges, and she is not afraid to fail.
- *Build coalitions and work collaboratively.* Flammang finds that women attribute their distinctive leadership styles to "[a]n insistence on mutual respect, consensus decision-making, validation of the feelings of others, and non-competitive power" (1985, 111). Baskerville's successful professional career is based on her ability to generate coalitions and to work collaboratively with those who would thwart her policy goals. In both her city council and House of Delegate roles, she made a point of working with the opposition, and there is evidence that doing so worked to the benefit of her constituents. She has always been a consensus seeker and is more than willing to share the credit for success.

In contrast to James McGregor Burns's famous research in 1978 that distinguished male leadership styles as either transactional or transformative, more recent studies on women's leadership styles suggest a more integrative, collaborative, and cooperative style of leadership (Fine 2007; Rosenthal 1998b). This integrative style is marked by power sharing, empowering those who come behind them, creating noncompetitive and inclusive environments, and consensus seeking in a participatory environment. Effectiveness is valued over status seeking (Rosenthal 1998b, 5). When she speaks of her experience on the city council, Baskerville's comments frequently refer to "coalitions" and "cooperation" and "communication"—all values characteristic of women leaders (Fine 2007).

- *Do the work.* This may be one of the most important lessons that we have learned from Viola Baskerville. She is meticulous in her research. She repeatedly affirms the importance of detailed preparation, and she enjoys doing it! Doing her homework, according to Baskerville, is a reason that she has engendered the respect of both her colleagues and her constituents, even when her support for a bill or policy has been unsuccessful.
- *Value lifelong learning.* This is not, of course, a lesson specific to women or to African Americans. Nevertheless, it is a value that is dearly held by Baskerville, and one that she has demonstrated in her own life. This is exemplified by her experiences as a scholarship student in Massachusetts, as a Fulbright scholar studying women writers in Germany, as a law student, and as an energetic supporter of policies to strengthen education in Virginia.

- *Mentor future leaders.* Women's mentoring role is important to bringing women into public life and to their success as leaders. Citing the characteristics inherent to good mentorship, including fostering autonomy, personal responsibility, and self-development, Porter and Daniel note that "Contemporary organizational theorists increasingly view such qualities as crucial for all leaders of effective organizations" (2007, 254). Citing Eagly, Johannesen-Schmidt, and Van Engen (2003), Porter and Daniel note further that "mentoring is a transformational behavior that serves women leaders well."

Central to Baskerville's lived philosophy is the importance of bringing along those who come behind. Baskerville values mentoring. She has experienced it in her career and is determined to extend the benefits of her experience to young women and African Americans who aspire to public leadership. For example, upon leaving her seat in the House of Delegates in 2005, Baskerville encouraged Jennifer McClellan, another young African American woman, to seek the seat that Baskerville was vacating, a seat that McClellan still holds today. Mentoring has a clear connection to a central tenet of representative bureaucracy: As more women and minorities are brought into leadership positions, constituents benefit. This is further supported by the representative bureaucracy literature that has become a part of the public administration discourse (see Keiser et al. 2002; Meier and Bohte 2001; Meier, Wrinkle, and Polinard 1999 for more on representative bureaucracy).

## CONCLUSION

In examining the strain of literature on leadership and on "the difference leaders make," Van Wart notes that "it is important to remember that leaders do not act in a vacuum—they are a part of the flow of history and set in a culture filled with crises, opportunities, and even dumb luck. In practical terms, however, the question of whether leaders make any difference gets translated into the questions of how much difference and when" (2003, 221). We must leave the "how much" question on Baskerville's leadership in Virginia until she is done trailblazing. However, the "when" question—the difference her leadership has made to women and people of color—can be addressed in the moment. Baskerville is a vanguard figure in Virginia public life, a model for young, aspiring women, one of the few African American women to serve in the Virginia State house in the state's history, and the first African American woman to run for statewide elective office. As Kelly so astutely concludes,

> The role of both elected and appointed leaders in promoting and supporting multiracial, multi-ethnic, and gender diversity can not be overstated. 'Being there' matters. If someone like oneself is not present, the likelihood of adequate substantive representation most likely will decline, and often decline sharply. When that happens, an inclusive democratic polity becomes less viable and less feasible. (1998, 204)

In breaking this new ground for women and people of color who follow, Baskerville personifies the model public servant. She marks a new and more hopeful future for public service in Virginia.

## REFERENCES

Baskerville, Viola O. 2006. Interview with the authors, March 6, May 1.

Bratton, Kathleen A., and Kerry L. Haynie. 1999. Agenda Setting and Legislative Success in State Legislatures: The Effects of Gender and Race. *Journal of Politics* 61 (3): 658–79.

Caiazza, Amy. 2002. Does Women's Representation in Elected Office Lead to Women-Friendly Policy? Publication no. I-910, Institute for Women's Policy Research. http://www.iwpr.org/pdf/i910.pdf [accessed September 22, 2008].

Cantor, Dorothy W., Toni Bernay, and Jean Stoess. 1992. *Women in Power: The Secrets of Leadership.* New York: Houghton Mifflin.

Center for the American Woman and Politics (CAWP). 2007a. *Fact Sheet: Women of Color in Elective Offices.* New Brunswick, NJ: Eagleton Institute of Politics, Rutgers University.

———. 2007b. *Fact Sheet: Women in Presidential Cabinets.* New Brunswick, NJ: Eagleton Institute of Politics, Rutgers University.

———. 2008. *Fact Sheet: Women in State Legislatures.* New Brunswick, NJ: Eagleton Institute of Politics, Rutgers University.

Center for Women in Government. 2001. *Women's Leadership Profile Compendium Report.* Albany, NY: Center for Women in Government.

Childs, Sarah, and Mona Lena Krook. 2006. The Substantive Representation of Women: Rethinking the "Critical Mass" Debate. http://www.psa.ac.uk/2006/pps/Childs.pdf [accessed September 22, 2008].

Crenshaw, Kimberlé. 1998. A Black Feminist Critique of Antidiscrimination Law and Politics. In *The Politics of Law: A Progressive Critique,* 3rd ed., edited by David Kairys, 356–80. New York: Basic Books.

Dahlerup, Drude. 1988. From a Small to a Large Minority: Women in Scandinavian Politics. *Scandinavian Political Studies* 11 (4): 275–98.

Dahlerup, Drude, and Lenita Freidenvall. 2005. Quotas as a "Fast Track" to Equal Political Representation for Women: Why Scandinavia Is No Longer the Model. *International Feminist Journal of Politics* 7 (1): 26–48.

Darcy, R., Susan Welch, and Janet Clark. 1994. *Women, Elections, and Representation.* 2nd ed. Lincoln: University of Nebraska Press.

Dolan, Julie. 2002. Representative Bureaucracy in the Federal Executive: Gender and Spending Priorities. *Journal of Public Administration Research and Theory* 12 (3): 353–75.

Dolan, Julie, Melissa Deckman, and Michele L. Swers. 2007. *Women and Politics: Paths to Power and Political Influence.* Upper Saddle River, NJ: Pearson/Prentice Hall.

Eagly, Alice H., Mary C. Johannesen-Schmidt, and Marloes L. van Engen. 2003. Transformational, Transactional, and Laissez-Faire Leadership Styles: A Meta-Analysis Comparing Women and Men. *Psychological Bulletin* 129 (4): 569–91.

Fine, Marlene G. 2007. Women, Collaboration, and Social Change: An Ethics-Based Model of Leadership. In *Women and Leadership: Transforming Visions and Diverse Voices,* edited by Jean Lau Chin, Bernice E. Lott, Joy K. Rice, and Janis Sanchez-Hucles, 177–91. Malden, MA: Blackwell.

Flammang, Janet A. 1985. Female Officials in the Feminist Capital: The Case of Santa Clara County. *Western Political Quarterly* 38 (1): 94–118.

Fox, Richard L., and Jennifer L. Lawless. 2004. Entering the Arena? Gender and the Decision to Run for Office. *American Journal of Political Science* 48 (2): 264–80.

Githens, Marianne. 2003. Accounting for Women's Political Involvement: The Perennial Problem of Recruitment. In *Women and American Politics,* edited by Susan J. Carroll, 33–53. New York: Oxford University Press.

Kanter, Rosabeth Moss. 1977. *Men and Women of the Corporation.* New York: Basic Books.

Kathlene, Lyn. 2001. Words That Matter: Women's Voice and Institutional Bias in Public Policy Formation. In *The Impact of Women in Public Office,* edited by Susan J. Carroll, 22–48. Bloomington: Indiana University Press.

Keiser, Lael R., Vicky M. Wilkins, Kenneth J. Meier, and Catherine A. Holland. 2002. Lipstick and Logarithms: Gender, Institutional Context, and Representative Bureaucracy. *American Political Science Review* 96 (3): 553–64.

Kelly, Rita Mae. 1998. An Inclusive Democratic Polity, Representative Bureaucracies, and the New Public Management. *Public Administration Review* 58 (3): 201–8.

Meier, Kenneth J., and John Bohte. 2001. Structure and Discretion: Missing Links in Representative Bureaucracy. *Journal of Public Administration Research and Theory* 11 (4): 455–70.

Meier, Kenneth J., Robert D. Wrinkle, and J.L. Polinard. 1999. Representative Bureaucracy and Distributional Equity: Addressing the Hard Question. *Journal of Politics* 61 (4): 1025–39.

Naff, Katherine C. 2001. *To Look Like America: Dismantling Barriers for Women and Minorities in Government.* Boulder, CO: Westview Press.

Porter, Natalie, and Jessica Henderson Daniel. 2007. Developing Transformational Leaders: Theory to Practice. In *Women and Leadership: Transforming Visions and Diverse Voices,* edited by Jean Lau Chin, Bernice E. Lott, Joy K. Rice and Janis Sanchez-Hucles, 245–63. Malden, MA: Blackwell.

Riccucci, Norma M., and Judith R. Saidel. 1997. The Representativeness of State-Level Bureaucratic Leaders: A Missing Piece of the Representative Bureaucracy Puzzle. *Public Administrative Review* 57 (5): 423–30.

———. 2001. The Demographics of Gubernatorial Appointees: Toward an Explanation of Variation. *Policy Studies Journal* 29 (1): 11–22.

Rosenthal, Cindy Simon. 1998a. Determinants of Collaborative Leadership: Civil Engagement, Gender or Organizational Norms? *Political Research Quarterly* 51 (4): 847–68.

———. 1998b. *When Women Lead: Integrative Leadership in State Legislatures.* New York: Oxford University Press.

———. 2000. Gender Styles in State Legislative Committees: Raising Their Voices in Resolving Conflict. *Women in Politics* 21 (2): 21–45.

Ruff, J.C. 2005. Effort to Right a Wrong Honored—*Good Housekeeping* Lauded Baskerville for Scholarship Push. *Richmond Times Dispatch*, July 4.

Scarborough, M. 2005. A Classic Choice for Virginia's No. 2 Job. *Washington Post*, June 5.

Selden, Sally Coleman. 1997. *The Promise of Representative Bureaucracy: Diversity and Responsiveness in a Government Agency.* Armonk, NY: M.E. Sharpe.

Seltzer, Robert A., Jody Newman, and Melissa Voorhees Leighton. 1997. *Sex as a Political Variable: Women as Candidates and Voters in U.S. Elections.* Boulder, CO: Lynn Rienner.

Swers, Michele, and Amy Caiazza. 2000. Transforming the Political Agenda? Gender Differences in Bill Sponsorship on Women's Issues. Publication no. I-906, Institute for Women's Policy Research. http://www.iwpr.org/pdf/transforming%20agenda%2010–00.pdf [accessed September 22, 2008].

U.S. Department of State. 1994. Report to UN on Status of Women 1985–1994. http://dosfan.lib.uic.edu/ERC/intlorg/Status_of_Women/s2.html [accessed September 22, 2008].

Van Wart, Montgomery 2003. Public-Sector Leadership Theory: An Assessment. *Public Administration Review* 63 (2): 214–28.

*Washington Post.* 2005. Kaine Names Cabinet Members. December 29.

# 11

## MANAGING THE "NEW NORMALCY" WITH VALUES-BASED LEADERSHIP

### Lessons from Admiral James Loy

### HEATHER GETHA-TAYLOR

The "new normalcy," or the contention that the nation cannot return to its pre–September 11 "normal" state, creates a vision of the future in which leaders must consider terrorist threats alongside a broad array of existing public governance concerns (Advisory Panel 2003). In the days following the September 11 attacks, this new paradigm created a dilemma for Admiral James Loy, who was then commandant of the U.S. Coast Guard. As summarized by Weinstock (2001), "How does he shuffle the deck to give adequate attention to the Coast Guard's myriad missions and at the same time continue to help maintain homeland security?"

In 2004, Loy clarified his thoughts on moving forward: "The terrorists hit us like a perfect storm. In so doing, they awakened us from our complacent nap and made us shockingly aware of new vulnerabilities. It's been said that the future arrives unannounced. Well, for us, the future arrived on 9-11-01. And there is no going back. This quest we often hear for a "return to normalcy"—there will be no such thing in our lifetime. We're constructing the new normalcy and our only choice will be to adapt" (Loy 2004a).

Following the 9/11 attacks, Loy assumed the role of administrator in the newly established Transportation Security Administration (TSA). He quickly, and successfully, implemented 36 congressional mandates for aviation security. Loy later accepted the role of deputy secretary in the Department of Homeland Security, an assignment that presented unprecedented opportunities in addition to considerable management obstacles. As a key public leader in the early years of the new normalcy, Loy's example offers important lessons.

From leading one multimissioned organization, the U.S. Coast Guard, to another, the U.S. Department of Homeland Security, one theme remained constant: Loy maintained a commitment to values-based leadership. By working to identify, communicate, and perpetuate organizational values in three organizational contexts, Loy spoke to the call from the General Accounting Office (now the Government Accountability Office) for public leaders to embed "*core values* in every aspect of the organization" (GAO 2003, 1; emphasis added).

This Administrative Profile examines Loy's efforts across three organizational contexts to address two primary questions: First, what is values-based leadership? Second, what process did Loy employ to identify shared values in three organizational settings? To answer these questions, this essay presents details on Loy's efforts in the Coast Guard, the Transportation Security Administration, and the Department of Homeland Security. It concludes with lessons learned on values-based leadership.

## WHAT IS VALUES-BASED LEADERSHIP?

Identifying organizational values is an important component of mission articulation. Values are enduring standards that involve cognitive and behavioral effects (Rokeach 1973). "Since values are prescriptive, they play an important role in determining the choices we make" (Russell 2000, 76). When leaders identify organizational values, they provide employees with an "internal compass" that allows them to act independently and responsibly (Kouzes and Posner 1993, 53). The need for such a compass was highlighted in House Select Committee reports that identified a lack of initiative and imagination as leadership failures in the responses to 9/11 and Hurricane Katrina.

Simply stated, core values provide the necessary guidance to help organizational members at all levels answer the question, "What should I do?" (Gawthrop 1998). This guidance has become even more important, says Walker, because of "recent scandals in both government and private industry" that "underscore the fact that ethics and integrity are an indispensable element of true leadership" (2007, xi). Identifying, promoting, and protecting values, then, is a critical job for leaders (Rowsell and Berry 1993). According to Russell, "[V]alues serve as the foundational essence of leadership" (2000, 78).

Values also represent an integral component of organizational culture. Managing organizational culture, says Van Wart (2005), is the leader's most important responsibility. Culture "defines for us what to pay attention to, what things mean, how to react emotionally to what is going on, and what actions to take in various kinds of situations" (Schein 1997, 498). Over time, values are "transformed into nondiscussable assumptions supported by articulated sets of beliefs, norms, and operational rules of behavior" (496). This transformation is aided by the integration of values into organizational philosophies, according to Schein, and "can serve as a guide and as a way of dealing with the uncertainty of intrinsically uncontrollable or difficult events" (497). As part of the organizational culture, values provide "a foundation for building goals, plans, and tactics" and an area for "consensus and agreement" (Kidder 1995, 508).

The area of "consensus and agreement" presents contemporary public leaders with a great challenge. As noted by Gawthrop, "[S]ociety is dependent on the career professionals in governments at all levels to lead it to the value vision of the common good. As a first step in this direction, public administrators must be willing . . . to reaffirm the values and virtues inherent in the notion of service" (1998, 101). Particularly in the era of new normalcy, identifying the relevant values that speak to an evolving notion of the common good is a timely and important task. Transferring ideals from "externally identified" to "intrinsically valued" is the key to connecting individual effort with collective goals: Responsiveness to public interest begins when individual values match broader ideals (see Bozeman 2007).

The practice of values-based leadership offers an opportunity to connect individual values and broader ideals. According to Kuczmarski and Kuczmarski (1995), values-based leadership helps ameliorate individual isolation and alienation in the workplace by identifying a foundation of beliefs to guide individual behavior and organizational efforts. This process, say the authors, supports organizational cohesion. Admiral Loy's efforts to build organizational cohesion by articulating broad ideals in three contexts are detailed in the following sections.

## U.S. COAST GUARD

In the early 1990s, a set of core values had not yet been articulated within the U.S. Coast Guard. Loy, then serving as chief of personnel and training, assembled a team representing three organizational member groups: civilians, enlisted members, and officers. The team was to identify a short list of core values that would serve as the basis for all future leadership development within the organization. This process was in line with Gawthrop's assertion that identifying the components that speak to the common good "requires serious reflection and intense discernment" (1998, 131). The team identified and refined a set of three core values: honor, respect, and devotion to duty (see appendix). These core values "demonstrate who we are and guide our performance, conduct, and decisions every minute of every day," according to the Coast Guard's core values and creed.

To determine the degree to which these three values accurately represented the organization, Loy embarked on a journey: "I went to the Chief's quarters and I went to the hangar decks and I went to the bilges of the ships of the Coast Guard to see whether or not we had gotten it right. I wanted to know whether it resonated well with people of the organization" (interview with the author, March 2008). While important, these conversations were not sufficient for cultural integration. To fully integrate the accepted values, Sashkin indicates that leaders must transform "cultural ideals into organizational realities" by "creating an explicit organizational philosophy and then enacting that philosophy by means of specific policies and programs" (1989, 406).

In the years following the adopting of the core values in 1991, the Coast Guard's core values were integrated into organizational documents and training. For example, the values are an important element of Publication 1 (2002), a foundational document for the U.S. Coast Guard. In addition, under Loy's leadership, the values "became the first thing kids learned in boot camp and the first thing kids learned at the Coast Guard Academy and at the OCS program" (interview with the author, March 2008).

In retrospect, Loy recalls a sense of broad agreement within the organization with regard to the values. "I knew we got it right, because it resonated so well in all the places that I knew leadership was important. It's almost as if those core values had been issued back in 1790 by Alexander Hamilton when the service was established" (interview with the author, 2006). Loy's contention is aligned with Kotter's reminder that visions and their associated value statements do not have to be "brilliantly innovative; in fact, some of the best are not" (1990, 117). Effective statements, says Kotter, "regularly have an almost mundane quality, usually consisting of ideas that are already well known. The particular combination or patterning of the ideas may be new, but sometimes even that is not the case" (117). Loy echoed the contemporary merit of traditional values: "I believe my service actually had those core values for a long, long time. They just hadn't bothered to pull them into a neat little package and write them down" (interview with the author, 2006). According to Kotter, "what's crucial about a vision is not its originality but how well it serves the interests of important constituencies" (1990, 117).

## TRANSPORTATION SECURITY ADMINISTRATION

In 2002, when Loy was tapped to serve as administrator of the newly established Transportation Security Administration, identifying shared values was a comparatively low priority. "When we were starting up TSA, there were no pencils, there were no pads of paper, there were no desks, there was nothing. All we had was an Aviation Transportation Security Act—a piece of legislation with 36 deadlines to get accomplished over the course of about 18 months" (interview with the author, March 2008).

The TSA's objectives included placing federal security directors in all major U.S. airports, deploying passenger screeners at all airports across the country, screening 100 percent of checked baggage for explosives, expanding the Federal Air Marshal Program, positioning law enforcement officers at screening checkpoints, reinforcing cockpit doors, and conducting background checks on airport employees (Loy 2003). What some would view as a potentially insurmountable management challenge, Loy viewed as an unparalleled opportunity: "We were going to start up the first twenty-first-century agency, not just another twentieth-century agency." The first priority for Loy was staffing: He ultimately was responsible for selecting, training, and placing 60,000 people in 541 worksites (also known as airports) over the course of 18 months. This considerable task was aided by the outpouring of "zeal" for public service in the weeks and months following the September 11 terrorist attacks.

Loy is convinced that it was this driving force, together with partnerships with industry, that propelled the TSA to achieve the mandated deadlines: "We met every one of those deadlines despite dramatic press . . . and other kinds of commentary along the way. Even at the point when we were cutting the ribbon on getting number 21 done, the headline the next day was, 'There's no way they can get number 22 done.' And we had to fight our way through that all the way through those two years. That in and of itself gets fatiguing" (interview with the author, 2006). The fatigue was mediated, Loy said, by an organizational commitment to performance. "I can tell you for the two years I was there the zeal was in the air. We were breathing it day after day after day . . . it was just a total commitment" (interview with the author, March 2008).

But Loy knew that the zeal that characterized the early days of the organization would not be sufficient to sustain commitment over time.

> I went off and took my leadership team and asked them . . . did they have core values? Had they even thought of that yet? And many of them said, 'Oh, yes. We do.' I said, 'Well how many do you have?' And they said, 'Well, I think we have eight.' And somebody else said, 'I think we have nine.' Somebody else said, 'I think we have seven.' I said, 'I'm going to make a list of them up here on the whiteboard. Tell me what they are.' And they could only produce about two or three of their list of eight or nine core values. So, they didn't have any. Because they didn't know them. They didn't believe in them. They hadn't even memorized them, let alone thoughtfully figured out what they meant. (interview with the author, 2006)

Motivated by his experiences in the Coast Guard, Loy helped the TSA identify and integrate a set of core values that were both relevant at the moment and would remain relevant over time. Particularly in an atmosphere that Loy equated with a "fishbowl," values serve not only as guides but also as sources of inspiration. "How do you continue to survive, how do you continue to go back to work the next morning in that kind of an atmosphere? You better have the foundation that is attendant to core values and character and recognize that in there lies the strength you need to press on with the work you're challenged to do" (interview with the author, March 2008).

The TSA's values—integrity, innovation, and team spirit—capture several qualities that may temper the effects of continual stress and scrutiny. Inherent in these three values are the qualities of accepting challenges, taking risks, being courageous, and standing ready for change. Time will illustrate the continued relevance and inspirational power of these values: "[E]ven the most inspiring values are not easy to sustain over time, when everyone is under a lot of pressure" (Boyatzis and McKee 2005, 20).

## DEPARTMENT OF HOMELAND SECURITY

In 2003, Loy was selected to serve as the deputy secretary of the Department of Homeland Security (DHS). Secretary Tom Ridge challenged Loy and the new department to breathe life into his slogan, "One Team, One Fight." This was no easy task, given that this "one team" would number approximately 180,000 individuals who were affiliated with 22 agencies or pieces of agencies. Loy indicated that the reorganization initiated by the Homeland Security Act of 2002 presented him with an enormous challenge: "Never before have we witnessed a full-scale government divestiture, merger, acquisition and start-up all coming together at once—certainly not on this scale" (Loy 2004b).

This change necessarily involved a transition that "required looking beyond old agendas, missions, cultures, histories, and processes, and coming together as one holistic enterprise. It required—and finally enabled—employees from many different organizations to rally around a single mission" (Loy 2004b). How best to identify shared values among a set of dramatically different agencies, however, presented a significant obstacle. For instance, some organizations within the DHS did not seem to "fit culturally" with others at the table. Agencies with a rich tradition and those that had just been established needed to be aligned. Loy considered the importance of honoring "the legacies of the past," while challenging leaders to think across boundaries with a shared focus on the future. In this context, Gardner's point is especially relevant: "Shared values are the bedrock on which leaders build the edifice of group achievement" (1990, 5).

To begin to build a bedrock of group achievement in the DHS, Loy again applied a consensus-building approach. He communicated with a group of individuals from the component agencies of the DHS to identify a set of shared values. However, the department's amorphous goals, constrained resources, and considerable external pressures contributed to an uncertain path. "The old aphorism about if you don't know where you're going any road will take you there . . . we didn't know where we were going and we had to define the road and we had to talk about and define what the light was at the end of the tunnel" (interview with the author, March 2008).

Overcoming agency-specific views to create a joint vision and a sense of values presented a considerable challenge during Loy's tenure at the DHS. As Gawthrop notes, service based on values must include "a faith in some transcendent good" (1998, 84). It was Loy's job to stress the DHS vision as the greater good; everyone had to be able to "see their puzzle piece fitting into the greater design effort" (interview with the author, March 2008). The task of aligning values for the department's "one team" vision was just as important as any externally mandated decree. Gardner warns that the absence of shared values can contribute to a situation in which members "believe in nothing strongly enough to work for it as a group" (1990, 5). In an attempt to counter this possibility, Loy facilitated a "three-day experience" during which he attempted to "push the thoughts of the organization to strategic goals that could manifest themselves and be articulated" (interview with the author, March 2008).

The result, Loy says, was the identification of six "magic words" that the members could agree on and identify with: awareness, prevention, protection, response, recovery, and preparedness. These core values became part of the DHS strategic plan, joined with strategic goals and action plans, which together are designed to guide organizational performance. "Describing who we are and what we do, it conveys the beliefs and values that govern our conduct" (Loy 2004b).

## LESSONS LEARNED

Loy's efforts to articulate values in three organizational contexts speak to the following broad questions and associated lessons learned.

### Does values-based leadership make a difference?

In the context of the U.S. Coast Guard, reports suggest that the organization's strong internal cohesion contributes to high levels of performance and employee engagement. For instance, the

Government Performance Project, according to Ingraham (forthcoming), "considered the Coast Guard an exemplar for the extent to which leadership talent and capacity was inculcated throughout the organization and the strength and clarity with which its top leadership demonstrated commitment to goals and mission." Indicators of performance and employee satisfaction at the Department of Homeland Security, however, are lackluster by comparison. Findings from the Partnership for Public Service's 2007 Best Places to Work in the Federal Government survey place the Department of Homeland Security next to last among 30 large agencies. This contrast speaks to the relevant question: Does values-based leadership make a difference?

Some would argue that Loy's efforts had minimal success in building a cohesive organizational culture in the DHS. In this context, a possible lesson learned is one of incomplete or inconsistent adoption. In applying values-based leadership, "[T]he only course for the leader is to build a vision that followers are able to adopt as their own" (O'Toole 1996, 10). Phillips and Loy remind leaders that they "have the skills to fashion an inspiring vision for the organization's future, to set goals that will achieve that vision, and to involve other people" (2008, 49). The combination of these efforts serves to "motivate people, focus their talent and energy, and, in the long run, generate results" (49). Values-based leadership necessarily begins with the efforts of one, but a lasting commitment can only be perpetuated through the continued efforts of individuals throughout the organization. In the DHS, an ongoing leadership vacuum (Peters 2007) makes such a commitment particularly difficult to maintain.

### What is the expected outcome of values-based leadership?

Loy's experiences illustrate Walker's point that "true leaders are unafraid to listen and learn from others at all levels of their organization" (2007, xi). However, value identification and cultural integration serves as just one side of the equation. Phillips and Loy (2008) identify values as the foundation of leadership. The purpose of leadership, however, "is to raise both individual and group performance to the highest possible standard of behavior, action, and achievement," (p. 86). The authors state that the ultimate measurement of leadership success, then, is "how an individual or an organization performs at the end of the day" (Ibid.). This illuminates a relevant and challenging question: how do we measure the outcomes of values-based leadership?

In the case of the TSA, Loy contended that value alignment within the organization contributed to an environment that supported the capacity for meeting the 36 congressional mandates for aviation security. "When you start with establishing a foundation of character and values, you yield performance, which is what it's all about, whether it's as an individual or as an organization. At the end of the day, it's 'did you get the job done?'" (interview with the author, 2006).

Beyond external performance metrics, the impact of values-based leadership should be measured in changes to organizational processes. For instance, Maierhofer, Rafferty, and Kabanoff stress the importance of infusing values into orientation activities. "Entry into an organization represents an important period for individual value acquisition" (2003, 7). Further, rewarding those leaders whose actions match the espoused values is symbolic and powerful. "When leaders demonstrate the desired norms and values on a daily basis they lend credibility and authenticity to them" (Kuczmarski and Kuczmarski 1995, 58).

Finally, the alignment between individual values and organizational values serves as a barometer of success. However, Brown and Treviño (2003, 155) note the paucity of studies that examine the acceptance of values by followers. If leaders are indeed "agents of influence," then the influence process should include internalization among organizational members. It is internalization, say Brown and Treviño, that will produce the most powerful and lasting effects.

**Which attributes contribute to an individual's effectiveness in practicing values-based leadership?**

O'Toole (1996) identifies four attributes of leaders who effectively engage in values-based leadership: integrity, trust, listening, and respect for followers. Values-based leadership, says O'Toole, presents a challenge to the traditional practice of hierarchical leadership by requiring leaders to overcome a "natural instinct" to lead by pushing others, instead leading by the "pull of inspiring values" (1996, 11). O'Toole goes on note that leaders who embrace this approach do so because they respect others in the organization and because "they honestly believe that the welfare of followers is the end of leadership (and not that followers are the means to the leader's goals)" (1996, 9).

The aforementioned desirable attributes speak to the connection between value legitimacy and the perceived moral character of the leader (Brown and Treviño 2003). This connection is reflected in Loy's commitment to building a sense of shared responsibility in responding to the challenges of the new normalcy. In all three contexts, Loy utilized a consensus-building approach to gain input, identify core values, and integrate the values into the organization. Work by Van Wart supports Loy's approach, noting that the most effective value statements are those that are "broadly conceived, widely understood, and have a real presence in the organization" (2005, 249).

## CONCLUSION

The paradigm shift to the new normalcy requires public sector leaders to continually consider how best to balance existing concerns with emergent needs, particularly as they relate to national security. Admiral James Loy's experiences as a prominent leader during the formative years of the new normalcy offer examples for public sector leaders in other organizations, particularly as they struggle with value identification and integration. According to Loy, balance is a primary concern for public managers in an age of new normalcy: "to press on securing our country and to protect those things we have always valued and will continue to value" (Loy 2004a).

A discussion of how to identify, inculcate, and perpetuate organizational values in an age of new normalcy is an important starting point, but Schein reminds us that even the best-intentioned value statements "may only reflect rationalizations or aspirations" (1997, 500). Careful attention to the ways in which organizational values accurately reflect reality is equally important to determine the values' continued organizational relevance. Particularly when a set of noble values have been identified and organizational dysfunction persists, Van Wart (2005) suggests a very prudent question: How successfully are our public organizations living up to their espoused values?

## REFERENCES

Advisory Panel to Assess Domestic Response Capabilities for Terrorism Involving Weapons of Mass Destruction (Gilmore Commission). 2003. Forging America's New Normalcy: Securing Our Homeland, Preserving Our Liberty. http://www.rand.org/nsrd/terrpanel/ [accessed November 24, 2008].

Boyatzis, Richard E., and Annie McKee. 2005. *Resonant Leadership: Renewing Yourself and Connecting with Others through Mindfulness, Hope, and Compassion.* Boston: Harvard Business School Press.

Bozeman, Barry. 2007. *Public Values and Public Interest: Counterbalancing Economic Individualism.* Washington, DC: Georgetown University Press.

Brown, Michael E., and Linda K. Treviño. 2003. Is Values-Based Leadership Ethical Leadership? In *Emerging Perspectives on Values in Organizations,* edited by Stephen W. Gilliland, Dirk D. Steiner, and Daniel P. Skarlicki, 151–73. Greenwich, CT: Information Age.

Gardner, John W. 1990. The Cry for Leadership. In *The Leader's Companion: Insights on Leadership through the Ages*, edited by J. Thomas Wren, 3–7. New York: Free Press.

Gawthrop, Louis C. 1998. *Public Service and Democracy: Ethical Imperatives for the 21st Century.* New York: Chatham House.

Ingraham, Patricia Wallace. Forthcoming. Leadership in the Unglued Organization. In *Public Sector Leadership: International Challenges and Perspectives*, edited by Jeffrey A. Raffel, Peter Leisink, and Anthony Middlebrooks. Northampton, MA: Edward Elgar.

Kidder, Rushworth M. 1995. Universal Human Values: Finding an Ethical Common Ground. In *The Leader's Companion: Insights on Leadership through the Ages*, edited by J. Thomas Wren, 500–508. New York: Free Press.

Kotter, John P. 1990. What Leaders Really Do. In *The Leader's Companion: Insights on Leadership through the Ages*, edited by J. Thomas Wren, 114–23. New York: Free Press.

Kouzes, James M., and Barry Z. Posner. 1993. *Credibility: How Leadership Gain and Lose It, Why People Demand It.* San Francisco: Jossey-Bass.

Kuczmarski, Susan Smith, and Thomas D. Kuczmarski. 1995. *Values-Based Leadership.* Englewood Cliffs, NJ: Prentice Hall.

Laurent, Anne. 1999. The Curse of Can-Do. *Government Executive*, March 1. http://www.govexec.com/gpp/0300cg.htm [accessed November 24, 2008].

Loy, James M. 2003. Statement before the Subcommittee on Aviation, Committee on Commerce, Science, and Transportation, February 5. http://www.globalsecurity.org/security/library/congress/2003_h/030205-loy.pdf [accessed November 24, 2008].

———. 2004a. Remarks delivered at the Maritime and Port Security Conference, February 4.

———. 2004b. Statement before the House Select Committee on Homeland Security, May 6. http://www.dhs.gov/xnews/testimony/testimony_0025.shtm [accessed November 24, 2008].

Maierhofer, Naomi I., Alannah E. Rafferty, and Boris Kabanoff. 2003. When and Why are Values Important in Organizations? In *Emerging Perspectives on Values in Organizations*, edited by Stephen W. Gilliland, Dirk D. Steiner, and Daniel P. Skarlicki, 3–32. Greenwich, CT: Information Age.

O'Toole, James. 1996. *Leading Change: The Argument for Values-Based Leadership.* New York: Ballantine.

Partnership for Public Service. 2007. Best Places to Work in the Federal Government. http://bestplacestowork.org/BPTW/rankings/ [accessed November 24, 2008].

Peters, Katherine McIntire. 2007. Management Chief to Fill in as DHS Deputy Secretary. *Government Executive*, October 19. http://www.govexec.com/dailyfed/1007/101907kp1.htm [accessed December 1, 2008].

Phillips, Donald T., and James M. Loy. 2008. *The Architecture of Leadership: Preparation Equals Performance.* Annapolis, MD: Naval Institute Press.

Rokeach, Milton. 1973. *The Nature of Human Values.* New York: Free Press.

Rowsell, Kate, and Tony Berry. 1993. Leadership, Vision, Values and Systemic Wisdom. *Leadership and Organization Development Journal* 14 (7): 18–22.

Russell, Robert F. 2000. The Role of Values in Servant Leadership. *Leadership and Organization Development Journal* 22 (2): 76–83.

Sashkin, Marshall. 1989. Visionary Leadership. In *The Leader's Companion: Insights on Leadership through the Ages*, edited by J. Thomas Wren, 402–7. New York: Free Press.

Schein, Edgar H. 2007. Uncovering the Levels of Culture. In *The Organizational Behavior Reader*, 8th ed., edited by Joyce S. Osland, Marlene E. Turner, David A. Kolb, and Irwin M. Rubin, 494–501. Upper Saddle River, NJ: Pearson.

Van Wart, Montgomery. 2005. *Dynamics of Leadership in Public Service: Theory and Practice.* Armonk, NY: M.E. Sharpe.

Walker, David M. 2007. *Foreword to Transforming Public Leadership for the 21st Century*, edited by Ricardo S. Morse, Terry F. Buss, and C. Morgan Kinghorn. Armonk, NY: M.E. Sharpe.

Weinstock, Matthew. 2001. Changing Course. *Government Executive*, December 1. http://www.govexec.com/features/1201/1201s6.htm [accessed November 24, 2008].

U.S. Coast Guard. 2002. U.S. Coast Guard: America's Maritime Guardian (Publication 1). http://www.uscg.mil/top/about/doc/uscg_pub1_complete.pdf [accessed November 24, 2008].

U.S. General Accounting Office (GAO). 2003. *Results-Oriented Cultures: Implementation Steps to Assist Mergers and Organizational Transformations.* Washington, DC: Government Printing O. GAO-03–669.

# APPENDIX

## U.S. COAST GUARD VALUES

*Honor*

Integrity is our standard. We demonstrate uncompromising ethical conduct and moral behavior in all of our personal actions. We are loyal and accountable to the public trust.

*Respect*

We value our diverse workforce. We treat each other with fairness, dignity, and compassion. We encourage individual opportunity and growth. We encourage creativity through empowerment. We work as a team.

*Devotion to Duty*

We are professionals, military and civilian, who seek responsibility, accept accountability, and are committed to the successful achievement of our organizational goals. We exist to serve. We serve with pride.

# 12

# NANCY ALFARO AS AN EXEMPLARY COLLABORATIVE PUBLIC MANAGER

## How Customer Service Was Aligned with Customer Needs

### KATHERINE C. NAFF

On February 12, 2004, Mayor Gavin Newsom of San Francisco made headlines across the country by ordering the county clerk to license and perform same-sex marriages. In doing so, he defied a state law, enacted by the voters in 2000, prohibiting marriage between anyone but a man and a woman. By the end of the second day after Newsom's order, 680 couples from around the country had been wed. The third day was a Saturday, Valentine's Day, which saw another 450 weddings take place.

This profile presents the administrator who was at the center of that storm, Nancy Alfaro, then county clerk. It will examine her work as county clerk and then assess her more recent role as director of San Francisco's 311 Customer Service Center. The profile is based on two hour-long interviews with Alfaro and conversations with seven of her colleagues who worked with her in her present or former capacity.

Both periods demonstrate a collaborative public management style, which is defined by O'Leary, Gerard, and Bingham as "facilitating and operating in multiorganizational arrangements to solve problems that can't be solved or easily solved by single organizations" (2006, 7). However, in this case, it is collaborative management with a twist—collaboration focused on customer service management. Customer service is more typically defined as the management of internal organization processes to satisfy customer (or citizen) expectations by providing information and solving problems in a timely and consistent manner (Wagenheim and Reurink 1991). As will be seen, the 311 Customer Service Center reconfigures much of the premise of how citizens access government for service delivery.

## THE EYE OF THE STORM

The tidal wave of marriage license applications at the county clerk's office was the result of pent-up demand among gay and lesbian couples who had been denied the right to marry under state law. It also was a reaction to legal challenges that threatened to shut down the entire operation at any time. (In fact, the state supreme court ordered an end to the marriages one month later.) "The line

From *Public Administration Review*, 69, No. 3 (May/June 2009): 487–493. Copyright © 2009 American Society for Public Administration. Used by permission.

on Saturday was so formidable, accompanied by daylong traffic congestion and happily honking cars on Van Ness Avenue, that it turned into a take-a-number event that at times resembled a Las Vegas wedding chapel," reported the *San Francisco Chronicle*. "Overwhelmed workers handed out numbers to 320 couples who couldn't be accommodated on Saturday, asking them to return [the following day] at scheduled times" (Kim and Asimov 2004).

It was Nancy Alfaro's responsibility to turn chaos into order. As county clerk, licensing and performing marriages was her responsibility. "That was very historical, very exciting." Alfaro recollected, "I absolutely believe in everything we did. I was supportive of the idea and the principle; it was the right thing to do." She described the time as "extremely emotional" as well. People were flying in from all over the country to get their licenses and camping out in the rain. Alfaro, her small staff, and volunteers worked 18-hour days and on weekends to accommodate the demand. "I know we made a difference in the lives of the 4,034 couples who [ultimately] got their licenses, and that is significant."

Alfaro is that kind of manager—one who can face the deluge enveloping her and her organization and channel it into positive action. It was like the typhoon in Burma, one former city administrator recounted—all of a sudden it was there. Consider thousands of forms and certificates that needed to be prepared with the new wording. The Department of Public Works put out portable toilets for the couples who waited in line for their turn (sometimes overnight). Another city staffer reprogrammed the lighting to illuminate the city hall exterior all night. Another brought love songs on CDs to play in the rotunda (Gordon 2004). Cakes and flowers showed up in city hall, sent in appreciation of what the clerk's office was doing.

How did she manage? Alfaro has an "uncanny ability" to calm people down and get the best out of them in hectic situations, according to the former director of administrative services for the city, who was responsible for her appointment. Alfaro and her staff further relied on dozens of volunteers from other city hall offices and from the community. The other officials were willing to pitch in because that is what Alfaro and her staff always do when they need additional support. Collaborative managers assemble and direct participants across organizational lines to address issues that are beyond the capacity of any one actor. While they aren't always able to order activity, they are responsible for the collective outcome (McGuire 2006). Alfaro is a collaborative manager's manager.

Alfaro also managed the flurry of wedding vows because she and her staff had already laid the groundwork. Early in her tenure as county clerk, they had taken a haphazard process, formalized it, and automated it. The practice had been that couples might show up to be married at noon when staff were all at lunch, or when they were occupied with other marriages. The staff wouldn't know whether to expect two or 22 couples, and the result, sometimes, was a long wait. Alfaro's team developed an online appointment scheduling system and ensured that she had sufficient people on hand to meet the demand.

Another of her proudest achievements was the development of a process for deputizing volunteers to perform marriages. Beginning with the recruitment and training of just two volunteers, the pilot project was so successful that Alfaro wrote procedures, put an ad in the paper, received 50 applications, and interviewed and "hired" 10 more volunteers. She insisted they be city residents, so that this would serve as a means for cementing the ties between the city and its citizens. Today, the clerk's office has some 23 volunteers with diverse cultural and language abilities. "Other counties have modeled programs after ours," Alfaro explained. "Its success depends on who you choose as volunteers. You have to interview them as though you are going to hire them as employees." One of her longtime volunteers, a retired school teacher, praised Alfaro's focus and clarity. She also commented that whether one marriage or 100 were to take place that day, Alfaro and her staff strove to ensure that each couple was presented with the time and environment to make their wedding special. (Is she always so proficient? Well, not once she gets in a car, the volunteer admitted—she has no sense of direction and can get lost just driving across the city.)

## WHO IS NANCY ALFARO?

Born in San Francisco, Alfaro moved at the age of six to El Salvador, her parents' birthplace. She lived there for nine years, returning to the San Francisco area in 1981 because of civil war in El Salvador. After graduating high school in the town of South San Francisco, Alfaro attended San Francisco State University and earned a bachelor's degree in business. From there, she went to work in the private sector. In 1992, Alfaro was hired as a management assistant by the San Francisco County Clerk's Office. She worked her way up, and was appointed county clerk in 1997. During her tenure with the city, elected officials have taken advantage of her dedication and organizing skills. She has served on the Customer Service and Efficiency Task Force and the Small Business Advisory Task Force. Alfaro also worked actively with the California County Clerk and Election Officials Legislative Committee to draft proposed language for amendments to the Family Law and Business and Profession codes.

Balancing her life between work and her husband and two young boys, Alfaro has also served as president of her son's school board. The inevitable stress that her workload brings is positive for her family, in her view, because it shows her sons that a woman can do anything. Always aware of stereotypes associated with Latinos, she consciously works to undermine them. If Alfaro has one regret, it is that she didn't pursue additional education. Her parents weren't in a position to provide financial support, and she did not have someone to point her toward academic programs or scholarships that she could have pursued.

Alfaro describes her management style as "very open door, approachable." Knowing how to assess people's strengths and weaknesses, she gives them projects that take advantage of their strengths at a level of responsibility they are ready for. She also ensures that people understand her expectations of them and are given clear direction. Alfaro meets with her employees on a regular basis to ask how they are doing and whether they still like their jobs. If she has one fault, those interviewed agreed, it's that she takes on too much—that she is reluctant to say no. Alfaro confessed, "I have come to realize I can't do everything, even though I would like to do everything."

## BIRTH OF A NETWORK

On March 29, 2007, Mayor Newsom announced the opening of a new customer service center that would allow city residents to call one telephone number—311—to inquire about any city service, make a request, or report a problem. Is there graffiti on a building near your home? Call 311 and the request to have it removed will be entered into the system. Want more information about a city event? Call 311. Did you lose your cane on a city bus? "We'll do our best to find your cane," a customer service representative promised a caller shortly after 311 was launched (Vega 2007). At the time, there were 2,300 different telephone numbers for local government services. Now, there are only two to remember: 911 for emergencies, and 311 for everything else.

Perhaps these telephone numbers illustrate the change in direction facilitated by collaborative management in government. Nye (2002) describes this in his introduction to Harvard University's study of global forces as governments move to governance. In Nye's view, the twentieth century was characterized by centripetal forces (hence the 2,300 telephone numbers that sprouted to respond to San Franciscans' every need and defined agency service domains). In the twenty-first century, centrifugal forces predominate (hundreds of separate telephone numbers have been distilled into just two with agencies linked and bureaucratic boundaries put aside).

The 311 customer service idea did not originate in San Francisco. Then-supervisor Newsom was inspired by a visit to the city of Baltimore. He had already set up the task force to address customer service and sponsored a ballot initiative that would require city agencies to formulate long-range plans that included customer service objectives, service standards, and customer satisfaction metrics. When Newsom was elected mayor, customer service remained a top priority.

Nancy Alfaro was appointed deputy director of the 311 Customer Service Center based on her record of providing customer service as county clerk and the wide array of contacts she had made across the city. San Francisco is the only consolidated city and county in the state, and comprises 50 departments that tend to work independently while competing for the limited resources apportioned by the Board of Supervisors (Friedrichsen 2006). Ensuring that a limited group of customer service representatives (CSRs) has the information to respond correctly and immediately to thousands of inquiries requires exceptional organizing ability. It requires a manager who will empower her employees and ensure they have the training and technology required to respond to customers (Wagenheim and Reurink 1991). Alfaro had proven her capabilities as county clerk, particularly during the month-long stampede for same-sex marriage licenses. She was pleased to be asked to work on 311: "I thought, if I am been able to [improve customer service] in this little [county clerk's] office and if I could do this for every person that touches San Francisco, I thought that would be very exciting." After six months, the previous director was appointed director of public works, and the mayor asked Alfaro to assume the directorship of 311.

Alfaro is operating a network, which is defined by O'Toole as a "structure of interdependence involving multiple organizations or parts thereof, where one unit is not merely the formal subordinate of others in some larger hierarchal arrangement" (1997, 45). This is another key feature of collaborative management: It disintermediates organizational fiefdoms. Alfaro has no authority to direct agencies to respond to the customers who call 311. Rather, the CSRs work across organizational boundaries to achieve common objectives. The 311 service is an example of informational, collaborative public administration (Argranoff 2006), but with a twist. The focus is not on solving social problems on a macro basis, but rather linking customers, one at a time, with service providers.

## FOCUSING ON CUSTOMER SERVICE AND BUILDING PARTNERSHIPS

The 311 enterprise makes a key assumption: that it ought to be easy for citizens to make requests for basic city services, and that the fast and efficient completion of those requests will allow agencies to focus on larger, more complicated problems. That statement, as a customer service concept in government, has generated controversy in public administration. The regulatory and accountability dimensions of many government programs have, in the past, focused service provision on eligibility determination and legal compliance.

However, in the context of 311, it simply means government understanding and responding to citizens' expectations for more convenient, timely, and responsive service delivery (Hyde and Olshfski 2008). A central conduit and agency network for service delivery isn't going to address homelessness, but it can aid one destitute person at a time as the appropriate agency is alerted by a concerned citizen's call to 311. It can enhance citizen engagement, one disaffected citizen at a time, when the CSR refers that citizen to the proper forum to weigh in on the proposed business expansion in her neighborhood. It can empower citizens who are alienated from city hall by the lack of response from city agencies to their concerns about graffiti or abandoned cars (Kathi and Cooper 2005).

Collaboration requires agencies to give up some of the control they once had over the service they provided themselves in the past. Giving up such independence can be a threat to an effective partnership (Ho 2002). Alfaro's team has encountered those concerns: "It requires ensuring the agency can see the benefit. We are not doing performance management—it is a partnership we are building. Ultimately, it is the customer that is getting the benefit. You have to really work with the agency to help them see we are not trying to take ownership. We are trying to help them fulfill their core mission. We are not going to do anything that is not directed by them. You have to build that trust and honesty," she said.

Because San Francisco is so decentralized, Alfaro had to use informal authority and collaborative skills to build a cross-government network. There is no established mechanism in the city for doing so. San Francisco is "about as far from a military hierarchy as you can get," according to one department head. The mayor's directives are sometimes ignored; that is part of the city's culture. It is a testament to Alfaro's collaborative skills that she was able to establish such a network.

## THE CALLS

The calls received by the 311 system run the gamut. About 4,000 calls are received each day from Municipal Railway (Muni) patrons trying to find out how to get from here to there or lodging a complaint. There is a serial caller known as the "graffiti wolf" who calls several times a day to report graffiti in all parts of the city. Others want to register for a Parks and Recreation Department program, report an abandoned mattress on the sidewalk, request a certified copy of a birth certificate, or find in-home health care for a grandfather (Colin 2007). Those who want to make their request in another language will find translation available in 175 languages.

The 311 Customer Service Center is "a service that resembles a kind of a Google hotline just for San Francisco" (Colin 2007). It allows citizens to ask any question of the CSR who takes the call, with a high likelihood of getting an answer. It is the kind of "one-stop service center" that has reemerged in recent years, facilitated by technology that makes it possible for CSRs to access a wide array of data (Ho 2002).

As Kettl (2006) reminds us, traditional public administration is built on stable structures with rigid boundaries—a configuration that is at variance with solutions to today's "wicked problems." The 311 service does not dismantle barriers, but rather makes them transparent to the citizen. The real issue is not necessarily that there is growing complexity in problems and increasing interdependence that makes solutions difficult. Actually, as Rittel, who coined the term "wicked problem" writes, the central dimension of the problem is confusion, especially among clients and decision makers, because of ill-formulated problems, poor information, and conflicting values (Rittel and Webber 1973).

Nancy Alfaro sees her role as working collaboratively with every city agency to acquire the information needed to answer questions and provide services. She has overseen the development of a database of 6,000 frequently asked questions and answers to those questions. This enables the 68 CSRs to respond to most calls directly. The initial expectation was that the center would handle 1.2 million calls annually. It is now predicting a volume of 5.6 million calls for the next fiscal year. Without any marketing, calls are increasing at a rate of 7 percent to 9 percent each month. Meanwhile, other city agencies are asking to become part of the network, so many that Alfaro has to say, "Wait, we're not ready for you yet!"

Alfaro is very clear: "311 is not a glorified switchboard." Representatives do not simply transfer calls to city departments. The goal is to satisfy the customer at the time of the call, and CSRs do so 95 percent of the time. If the answer isn't in the knowledge database at the time of the call, the question is referred to the content team, who will research the issue, get back to the caller, and add the question to the database. Moreover, unlike most city departments, 311 is up and running 24/7. Only 45 percent of its call volume occurs during the standard Monday through Friday workweek. "So it shows clearly that people need access to government at all hours," Alfaro commented. "At midnight and 1:00 in the morning, we are still getting over 200 calls an hour."

Moreover, the benefit provided by 311 doesn't stop there. When a caller requests a service—for example, that a pothole be filled—the request is given a tracking number and routed directly to the Department of Public Works, which will service the request. When the request has been met, that information is routed back to 311 so that citizens can learn the status of their requests simply by calling 311 again.

## EVIDENCE OF SUCCESS

Such a process simply didn't exist before. Citizen requests for service often fell through the cracks, and citizens had no way of knowing when or if their request or complaint would be heeded. Alfaro's team set up a process that improved the front-end customer experience. The process is tighter and more professional, according to one department head. Previously, at the Housing Authority, for example, with only one person taking service requests, many work orders would be input late in the day, causing the agency to incur overtime charges. With 311 now taking the requests, overtime costs have been reduced by 15 percent to 20 percent.

At the Municipal Transit Agency (MTA), a request that a curb be painted red for a no-parking zone or white for a commercial zone used to be a paper process. Citizens would complete a paper form and mail it to the MTA. An MTA representative would call them to discuss the request and then ask the customer to mail in payment. Now 311 takes the requests, reducing a several-step process to just two. Information about transit schedules and routes is now available 24/7, hours longer than it was when the MTA handled the calls. The MTA is currently working with 311 to identify locations where requests for the arrival time of the next transit vehicle are most frequent. With this information, the MTA can post signs displaying this information where there is the greatest demand. This benefits patrons, who know how long the wait will be at their stop; the MTA, which knows where to invest funds; and 311, which can reduce the number of callers requesting this information. "Nancy is always nudging us toward progress," reported an MTA manager.

Another example is the Department of Public Works, which has now developed service-level goals so that it can make the commitment that potholes will be filled in two days. A backlog of 30,000 open cases at the department has been reduced to 4,000, many of which are within service-level goals.

One satisfied customer is the San Francisco Bicycle Coalition, an important advocacy group in a city where nearly 30,000 people use bikes as their primary means of transportation. A priority for the coalition has been to improve pavement quality to reduce the number of accidents caused by potholes and other such hazards. Volunteers routinely canvass the city to identify the hazards and report them to 311. According to the director, 311 staff have not only efficiently fielded their calls, they also have worked with the coalition to streamline the process. For example, at the suggestion of 311 staff, the coalition now uses an e-mail address to submit their multiple reports and tags them as coming from the coalition. That way, 311 can provide them with a report detailing the number of complaints that are still open and those that have been attended to.

## MORE THAN CUSTOMER SERVICE

Alfaro takes the collaborative effort one step further. In Moore's parlance (1995), she manages outward and inward. She meets with larger departments once a month to go over outstanding service requests received at the center. The department head is asked when the service will be provided, and he or she is reminded that citizens often are satisfied simply by knowing when they can expect their request to be met. "If it is graffiti on a public property, it might take 48 hours [for it to be removed]; if it is graffiti on private property, that might take 30 days," she suggested as an example. At least the customer knows not to expect results before that time.

Under Alfaro's direction, 311 has become more than a hotline—it is a method for building accountability into processes where it didn't exist before. Department heads are presented with clear  data about service requests or complaints that have come in and have not been resolved. This is where the reciprocity in the collaborative relationship comes in: Department officials use the reports that Alfaro provides to follow up on service requests. The systematic information they receive from 311 enables them to provide better service. They can also use the information to spot trends. If there is a spate of calls coming in about graffiti in a particular area, the department head may realize that a partnership needs to be developed with the police department in response. The Department of Public Works is beginning to use the data provided by 311 to track which parts of the city record lower response to pothole requests, so that problems can be identified and addressed.

The 311 operation is funded by the city's general fund. However, in some cases, funding and personnel are transferred from other agencies that no longer need to staff caller response centers themselves. This was the case with the MTA passenger center and public works call centers, which were transferred in their entirety to 311. The center is also getting some funding from other enterprise agencies, so the portion of the budget funded by the general fund declined from 2007 to 2008. When it first agrees to establish a partnership with an agency, the 311 team does a business process analysis, including an examination of staffing. If the agency has staff taking calls from customers, the 311 team "has a conversation with them" about moving those staff to the 311 center.

A unique set of skills is required to manage such networks—negotiation and collaboration (Goldsmith and Eggers 2004)—and Alfaro has them. The process of collaboration has to be mutually beneficial to succeed (Thomson and Perry 2006). Why should these department heads cooperate with her? "We all agree that we are here to achieve that ultimate goal—to serve customers," Alfaro responded. The consolidated information about service requests helps department directors follow up with their own staff. They also may use the reports to show the budget office that they require greater resources or staffing. Department heads are aware that at any time, the mayor can look at those reports. In my opinion," said Alfaro, "it's a win-win for everybody."

## MOVING FORWARD

Alfaro's short-term objectives for 311 include developing its online counterpart, so that the full knowledge base will be available to the public online. "So," Alfaro explained, "if you wanted a new parking sign in your neighborhood, you would know where to find out how to request it." The problem with online government service now is that the service people want may not be online, or they may make the request and never hear back. The 311 online service will provide citizens with a tracking number so that they can follow the progress of their requests. It is already providing that service on behalf of the MTA, and it has plans to expand the service to the Departments of Public Works and Parks and Recreation in the fall. "We need to find alternative ways of communicating with 311 and still building transparency out there," Alfaro said.

If there is a downside to 311, it is that the calls are increasing, but Alfaro's staffing levels are not. "Our goal is to answer 80 percent of the calls within 60 seconds," Alfaro affirmed. "For the past four months we have not met that goal. We are answering only about 60 percent of calls in that time frame." So, moving some of the traffic from the telephone to the Internet will improve efficiency. Alfaro is also developing a multipurpose form that will facilitate the transmittal of reports and requests to most city agencies. Eventually, a citizen who wants to open a business, for example, will be able to complete just one form, which will then be routed to all of the agencies that may be involved in the approval process. The prospective business owner will be able to check the status of his or her request with each of the departments at any time.

In recognition of their exceptional work in launching the 311 center and building the knowledge base, Alfaro and her team received a 2008 Managerial Excellence Award from the Municipal Fiscal Advisory Committee. "This is the biggest recognition you can receive as a city employee, and I was very proud of getting that." Alfaro said. The Municipal Fiscal Advisory Committee comprises business representatives and community leaders who provide pro bono management and consulting services to the mayor of San Francisco. Each year, it recognized a limited number of San Francisco managers for their exemplary job performance and leadership.

The 311 Customer Service Center represents a flourishing network and a testament to Nancy Alfaro's skills as a collaborative manager. In a city where departments are accustomed to going their own way, she has successfully built a cross-government alliance that provides a single point of access for information and service requests. This required Alfaro to know what is reasonable to ask of people, and to use her experience and reputation to find the right people to work with. Could another city replicate 311? In a city with a city manager who has direct authority over departments, using today's technology, it should be easy. In a city as decentralized as San Francisco, a unique kind of collaborative manager is needed.

Recently, the California Supreme Court ruled on a challenge to the state law banning gay marriages that had been filed at the time San Francisco was ordered to halt the issuance of marriage licenses to same-sex couples. The challenge asserted that the law was a violation of state residents' constitutional right to equal protection. The court agreed, and on June 17, 2008, San Francisco and other counties statewide began issuing licenses to same-sex couples. Nancy Alfaro was on hand to help.

## POSTSCRIPT

In late 2008, California voters passed an initiative to amend the state constitution to ban same-sex marriage, effectively overwriting the California Supreme Court's decision. A week after thousands of people took to the streets to protest the amendment, the high court agreed to hear challenges to it. Opponents of the ban claim that the amendment makes a fundamental change to individual rights and judicial responsibilities, and therefore amounts to a revision of the state constitution, not just an amendment. A revision would require a two-thirds vote by the legislature to appear on the ballot, instead of the roughly 700,000 signatures of registered voters required for an amendment. Also left for the court to resolve is whether those marriages that took place after its ruling can remain in effect.

## REFERENCES

Argranoff, Robert. 2006. Inside Collaborative Networks:Ten Lessons for Public Administrators. Special issue, *Public Administration Review* 66: 56–65.

Colin, Chris. 2007. Pig Balls and Stuck Skunks: A 322 Customer Service Rep Has a Window onto San Francisco's Secret Heart. *San Francisco Chronicle*, September 4.

Friedrichsen, Sharon. 2006. Collaborative Public Management in San Francisco. Special issue, *Public Administration Review* 66: 150–51.

Goldsmith, Stephen, and William D. Eggers. 2004. *Governing by Network: The New Shape of the Public Sector.* Washington, DC: Brookings Institution Press.

Gordon, Rachel. 2004. City Hall Is "Can Do" Spot for "I Do's." *San Francisco Chronicle*, February 4.

Ho, Albert Tat-Kei. 2002. Reinventing Local Governments and E-Government Initiative. *Public Administration Review* 62(4): 434–44.

Hyde, Albert C., and Dorothy Olshfski. 2008. Service Quality in the Public Sector in the Internet Economy. In *Entrepreneurial Management and Public Policy*, 2nd ed., edited by Van R. Johnson, 251–74. New York: Nova Science Publishers.

Kathi, Pradeep Chandra, and Terry L. Cooper. 2005. Democratizing the Administrative State: Connecting Neighborhood Councils and City Agencies. *Public Administration Review* 65(5): 559–67.

Kettl, Donald F. 2006. Managing Boundaries in American Administration: The Collaboration Imperative. Special issue, *Public Administration Review* 66: 10–19.

Kim, Ryan, and Nanette Asimov. 2004. The Battle over Same-Sex Marriage. *San Francisco Chronicle*, February 15.

McGuire, Michael. 2006. Collaborative Public Management: Assessing What We Know and How We Know It. Special issue, *Public Administration Review* 66: 33–43.

Moore, Mark H. 1995. *Creating Public Value: Strategic Management in Government.* Cambridge, MA: Harvard University Press.

Nye, Joseph S., Jr. 2002. Information Technology and Democratic Governance. In *Governance.com: Democracy in the Information Age*, edited by Joseph S. Nye, Jr., and Elaine Ciulla Kamarck, 1–16. Washington, DC: Brookings Institution Press.

O'Leary, Rosemary, Catherine Gerard, and Lisa Blomgren Bingham. 2006. Introduction to the Symposium on Collaborate Public Management. Special issue, *Public Administration Review* 66: 6–9.

O'Toole, Laurence J., Jr. 1997. Treating Networks Seriously: Practical and Research-Based Agendas in Public Administration. *Public Administration Review* 57(1): 45–52.

Rittel, Horst, and Melvin Webber. 1973. Dilemmas in a General Theory of Planning. *Policy Sciences* 4(2): 155–69.

Thomson, Anne Marie, and James L. Perry. 2006. Collaboration Processes: Inside the Black Box. Special issue, *Public Administration Review* 66: 20–32.

Vega, Cecilia M. 2007. Dial 311—For Everything but Emergencies. *San Francisco Chronicle*, March 30.

Wagenheim, George D., and John H. Reurink. 1991. Customer Service in Public Administration. *Public Administration Review* 51(3): 263–70.

# 13

## CHRIK POORTMAN

### A World Bank Professional

### XU YI-CHONG AND PATRICK WELLER

On October 26, 2006, a crowd of former and current Word Bank staff packed the area outside the Preston Auditorium in the Bank's main complex to attend the farewell for Christiaan Poortman, universally known as Chrik. "The pain, the anger and the anguish were just unbelievable," recalled one former Bank staffer. "Meanwhile, there was this pride for this man who was the best of the institutional insiders, who would not want to see the institution go down the drain or his boss screw up his client countries or his colleagues." For those in the lower ranks, the dismay was apparent: "Chrik is of the absolute highest integrity; he was not a rebel or defiant or trying to undermine the president. If this can happen to someone so smart with such a strong career and such an institutional guy," colleagues asked, "what could happen to me?" "Then and there," a former official observed, "I just saw the institution reject Paul Wolfowitz, the president of the World Bank."

Poortman had been vice president for the Middle East and North Africa (MENA) for three years. In the 13 months he had served under Paul Wolfowitz, there had been a number of disagreements over Palestine, Iraq, and issues of anticorruption in general. The straw that broke the camel's back was Lebanon—whether the Bank should have high-level representation at a donor conference in Rome, convened by Secretary of State Condoleezza Rice, to discuss the rebuilding of Lebanon, while bombing continued with U.S. acquiescence. "To me this is hypocrisy to the extent of hypocrisy," said Poortman. Wolfowitz thought otherwise. Soon after, Poortman was offered the position of country director in Central Asia as a demotion, an insult, and a way to force him out. Poortman resigned. To assist in a smooth transition, he was prepared to stay on for a few more months. Against all norms and practices, and with a blatant lack of respect, the Bank president immediately announced a replacement, and Poortman was asked to clear his desk in a matter of days. Disrespect for a veteran Bank senior officer, the staff in general, and the institution as a whole led to the downfall of Wolfowitz. Respect is what everyone we interviewed had for Poortman.

Poortman was an international civil servant, working for a World Bank that provides assistance to more than 100 countries around the world. Its staff work with shareholders (donors) and clients (recipients), all of which are independent sovereign states. They interact with nongovernmental organizations and the general public, work with the poor in the field, and negotiate with the powerful in international forums. Like all international civil servants, they share a number of managerial

From *Public Administration Review*, 69, No. 5 (September/October 2009): 868–875. Copyright © 2009 American Society for Public Administration. Used by permission.

functions with their domestic counterparts, but their tasks are made more complex when they can only negotiate with, and never dictate to, their clients. Their power is the power to persuade: with knowledge, with experience, and with offers of assistance. International civil servants are thus a distinct class of public servants whose position and capacity need to be examined.

This profile uses the career and experiences of Poortman to illustrate the functions and roles played by Bank staff at each level of its flat hierarchy and the capacities needed to face challenges that are unique to their ilk. Each section explores a different range of functions:

- Working on development in the field, Poortman had to provide assistance in difficult circumstances and often with corrupt regimes.
- Working as a country director, Poortman was responsible for building bridges between the country's need and donors' willingness to help, among different factions so that the Bank could provide effective assistance, and among the Bank staff working in Washington and in the field.
- Working as a vice president, Poortman provided leadership and strategic planning.
- As a member of the Bank's senior management team, he advised American-appointed presidents, who often brought their own agenda. Speaking truth to power is the most serious challenge senior officials face, and it ultimately can determine their career.

## POORTMAN AS EXEMPLAR OF A WORLD BANK PROFESSIONAL

While the circumstances of Poortman's departure may be unique, he was neither the first nor will he be the last professional official to clash with a president who has a political agenda. His departure nonetheless was significant because he stood for, and was taken as an exemplar of, professionalism and staff traditions.

First, Poortman was an exemplar of a generation in the Bank that was interested in and did development work before joining the Bank in the 1970s, was passionately committed to development, and served several presidents and many rounds of executive directors. He and his colleagues spent their careers working in the poorest and sometimes conflict-stricken regions, having an ever-widening range of responsibilities and autonomy, and facing challenges beyond those that most domestic civil servants could conceive. His career is thus the story of a group of talented, dedicated international officials. It provides insights into the way the Bank operates, the development work it undertakes, and, more importantly, the life of international civil servants.

Second, Poortman's career followed the normal trajectory for successful staff. Once in a senior management position, Poortman, again with his colleagues, was presented with new challenges, especially the potential for tension between the senior career officials and U.S.-appointed presidents. Clashes and resignations are not abnormal. Every president wants to make a mark, but must work with and through career officials who are no ciphers. Senior officials, in turn, have to assess their own positions in determining, consistent with their professionalism and their perception of the responsibilities, what they can accept, and where they draw the line, in responding to presidential demands.

The Bank may appear as a presidential institution when its presidents, Lewis Preston (1991–95), James Wolfensohn (1995–2005) or Paul Wolfowitz (2005–7), all international figures, were the focus of interest and the subject of media coverage. This creates an impression that the presidents could direct and the Bank would follow. The reality is never that simple. Its presidents might make the Bank thrive or fall into disarray (Kraske et al. 1996; Mallaby 2004); they can never *be* the Bank. It may have a formal hierarchical structure, yet it operates in a quite flat manner in which ideas are sought and contested and everyone makes contributions (Kapur, Lewis, and Webb 1997; Mason and Asher 1973). As Inis L. Claude, Jr., pointed out nearly five decades ago, "members, stockholders, or citizens may control the organisation, but they cannot *be* it; the staff, in a fundamental sense, *is* the organisation." The identity of the organization is "lodged in its professional staff" (1971, 191). They *are* the Bank.

Indeed, what makes the World Bank a "global institution up to the monumental task of translating global [knowledge] into global plans of action" (Goldman 2005, 10) are the 10,000 *people* serving this institution, with nearly two-thirds of them well-educated and highly qualified professionals. They have extensive experience working on development, and serve more than 100 client countries in areas from agriculture, health, education, infrastructure, and, increasingly, governance. In an integrated world, these international professionals require the same attention and analyses as domestic civil servants traditionally have received.

## WORKING FOR DEVELOPMENT

Poortman joined the Bank in 1976 after working for four years as an economist at the Ministry of Finance and Planning in Swaziland, helping to establish the ministry following the country's independence in 1969. He was one of the elite recruits in the Young Professional program (YP) at the Bank. Created in 1963, the YP program has always been very competitive. Each year, the Bank recruits about 35 bright, enthusiastic, and well-educated YPs under the age of 30 out of approximately 10,000 applicants. They come from both developed and developing countries, but overwhelmingly receive their postgraduate degrees from leading universities in the United States or the United Kingdom. Harvard, MIT, or the London School of Economics are the most common alma maters, and economics the most popular discipline. Poortman was an exception, trained as a development economist but without a doctorate, a graduate from the Netherlands, and, at 30, older than most of his cohort. What he brought was experience in the field.

In their first year, YPs are rotated around the Bank. Poortman's first assignment was to work on an irrigation project in Indonesia, where he had spent the first 10 years of his life and where his father, a second-generation Indonesian-born Dutchman, had practiced as a doctor. He went from village to village, talking to farmers, developing farm and community budgets, calculating crop yields, and trying to discover how best support could be given. This activity might be basic, but it was necessary for the local people and the Bank projects. There was supervision and assistance, but he was trusted to get it right. That was the way the Bank, at its best, developed its staff.

After completing his YP rotation, Poortman spent six years as an economist working on the Philippines and giving advice on fiscal reform, balance of payments, trade policy, and debt management. The work was led by the director of the Country Programs Department in the East Asia and Pacific region, Kim Jaycox. A YP himself in 1964, Jaycox had already built a reputation in the Bank as a no-nonsense, hard-driving, and extremely dynamic manager. He impressed Poortman: "Jaycox was a very dynamic leader with a lot of charisma." It was reciprocal. "Chrik was a very good economist and an outstanding performer there," recalled Jaycox, who became Poortman's mentor. In the Bank, career development is left to the individual. Mentoring is invaluable for younger staff who are thrown straight into the fray.

Just as Poortman was finishing his assignment in the Philippines, "the house came down." Benigno Aquino was assassinated; foreign creditors pulled out of the country; and all of a sudden, the Philippines plunged into a big hole of debt that it could not repay. The Bank was very exposed. The Philippines taught Poortman, as a macroeconomist, his first lesson: "Economic management is not just a matter of tinkering here and there; there are fundamental principles that have to be obeyed; as a banker, one has to be careful and be aware of the broad economic, social and political context into which one is lending." He took that basic lesson to the places where he later worked as country director and vice president—understanding the client countries, particularly their political situation, and working with them.

As incoming vice president for Africa, Jaycox brought Poortman back to his initial passion, Africa. "I did not need much encouragement," recalled Poortman. For Jaycox, known as Mr. Africa in the Bank, the African region needed people like Poortman who were not only good economists and high performers, but also "had a lot of humility and respect" for the client countries. For Jaycox, Africa was the acid test for those who wanted a career in development; he thought every high-flier in the Bank hierarchy should work there for several years. In hindsight, he was right—five of the current six regional vice presidents in the Bank were recruited through the YP program, and all worked in Africa for some time.

Poortman went to Africa in 1984, working as a senior country economist and then as a division chief for industry and energy operations in West Africa, covering a number of Sahelian countries such as Mali, Burkina Faso, and Niger, where people were not just poor—they were "absolutely and totally poor." Some places "were utterly destitute." There, Poortman received recognition from the senior management, not just for developing new projects, but also for his willingness and ability to work in very difficult environments. He also learned how to become a good manager: "If your manager is asking you to do something that is necessary but may not be in the spotlight, you will do it if you have a certain amount of trust that he or she is a person who will look out for you and your career in the future." It was a philosophy he later sought to apply in senior positions.

In those years, Poortman worked, as almost all the Bank staff did, out of Washington and traveled on missions, often for weeks on end, to the countries he served. Few Bank staff worked in the field, and those who did were granted little authority. Field offices were no more than post offices; the power was in Washington. This was the case in Zimbabwe when the Bank opened its office in 1986. In 1990, the Bank significantly expanded and changed its activities there when the government wanted to undertake economic reforms and sought the Bank's assistance. Seeing Zimbabwe as a potential development "success story," Jaycox brought Poortman to Harare as the resident representative because of his reputation of working successfully in difficult countries in West Africa. He moved to Zimbabwe with his family in 1990. Although President Robert Mugabe was suspicious, even hostile, to any international organization, Poortman worked closely with the finance minister, who wanted to open up the country's economy and adopt structural reform measures. "Being a resident in Harare was very important then because the government was making big decisions requiring technical input and advice on a real time basis." Being in the field, Poortman was given a lot of trust, discretion, and support by his country director and regional vice president.

The first two decades of Poortman's career reflect the pattern that successful Bank staff followed—that is, there are no ordained career structures; they have to manage their own careers and mentors are an asset. They also demonstrate some of their challenges working on development. *They have to come to terms with the difficulties and frustrations of development work; whatever they seek to achieve, they have to work with a government as given, not as they desire; they have no control over the domestic crises of their client countries.* Development work therefore requires commitment and dedication. Working with client countries, they also need to be trusted by their superiors, because often they alone have the access to people and information.

## BUILDING BRIDGES BETWEEN DONORS, CLIENTS, AND FACTIONS

Country directors are the principal links between the Bank in Washington and the client countries. They represent the Bank in the countries where they are entrusted with authority and resources to decide, provide, and deliver the assistance needed there. They represent the countries in Washington, conveying their demands, needs, and expectations. Country directorships are often described as "the best jobs" in the Bank (Gill and Pugatch 2005) because country directors can shape the country's development and the Bank's policies and operations on a daily basis (Weller and Xu, forthcoming).

In 1997, Poortman was appointed country director for Southeast Europe, which initially covered Bosnia-Herzegovina, and later Kosovo, Macedonia, Serbia/Montenegro, and Albania. Poortman's challenge in this region was to "manage the Bank's crucial involvement in post-conflict reconstruction of the Balkan states" (Gill and Pugatch 2005, 197) and then help manage the transition from post-conflict reconstruction to development. After leaving Zimbabwe in 1994, Poortman had worked in the Europe and Central Asia region as a division chief and then as acting country director. During the reorganization of 1997, the regional senior management team met regularly, allowing then-regional vice president Johannes Linn to assess his performance. According to Linn, Poortman "just seemed to be the natural person for the job." He had this "rare" combination of being a good economist and an effective manager, level-headed, and efficient. He had also had hands-on operational experience in difficult situations. By then, the program for Bosnia-Herzegovina had already been set up; it was a complex operation under the joint management of the World Bank and the European Union. Given that the Bank had to work closely with the European Commission and that the Dutch executive director represented Bosnia on the Bank's board, Poortman's Dutch nationality was an asset.

As a country director, Poortman was responsible for formulating the Country Assistance Strategy, selecting and determining the composition of the lending program, allocating the budget for various projects and programs, and supervising the country office with both international and local staff. His job was as much about politics as economics: "From a technical point of view, dealing with such issues as fiscal policy, privatization or banking reform was straightforward but getting together different factions, who had not long ago been killing each other and would have had little hesitation in doing so again, turned out to be extremely difficult." Yet integrating all parties and sharing power was the precondition for establishing a common economic space—the linchpin for strengthening the new single state created by the Dayton Accord. "My training in economics revealed its limitation when the solutions most often available were not second best, but fifth or sixth best" (Poortman 2005, 200).

The Dayton Accord created a joint multiethnic and democratic government charged with conducting foreign, diplomatic, and fiscal policy, but it also established a second tier of government composed of the Bosniak/Croat Federation of Bosnia and Herzegovina and the Bosnian Serb-led Republika Srpska (Bosa 2002; World Bank 1996). "It was a very tense situation in which you had a three ring circus where everyone tried to bull and get out of the ring," explained Poortman. "In that kind of environment, it was a complete nightmare to help put together an economic policy and economic reform." The hatred among the parties ran deep, and many had no hesitation in embarrassing the Bank people either. "Our role at the Bank was the difficult one of ensuring joint responsibility for the debt, while at the same time being careful not to take sides in the underlying political dispute" (Poortman 2005, 204). The donors did not make the job any easier.

Poortman co-chaired the international community's donor conferences with an experienced official from the European Commission. The Bank later set up an office in Brussels to coordinate its actions and those of the donors. The challenge was to ensure that the donors would pledge sufficient amounts of assistance for the right projects for reconstruction, the pledges would materialize, and, more importantly, the assistance would be provided even-handedly. The latter turned out to be very difficult. Donors had pledged $5.1 billion for repairing damaged infrastructure and utilities, clearing mines, providing employment and demobilizing combatants. Some donors insisted on reimposing sanctions against the Bosnian Serb republic for its failure to meet obligations stated in the accord. Poortman had to convince the donors that "the peace dividend" must be widely shared and "the Serb minority was not shut out of development." Many Bank staff think it is often more difficult to work with donors than client countries.

Poortman internalized the lessons he had learned in Africa and applied them when he became the country director for Southeast Europe. "Chrik was an inclusive manager," recalled a staffer working for him, "a new style of people manager; giving a great deal of trust to the people who worked in the field." He delegated responsibilities to the field officers, and expected them to tell him what they thought was right and wrong. He wanted no surprises. The work could be dangerous for the Bank staff working in the field. "Part of my time was being worried about my staff being in the wrong place at the wrong time and caught up in protest," recalled Poortman. "When I traveled to eastern RS and encountered angry residents trying to stop or stone my car and that of other foreigners, I could not but think that political conditionality was a very blunt policy tool" (2005, 202).

The situation did improve over time. More countries were then added to Poortman's portfolio—Kosovo, Albania, and Macedonia. When the Bank was asked by the United Nations and the European Union to help Kosovo rebuild itself, the first question Poortman and his colleagues asked was, "What have we learned so far?" Learning lessons from self-evaluation is one of the attributes of the Bank as a "knowledge bank." Poortman and the same team that worked on Bosnia and Herzegovina handled development issues in Kosovo "with much greater appreciation of the political constraints involved." After 2000, Slobodan Milosevic was toppled in a bloodless democratic coup. "I could only smile when the Bank had me assume the additional role of country director for Serbia and Montenegro" (Poortman 2005, 208).

The Bank is an institution that offers opportunities for its staff to exercise imagination and initiative. To build trust and cooperation, Poortman and his team undertook a major symbolic project in which the Bank normally would not get involved—reconstructing the historic Mostar Bridge. Getting the agreement from Bosniaks, Bosnia-Croats, and Bosnia-Serbs turned out to be much more difficult than pooling funds from the International Development Association, UNESCO, and various bilateral organizations. The bridge was opened on July 23, 2004, after Poortman had already moved on to become the vice president for the MENA region. Even though the Bank does not normally "do" reconstruction of old bridges and towns, "putting the bridge and its surroundings back together again provides an extraordinary opportunity for reconciliation among the people of Bosnia-Herzegovina," Shengman Zhang (2004), the Bank's then managing director, told the audience at the opening ceremony. "This kind of reconciliation is a prerequisite for revitalizing the economy and rebuilding the social fabric of a land that was a synonym for suffering and conflict less than a decade ago." Poortman still keeps a piece of stone from the old bridge in a glass box in his office because the bridge "is a powerful symbol not only of the country's history and recovery, but also of the catalytic role that we in the World Bank can play in promoting development" (2005, 212).

Country directors are the pivots of the Bank, linking the Bank with clients, clients with donors, country teams and sector people, and management and staff in the field. They also bring together the factions in the client countries to make development work. They are thus diplomats, advisers, decision makers, administrative leaders, and technical experts; it is a challenging position.

## PROVIDING LEADERSHIP, SUPPORT, AND STRATEGIC DIRECTION

As the country director in the Balkans, Poortman received exposure to the Bank's president and the Executive Board. In 2003, he returned to Africa to become the director for operations. Just four months later, he became the vice president for the MENA region. Among 30-some positions at the vice president level, some Bank staff argue, "only the 6 regional VPs are real VPs." They are often internally promoted and have had long experience working on development. As vice president, they understand that they now serve at the pleasure of the Bank's president. Their good relationship with their colleagues and the executive directors may help them go through difficult times. No one is in a position to provide them with political protection.

The selection of vice presidents is in the hands of the president and the managing director. In the case of Poortman, his appointment as vice president for MENA was a surprise to many, but a natural choice for Shengman Zhang, who later described the process:

> In 2003, the Bank had to select a Vice President for the Middle-East and North Africa. After going through the search and review processes, we decided on two candidates. To be cautious, I went to the field to see how they worked. One was young while the other older. Each had his own specialties and advantages. Balancing everything, I thought the older one was more suitable for the job, while the departing VP wanted the younger one to succeed him. At the end the selection committee agreed with me. That departing VP went to see the President, asking for help. Wolfensohn then called me. I explained to him the process, and later to the departing VP too. The day before the announcement, Wolfensohn came to my office, asking me to reconsider the decision, because the departing VP had gone to him again, trying to sell his idea. I told the President, "Let's ask this VP to come to my office now." He came. In front of both of them, I explained my decision and then said, "The committee has made a decision. We are not going to change it even if the President disagrees. Of course, he can veto it." (2006, 113)

Poortman was aware neither of this drama nor that he had been observed in the field. He got the appointment because of his experience and ability to "settle things down, deal with the conflicts and tensions and be sensitive to the political issues on the ground." Wolfensohn needed somebody to navigate the minefields in the region among its shareholders while respecting the interests of its stakeholders. Poortman's years in the Balkans made him an obvious choice. Again, it helped that he was not from any of the countries embroiled in the region.

Poortman's appointment as vice president for MENA surprised him and many who had never considered him as a "political player," who would not speak up unless it was to his advantage. He was a straightforward, competent manager and a good technocrat. It surprised even his former boss, who had discussed his career just a few months earlier. Outside his immediate circle, Poortman's promotion received extensive approval. One senior officer who had not worked closely with Poortman commented, "His appointment was seen as part of a process in which more weight was given to technical excellence and contributions to development."

Regional vice presidents have at times developed into little barons within the Bank, partly because of their long experience across regions and sectors, and often because of the inability of some presidents to work with them as a team. In general, they do not deal with day-to-day operations in the region; they act as diplomats, mixing with government officials and regional leaders, set the strategies, and oversee the operations and budgets. Chemistry between the vice president, country director, sector directors, and the staff in general is extremely important for the success of the vice president and the Bank programs. When Poortman was appointed, he had to build those links.

"When I got there, clearly the mood was not of great jubilation." Poortman replaced a vice president who was well liked by the staff in the region and who did not want to leave. He understood that he needed to be extremely careful, modest, and humble. He told his staff, "I am not going to come in here and pretend I know everything, I need everybody's help, we have a job to do and we will pull together and do it." Poortman was good at listening and seeking others' views. He wanted to know what people thought, especially those who had been in the region for some time, on the important regional and country issues. In addition to many formal meetings and consultations, "Chrik, being Chrik, also had a lot of informal interactions with people, every hallway and every cafeteria line was an opportunity for communication." He traveled frequently, listening to government officials and people working in the field. After 14 months on the job, he had visited all his countries except Syria, where there were some difficulties. He made an effort to know "what was going on in the trenches" and to "understand and listen to the frustration and problems facing the staff, not just about the office work but about their families and their long absence from home."

New vice presidents often change personnel to provide opportunities to build their own teams. MENA had just gone through several rounds of reorganization under his predecessor. Poortman kept the regional operations director, equivalent to a deputy vice president, and the regional chief economist. In a short period of time, mutual trust between him and the team was built—"he had this trust in you that you are willing to do a lot," one staff member commented. He had unreserved confidence in his deputy, Hasan Tuluy, who acted in his place in Washington for the 40 percent of the time he was away in the region.

All the country directors in the region had been there before Poortman arrived. He understood that country directors were on the front line dealing with the government in client countries and managing the Bank programs; they needed discretion and autonomy as well as trust. He also understood that trust from either his colleagues or the government would not come overnight or by virtue of the position. He pretty much "left me alone" and seldom intervened, a country director said; but he was very supportive and gave his advice if needed. He listened, sought others' opinions, and then made decisions when it was required. "That is the kind of leadership you are looking for," one country director said. "You want to be heard and you want a decision to be taken too. It may or may not be the decision that I or somebody else would have taken, but that is okay because no one is right all the time. Chrik was very good at this."

Executive directors at the Bank are often either overestimated by those who see the Bank as an instrument of rich countries or dismissed easily as puppets of the Bank's president, who, in turn, is the puppet of the American government. In reality, executive directors are neither all powerful nor powerless. With this understanding, Poortman established regular interaction with the executive directors that represented the region, who "first looked at me with big eyes, wondering whether they were given an amateur to handle the region." They soon struck a mutual respect. In both the Balkans and MENA, Poortman interacted closely with the executive directors inside and outside the board room. "I felt responsible vis-à-vis the Bank, and also vis-à-vis the international community that was putting a lot of money into the place and fully expecting the Bank to be in the driver's seat, to be able to show that there was progress and improvement in the situation." Briefing, reporting, and seeking advice and support from executive directors was necessary for the success of the Bank program. Even though the relationships sometimes were trying or even difficult, communication allowed the executive directors to understand and appreciate the work the Bank was undertaking in the region. In MENA, according to his colleagues, "because he communicated with the executive directors frequently, a lot of preventive work was done before the crises hit." Later, these executive directors effectively became colleagues, people whom Poortman could go to for information, wisdom, and guidance—even his close allies during the most difficult time with Wolfowitz.

The MENA region covers some 20 countries, from Morocco to Iran, including the Gulf countries. It has the "poorest of the poor" (Yemen, Djibouti); middle-income countries (Morocco, Algeria, Egypt, Jordan, Iran); countries in conflict (Iraq, Palestine, Lebanon); and high-income countries (Gulf countries, including Saudi Arabia). Poortman had his hands full from the beginning. Working in the field in the region had always been dangerous, but the Bank staff had never been the target in the past. In August 2003, soon after Poortman became vice president, a truck bombing in Baghdad targeted the UN headquarters and killed 22 UN staff, including its special representative in Iraq. A Bank official was killed, too. A month later, another suicide bombing targeted the UN office in Iraq. The Bank had pulled its staff out because, according to the Articles of Agreement, it was prohibited from working in conflict regions. There was no development to talk about if fighting was still going on. This became one of the focal points of disagreement between Poortman and Wolfowitz.

In all difficult situations, whether in Bosnia, Kosovo, the West Bank and Gaza, or Lebanon, Poortman was willing and able to make difficult decisions—a necessary quality for a senior manager at the Bank. For example, because, to a large extent, the Israeli government controlled the destiny of Palestine's economy, the Bank could not begin to support economic development for Palestinians without talking to the Israeli government. To approach Israel about the development in Palestine, the Bank people had to present the issue to them from their security point of view—"their security considerations ruled a lot of decisions about movement of people and goods." Making a decision to negotiate with the Israelis on development issues in the West Bank and Gaza was making a political calculation. It was never easy. Poortman was able to do so.

He was comfortable, often relaxed, on the job. Concerned about the birds nesting on the top of the building opposite, he could suddenly jump up from his chair in the middle of a meeting in Washington, grab his binoculars to watch a bird across the roofs: "Oh boy, did you see that hawk!" Then he would plunk himself back down on the chair and say calmly, "Now, let's transfer $500 million to. . . ." A colleague commented that "Chrik was not a person for shoulder slapping and that sort of stuff," but he always took personal interest in his people. He would reach out to people, whether it was a celebration of a wedding or a birth of a baby, a sickness or a retirement. He would always be there, and he genuinely cared about people. That earned him the trust of his colleagues at the Bank.

Vice presidents are executive leaders, not cogs in a machine. They are required to manage a large group of diverse staff and negotiate political minefields with the executive directors, client governments, the president, and the management team. Their personal reputation, interpersonal skills, and the willingness and ability to delegate, as well as to decide, are necessary for the smooth operation of a region. Regional vice presidents may come to the job with a lot of experience working on development but little knowledge about the region. Their desire to learn often is the first step for success. Their appreciation of political nuances is crucial because, in many ways, they are diplomats with the client governments and negotiators with the donor community. As members of the senior management team, they also participate in the broader Bank-wide decision making.

## SPEAKING TRUTH TO POWER

In the late summer of 2006, when he resigned, Poortman was considered one of the heroes at the Bank, standing up for the Bank's staff, clients, and mission. He did not seek to be a hero or to represent any broader movement. He was not defiant, nor did he orchestrate any revolt against the senior management. He simply said what he thought to the president. Speaking truth to power is a perennial challenge for all civil servants, domestic or international. Vice presidents at the Bank serve at the pleasure of the president, but they also serve the client countries, which are the ultimate principals of the Bank. They have the responsibility to take the interests of the client countries into consideration, whether or not the president is aware of them. Representing the interests of the client countries, even in the interest of the institution, may or may not be welcome. This is the dilemma facing all civil servants.

Chrik Poortman, said a number of his colleagues, was "Dutch," as though that explained everything about him. What they meant was that he was straightforward, never shy about telling his boss his views; he could be very persistent but was never confrontational. "When he felt that the things were not going right, he would come and tell me not in a confrontational way, but in a clear and concerned way," said a former boss, Johannes Linn. "He would say what he thought and thought what he said," whether talking to superiors or colleagues. He did not see why he should kowtow to superiors just because of their position. He expected the same from the people who worked for him. Most appreciated his frank views because Poortman was an institutional man—he would not do anything to undermine the institution. When he expressed disapproval of certain actions or policies of the Bank, he did it because he believed that was right for the client countries, or for his colleagues or the Bank as an institution.

Poortman was passionate and cared deeply about the countries he served. That passion and commitment could be both a strength and a weakness. He was an insider, steeped in the Bank's history and its beliefs. That could make him cautious and careful, as he saw development tasks through the lens of the Bank and its way of working, whether in structural adjustment lending or concepts of country ownership. There is often a Bank orthodoxy, perhaps no more than the current appreciation of best practice, but nevertheless a position from which he would start. On arriving in Bosnia, "I expected to be successful if I could apply the Bank's general approach to transition in its broad outlines, with some adjustment to suit the postconflict reality." Political difficulties limited the possibility of designing any economic policy based on preexisting formulae. "Policies that we think are right at one point in time or space may be inappropriate in other situations," Poortman stated. "Our approach can veer into dogma if we do not account for the role of luck" (2005, 210).

This passion, however lofty, could bring him into conflict with his superiors. In Harare, when the Bank president visited, Poortman thought Preston ruffled some local sensibilities by using apartheid South Africa as an example for best practice; further, he did not show sufficient respect to the Bank staff who had worked hard to prepare for his visit. Poortman felt he had to mollify some of his government contacts and his staff. He told Preston, however tactfully, about his concerns. Preston then consistently blocked his reintegration into Washington. To have a president as an enemy is not career enhancing.

Straightforward and frank advice is regarded as constructive only when those in power see themselves as part of, not above, the institution. Poortman eventually developed a good relationship with Wolfensohn because of their shared concern for the institution and the commitment and passion for development. Wolfensohn was known both for his short temper, his self-centeredness, and his egotism, as well as for his charm, talent, and managerial skills (Ferguson 2004; Mallaby 2004; Zhang 2006). Poortman was skeptical when Wolfensohn came to the Bank, and he was particularly critical about his first trip to Africa and his treatment of Jaycox. His views were known to Wolfensohn, too. "I received a phone call from Jim Wolfensohn, asking me to become the VP for MENA. I was very surprised because I never really thought that was anywhere near possible. When I went to his office for a discussion, he asked me whether I could work with him as he had heard that I was not always in favor and sometimes even critical of what he had been doing."

In the following two years, they worked together on the Middle East at a difficult time when Wolfensohn was under pressure from the Coalition of the Willing to provide funding and other assistance to Iraq, while the Germans and the French made it explicitly clear that "those that do the damage carry the main burden for reconstruction." He wanted to improve the relationship with the George W. Bush administration, and "he also had to respect the feelings of his other Board members" (Mallaby 2004, 264). When the Bush administration demanded that the Bank "enter into Iraq on the back of American tanks," Wolfensohn and Poortman both thought that would drive the Bank backward in its relationship with the Arab countries for years to come. This was symptomatic of the many political minefields that Poortman had to navigate among donors and regional partners. "At the end I was genuinely sorry not to be able to work with Wolfensohn any more when he left," recalled Poortman. "It was a lot of difficult work, but we worked together very well."

This relationship was in sharp contrast to the one he had with Wolfowitz, who, during Poortman's tenure, never visited the region and never gave specific instructions. Despite his promise that he would start his job at the Bank by "listening" (*The International Economy* 2005, 20), Wolfowitz was never prepared to take responsibility for providing specific directions. This made the job for vice presidents almost impossible. On the issue of the Bank's presence in Baghdad, Poortman and his team sent briefings to the president, with recommendations and requests for decisions. Wolfowitz never gave them one. Messages were sent out indirectly through his advisor without explanation. When confronted, Wolfowitz simply refused to talk about it. After he left the Bank, Wolfowitz explained in an interview, "It is easy to think of supervising contracts long distance, but when the real purpose is dialogue with policy makers it is hard to do that long distance" (Cassidy 2007). It was too late: Poortman had already been forced out for not being willing to make the decision on Wolfowitz's behalf.

The links between a vice president and the president will always depend on a degree of chemistry. While presidents are responsible for the management of the institution, they must rely on a group of long-serving professionals who have their own ideas about what the Bank could or should do. Wolfowitz seemed to regard the Bank as an alternative Pentagon whose senior officers were political appointees. He did not understand until the day he departed that, senior or not, the Bank staff are professionals; they make decisions every day and often express their opinions freely. Poortman, like his colleagues, was prepared to work with his new president and understood that vice presidents serve at the president's pleasure. He was not prepared, however, to be a "yes man," regardless of the interests of his clients or his staff. "I made a decision soon after Wolfowitz came on board that, if I wasn't going to speak up, how could I expect younger managers to do so who had much more at stake in terms of their career, their children at school or their pension? So I decided it came with the territory that I must speak up for my client countries and for the Bank." He duly spoke up, so he had to leave.

Speaking truth to power is always a challenge in the Bank. Presidents are appointed by the U.S. president; they have never had experience working at the Bank and seldom even in development, but they almost always bring a political or a personal agenda. Presidents have authority and, initially at least, legitimacy. Serving at the pleasure of the president, senior Bank staff must translate what the presidents want into practice while upholding their professional values and their perception of the Bank's standing. When clashes loom, they must decide how far they are prepared to go. At what stage do they think their sense of professionalism and dignity, their responsibility to staff and clients, and their sense of institutional commitment are so offended that they must go? That may be a personal choice, but it is created by an institutional dilemma.

## CONCLUSION

Poortman's distinguished career at the Bank lasted 30 years, spanned three continents, and touched a wide variety of countries and a massively diverse set of programs. At each level of the organization, he had to learn sets of skills that are unique to the processes of international governance and develop the capacity to work across national boundaries and sectors. His experience is not unique. In order to understand the Bank, we need to appreciate the role played by these international civil servants. Although often anonymous, these well-educated and highly qualified professionals shape the programs of the Bank, working in an environment in which both their patrons and clients are sovereign states, and in which their success depends on their ability to educate and persuade. Most of the career vice presidents and many country directors at the Bank have had similar career paths and faced similar challenges. To succeed, they have to be leaders: to back their judgment, to assess the opportunities, and to make tough decisions. Despite the image of the World Bank as a presidential institution, the senior staff within the Bank cannot just react within bureaucratic rules and instructions. Nor can they live without bureaucratic risk. By the time they reach vice presidential status, the position is challenging, but potentially precarious. That is the life of an international civil servant at the Bank.

And Chrik? He is now director of global programs for Transparency International in Berlin.

## ACKNOWLEDGMENTS

This profile is based in part on interviews with Chrik Poortman and with 12 other World Bank officers whom he worked for, who worked with him, and who worked for him: a 360-degree perspective. The interviews were undertaken on the basis that they would not be attributed without permission. All quotations are taken from these interviews. We have also drawn from a further 100 interviews with World Bank staff undertaken for our forthcoming book, *Inside the World Bank* (Palgrave, 2009). The quotes from Shengman Zhang's book were translated by us, and therefore we are responsible for any infelicities of style or misinterpretations.

## REFERENCES

Bosa, Sumantra. 2002. *Bosnia after Dayton: Nationalist Partition and International Intervention.* New York: Oxford University Press.
Cassidy, John. 2007. The Next Crusade: Paul Wolfowitz at the World Bank. *The New Yorker*, April 9.
Claude, Inis L., Jr. 1971. *Swords into Plowshares: The Problems and Progress of International Organization.* 4th ed. New York: Random House.
Ferguson, Niall. 2004. The Real Mr. Wolfensohn. *The Washington Post*, October 3.
Gill, Indermit S., and Todd Pugatch, eds. 2005. *At the Frontlines of Development: Reflections from the World Bank.* Washington, DC: World Bank.
Goldman, Michael. 2005. Tracing the Roots/Routes of World Bank Power. *International Journal of Sociology and Social Policy* 25(1–2): 10–29.
*The International Economy.* 2005. If the New World Bank President Calls . . . 19(2): 20–31.
Kapur, Devesh, John P. Lewis, and Richard Webb. 1997. *The World Bank: Its First Half Century.* Washington, DC: Brookings Institution.
Kraske, Jochen, William H. Becker, William Diamond, and Louis P. Galambos. 1996. *Bankers with a Mission: The Presidents of the World Bank, 1946–91.* New York: Oxford University Press.
Mallaby, Sebastian. 2004. *The World's Banker: A Story of Failed States, Financial Crises, and the Wealth and Poverty of Nations.* Sydney, Australia: University of New South Wales Press.
Mason, Edward S. and Robert E. Asher. 1973. *The World Bank since Bretton Woods.* Washington, DC: Brookings Institution.

Poortman, Christiaan. 2005. Leadership, Learning, and Luck: Reflections on the Balkan States. In *At the Frontlines of Development: Reflections from the World Bank*, edited by Indermit S. Gill and Todd Pugatch, 199–212. Washington, DC: World Bank.

Weller, Patrick, and Xu Yi-chong. Forthcoming. Agents of Influence: Country Directors at the World Bank. *Public Administration*.

World Bank. 1996. *Bosnia and Herzegovina: Towards Economic Recovery*. Washington, DC: World Bank.

Zhang, Shengman. 2004. Opening Ceremony for Stari Most (Mostar Bridge). http://web.worldbank.org/wbsite/external/countries/ecaext/bosniaherzextn/0,contentmdk:20251716~menupk:362049~pagepk:2865066~pipk:2865079~thesitepk:362026,00.html [accessed May 30, 2009].

———. 2006. One Step at a Time. Shanghai: Wenhui Press.

# 14

# THE PRACADEMIC AND THE FED

## The Leadership of Chairman Benjamin Bernanke

### ANNE M. KHADEMIAN

If you want to build a factory, or fix a motorcycle, or set a nation right without getting stuck, then classical, structured, dualistic subject- object knowledge, although necessary, isn't enough. You have to have some feeling for the quality of the work. You have to have a sense of what's good. That is what carries you forward . . . It's not just "intuition," or unexplainable "skill" or "talent." It's the direct result of contact with basic reality . . .

—Robert M. Pirsig, *Zen and the Art of Motorcycle Maintenance*

There are no atheists in foxholes and no ideologues in financial crises.

—Benjamin Bernanke, 2009[1]

Following President George W. Bush's appointment of Ben S. Bernanke in October 2005 to chair the Federal Reserve Board, commentators labeled him the "safe choice," the "most predictable" in his approach to monetary policy, and an economist "closely aligned with the president" (Andrews et al. 2005; Godt 2005). As a Federal Reserve Board governor from 2002 to 2005, and chair of the President's Council of Economic Advisers for a brief time beginning in June 2005, Bernanke was well known in the financial markets, among policy makers, and in the financial press. Following his nomination as Fed chairman, Bernanke told the press that, if confirmed, his plan was "to maintain continuity with the policies and policy strategies established during the Greenspan years" (Teather 2005). His commitment to the policies of former Fed chairman Alan Greenspan was met with relief by many, and with consternation by a few Greenspan critics such as Senator Jim Bunning (R-KY), who cast the lone Senate vote of opposition to Bernanke's appointment (Harris 2008, 1; Kudlow 2008).

In addition to the expectation of policy stability, Fed watchers anticipated that Bernanke's leadership would be driven by the day-to-day exercise of central bank technocratic expertise rather than the drama of celebrity and lyrical commentary on the markets. In a letter published by the *American Economic Review* in 2006, Harvard economist Gregory Mankiw suggested that Ben Bernanke continue the policies of Alan Greenspan, with a few tweaks, but, more importantly, that he lead the Fed with a low profile to foster institutional "stability, not excitement." One way

From *Public Administration Review*, 70, No. 1 (January/February 2010): 142–150. Copyright © 2010 American Society for Public Administration. Used by permission.

to accomplish that, Mankiw continued, "is to increase confidence in the institution of the Federal Reserve and to educate the public that the institution matters more than the individual who happens to be leading it at the moment. It would be ideal if, after a long, successful tenure, your retirement as Fed chairman were a less momentous event than your arrival" (2006, 184).

More than three years into his tenure as chair, in the midst of a tsunami of subprime mortgage defaults and toppling asset values that daily erode the balance sheets of financial giants across the globe, Bernanke, the "safe choice," has led a revolution in the exercise of the Federal Reserve's bureaucratic muscle. "Excitement," to put it mildly, has trumped "stability" at the Fed. Chairman Bernanke has dramatically broken with the policies of Alan Greenspan, has authorized actions that have stretched the mandate of the Federal Reserve, and has enacted an aggressive approach to the credit crisis aimed at avoiding the policy mistakes of the Great Depression.

It was perhaps the observation of *The Independent* regarding Bernanke's October 2005 appointment that was most prescient: "[O]f all the jobs in the world, this is one where the incumbent grows in office" (McRae 2005). Chairman Bernanke has certainly grown in the office of Federal Reserve chairman, but his exercise of leadership goes beyond personal growth, success, or failure. As Donald F. Kettl points out in his work *Leadership at the Fed*, "the Fed's power has depended on the chairman's leadership" (1986, 13), and Bernanke's leadership efforts during this time of financial crisis are critically linked to the long-term institutional integrity of the Federal Reserve. This essay will examine Bernanke's evolving leadership style, and the relationship between his leadership and Federal Reserve autonomy and distinctive competence. We turn first to an overview of the dramatic events and Fed actions that have defined Bernanke's early tenure.

## THE SUBPRIME CONTAGION AND THE FED'S RESPONSE

On April 2, 2007, New Century Financial, a leading subprime mortgage lender, declared bankruptcy. Several weeks before bankruptcy was declared, New Century accountants and the company's auditing firm, KPMG, informed the board of directors that reserves for high-risk home loans had been calculated incorrectly; bottom line, $300 million in profits for the second half of 2006 were now gone (Bajaj and Creswell 2008). In addition to the tricky accounting, New Century was highly leveraged, using just over $2 billion in equity to control more than $25 billion in assets. New Century's failure ricocheted into the balance sheets of other financial firms that were creditors to the subprime lender; Bank of America, Citigroup, UBS, Morgan Stanley, and others had extended more than $8 billion altogether in loans to the failed company. As part of the bankruptcy restructuring, New Century, the largest independent provider of home loans to people with poor credit ratings, announced that the company would cut 3,200 jobs from its workforce (CNNMoney.com 2007; Federal Reserve Bank of St. Louis 2009).

The New Century failure was an early manifestation of the problems that now define the financial crisis: questionable accounting, complex assets built on subprime mortgages for a teetering real estate market and a growing number of foreclosures, highly leveraged positions (companies controlled assets worth as much as 35 times the equity held), intricate and devastating connections with balance sheets across the global financial world, contracting credit, layoffs and job losses, and more home foreclosures. Many troubled institutions followed a similar path, from American Home Mortgage Investment Company and Countrywide Financial Corporation to the investment banks Bear Sterns and Lehman Brothers, to the financial giants Bank of America, Citigroup, and insurance behemoth AIG. Some, such as Lehman Brothers, collapsed; others, such as Countrywide and Bear Sterns, found a white knight to rescue them with support from the Fed, and others, such as Bank of America, Citigroup, and AIG, took billions of dollars from the Troubled Asset Relief

Program to prop up capital positions through U.S. Treasury purchases of bank stock and loans from the Fed (Cassidy 2008; Federal Reserve Bank of St. Louis 2009; Harris 2006; Lowenstein 2008a, 2008b).

The Federal Reserve Board of Governors was initially slow to react to the oncoming crisis. In a June 5, 2007, speech to the International Monetary Conference in South Africa, two months after the failure of New Century Financial, Chairman Bernanke reassured the audience that the Fed would "follow developments in the subprime market closely." Yet, he continued, "solid growth in incomes" and "low mortgage rates" would "ultimately support the demand for housing, and at this point, the troubles in the subprime sector seem unlikely to seriously spill over to the broader economy or the financial system" (Bernanke 2007). This cautious optimism was reflected in the policy moves of the Fed throughout the summer of 2007. In June 2007, the Federal Open Market Committee (FOMC, the monetary policy-making arm of the Federal Reserve) voted to keep the targeted federal funds rate (the interest rate for balances traded between depository institutions for overnight loans) at 5.25 percent. The August 2007 FOMC meeting also concluded with the decision to maintain the target federal funds rate at 5.25 percent, reflecting in large part Bernanke's concern that inflation was a larger threat to the economy than an economic slowdown (Peters and Bajaj 2007).

Through its daily open market operations (the buying and selling of primarily short-term government securities by the Federal Reserve Bank of New York), the Fed targets and influences the federal funds rate. Purchases of government securities by the Fed increase the amount of money in the banking system—investors sell the securities to the Fed in return for cash, and the increased supply of money is reflected in a lower federal funds rate. When the Fed sells government securities, the reverse happens—the amount of money in the system decreases and the federal funds rate trends upward. The federal funds rate, in turn, affects other interest rates, such as the rates at which borrowers can secure home mortgages, car loans, and student loans.

By September 2007, however, additional bankruptcies and liquidity problems, the continued collapse of real estate markets and downward spiral for mortgage-backed securities, and consequent credit-rating downgrades prompted the Fed to reduce the targeted federal funds rate by 50 basis points (0.5 percentage point) to 4.75, then to 4.50 percent in October, and to 4.25 in December 2007. A year later, the federal funds rate would hover just above zero at 0.25 percent (with little change in the liquidity of the financial system), technically maxing out the federal funds rate as a tool for lowering interest rates and increasing the flow of money in the economy. In a December 2008 speech before the Greater Austin Chamber of Commerce, Bernanke described the unprecedented moves to lower the federal funds rate:

> By way of historical comparison, this policy response stands out as exceptionally rapid and proactive. In taking these actions, we aimed not only to cushion the direct effects of the financial turbulence on the economy, but also to reduce the risk of a so-called adverse feedback loop in which economic weakness exacerbates financial stress, which, in turn, leads to further economic damage. (Bernanke 2008)

In that same speech, Bernanke detailed two additional strategies pursued by the Fed to provide liquidity to the private sector. The first was to increase the amount of credit extended to the banking system by the Federal Reserve though direct purchases of assets by the Fed, and through direct lending by the Fed. The Fed lowered the discount rate, or the rate at which banks can borrow from the Federal Reserve, and extended the term, or the number of days banks could borrow the funds. The Fed also created the term auction facility to auction off billions of dollars in fixed amounts of credit with specific terms (loan limits) to institutions in need of liquidity, and the term securities lending facility to encourage lending and borrowing in Treasury securities markets. The second overall strategy has been to support dollar-funding conditions in foreign markets through bilateral currency swap agreements with other central banks. As described by Bernanke, central bank swaps, or the borrowing of foreign currency between central banks, allows central banks in Europe, Japan, and England, for example, which "have borrowed dollars from the Federal Reserve[,] to re-lend to banks in their jurisdictions. Because short-term funding markets are interconnected, the provision of dollar liquidity in major foreign markets eases conditions in dollar funding markets globally, including here in the United States" (Bernanke 2008).

The Fed has lent more than $1.5 trillion based on the collateral of banks and nonbanks, and provided another $1.5 trillion in financial guarantees to banks, investment companies and insurance companies flailing in the current crisis (Cassidy 2008). The Federal Reserve Board made decisions to support the rescue of the investment bank Bear Sterns in the summer of 2008, and the insurance giant AIG, while Lehman Brothers was left to declare bankruptcy. The Fed has accepted subprime mortgages and other troubled assets as collateral, and has purchased more than $1 trillion in mortgage-backed securities (Board of Governors 2009a). Fed purchases of debt (called "agency debt") issued by Freddie Mac and Fannie Mae have topped $200 billion, and in March 2009, the Fed announced it would purchase $300 billion in long-term Treasury bonds as a means to further reduce interest rates and stimulate the credit markets (Board of Governors 2009b; Duke 2009). Paying for this bold and controversial purchase of Treasury debt may stimulate lending by lowering interest rates, but it may also be highly inflationary. The monetization of fiscal policy, as Fed watchers have labeled the long-term Treasury bond purchase, continues a trend of essential, gutsy, or reckless steps by the Fed—the appropriate adjective depends on the assessment of the leader—with Bernanke at the helm (Pender 2009).

## DEVELOPING A LEADERSHIP STYLE: TRANSPARENCY, LEARNING, AND THE "REAL" ECONOMY

Benjamin Bernanke grew up in the small town of Dillon, South Carolina, where his parents owned and operated Jay Bee Pharmacy on Main Street. Described as a "brainy boy who obsessed over baseball statistics, played the saxophone, taught himself calculus and scored 1590 out of 1600 on his SATs, the highest in the state that year," Bernanke was an academic superstar (Kessler 2005). Despite his parents' reservations about the distance and the cost, Bernanke attended Harvard as an undergraduate and graduated with top honors in 1975, and he attended MIT to earn his PhD in economics four years later. By 1985, at the young age of 31, Bernanke was a full professor at Princeton, and was eventually named chair of the economics department. His research specialty has been macroeconomics, and his passion, the study the Great Depression—what Bernanke calls "the Holy Grail of macroeconomics" (Bernanke 2000, 5). In the preface to his book, *Essays on the Great Depression*, Bernanke writes,

> Fascinating, and often tragic, characters abound in this period, from hapless policymakers trying to make sense of events for which their experience had not prepared them to ordinary people coping heroically with the effects of the economic catastrophe. For my money, few periods are so replete with human interest.

The human interest, as well as the potential policy lessons of the Great Depression drove Bernanke's early scholarly interests. "Those who doubt there is much connection between the economy of the 1930s and the supercharged information-age economy of the twenty-first century," he wrote, "are invited to look at the current economic headlines—about high unemployment, failing banks, volatile financial markets, currency crises, and even deflation. The issues raised by the Depression and its lessons are still relevant today" (2000, viii)—and, one might add nine years later, today in 2009. Of particular interest to Bernanke was the role of the Federal Reserve in the 1930s, which he and others have argued contributed to the Great Depression through its contraction of the money supply and its failure to save the banks.

Chairman Bernanke began his term as leader of the Federal Reserve Board in late 2005, firm in the belief that the institution of the Federal Reserve "matters more than the individual who happens to be leading it at the moment." Bernanke's long-standing research efforts provided the lessons of Federal Reserve Board action and inaction, and his early descriptions of the chairman-ship position demonstrated a scholarly assessment of the challenges the work posed and the role of his academic training in approaching the work:

> The Federal Reserve's responsibilities are quite broad, including not only monetary policy but the regulation and supervision of banks, oversight of the payments system, the making and enforcement of various regulations to protect consumers in their financial dealings, and the promotion of financial stability generally, among others. Getting up to speed on these diverse topics required some concentrated effort on my part. Much of what I had to absorb was insti-tutional detail—some interesting, some less so—but I have also come to appreciate that the dictum that "the devil is in the details" applies with great force to all serious policy work. My academic training has helped considerably by leading me always to focus on the underlying conceptual framework on which the legal, procedural, and institutional details depend. With an underlying framework in mind, seeing what is at stake and making a reasonable and coherent decision on a policy issue becomes easier, though rarely easy. (Bernanke 2005)

In addition to the scholarly approach that placed institution before celebrity, many observers expected Chairman Bernanke to focus like a laser on fighting inflation as a means to establish the essential "inflation-fighting credibility at the beginning of this term, in order to take a more relaxed approach later on" (quoted in Kessler 2005; see also Wray 2007). Yet as the Fed's plan to purchase $300 billion in long-term Treasury bonds indicates (among other dramatic policy actions), the balance between a scholarly approach to leadership at the Fed that draws on a "legal, procedural, and institutional" conceptual framework, and the pressure to take action in the eye of an economic storm can create leadership contradictions that are not easily reconciled by applying a set of guiding principles or research-based understandings. Many view the $300 billion purchase as a dangerous race toward inflation that the Fed may have little capacity to halt (El-Erian 2009; Frisby 2009). More broadly, the Fed's purchases of long-term Treasuries, as well as more than $1 trillion in mortgage-backed securities (primarily securities issued by the government-sponsored entities Freddie Mac and Fannie Mae), place the Fed in the awkward position of propping up fiscal and housing policies. Bernanke's June 3, 2009, testimony before the U.S. House Committee on the Budget suggests that he is not comfortable with this shift in Fed priorities, nor does he see full economic recovery unless Congress and the Barack Obama administration find long-term fiscal solutions that do not involve the Fed (Bernanke 2009b). Addressing the Congress, administration, and the American people, Bernanke argued that "[u]nless we demonstrate a strong commitment to fiscal sustainability in the longer term, we will have neither financial stability nor healthy economic growth" (Bernanke 2009b).

Just how the Fed's bold actions to meet the economic crisis head-on will affect the institution-alized practices and policies of the Fed will depend in large part on Bernanke's leadership. The edge to Bernanke's June 3 testimony, pushing back on Congress and the administration to take ownership of the fiscal challenges, indicates the difficulty of this balance. Recent history demonstrates the tendency of elected officials to rely more heavily on regulatory expertise in times of uncertainty and crisis, particularly when the policy intervention could have significant financial implications with political blowback (Khademian 1992). As a highly competent institution with the distinct record of managing monetary policy, as well as expertise in supervising some of the largest banks and bank holding companies, the Fed has become the go-to institution in the current crisis; proposals to make the Fed the systemic risk regulator across the economy are indicative (U.S. Department of the Treasury 2009). In anticipation of these proposals, Bernanke has sought to balance Fed authority with capacity in order to maintain the Fed's competence. In a speech in May 2009, Bernanke noted,

> We must ensure that we continue to increase our expertise so it is properly matched with the problems and challenges we will face in both our bank supervisory role and in meeting our traditional financial stability mandate. (Bernanke 2009c)

Bernanke is at once the cautious academic, considering the possible new sources and quantities of expertise required by the Fed under the legislative microscope, the savvy political leader assessing the vital balance between capacity and political expectations essential for institutional autonomy, and the entrepreneur pushing the Fed to engage in aggressive actions to minimize the reverberations of the current financial crisis. It is a style that has its roots in part in his academic career. As Bernanke moves to exercise Federal Reserve authority more dramatically than any predecessor, his leadership is defined by a commitment to transparency and an effort to incorporate learning into the basics of economic theory and practice.

Perhaps more significant, however, his leadership has been defined by the reality of the financial crisis and by his close connection to and understanding of Main Street. As the epigraph to this article states, if you want to "set a nation right without getting stuck. . . . It's not just 'intuition,' or unexplainable 'skill' or 'talent.' It's the direct result of contact with basic *reality*" (Pirsig 2005). In his governance of Federal Reserve Board activities, Bernanke's leadership represents a sense of "what is good," grounded in his experience with the "real" economy.

## WORKING WITH THE LEARNING CURVE: TRANSPARENCY AT THE FED

In a 2004 speech to the American Economics Association in San Diego, California, Bernanke made the case for translating "Fedspeak" into clear, transparent signals:

> [A]lthough monetary policy cannot be made by a mechanical rule, policy can and should have "rule-like" features. Obviously, the more systematic and the more consistent with a few basic principles the conduct of monetary policy becomes, the easier it will be for the public to understand and predict the Fed's behavior. However, because the world is complex and ever changing, policy actions alone, without explanation, will never be enough to provide the public with the information it needs to predict policy actions. Words are also necessary. (Bernanke 2004)

"Predicting" the Fed's behavior in the current crisis might be a stretch for even the most savvy market players. However, Bernanke has worked to make Fed actions more "understandable," primarily by working to make the Fed more transparent. First, Bernanke works to *communicate* Fed policy and actions clearly to investors and market players, other central banks, elected officials, and the general public. As noted by a blogger recently considering Bernanke's leadership, "What he says seems to be what he actually thinks and plans to do—quite a revolutionary approach to central banking" (Werner 2009).

Connections between Bernanke's public statements (before Congress, in speeches, and in statements to the press) and the actions of the Fed are considered more explicit than evidenced by previous chairmen, who often engaged in "blowing smoke" or the exercise of "constructive ambiguity" (Harris 2008, 2). Many observers attribute Bernanke's efforts to couple clear information and actions by the Fed to his belief in "rational expectations," a theoretical assumption that the public will utilize all available and useful information to predict the economic future, including the anticipated actions of the government. To the extent that these expectations do not change significantly over time or in response to new information, they are "anchored," or established. Efforts to model anchored expectations for inflation, for example, provide a means to forecast or control inflation. In terms of Federal Reserve Board policy making, rational expectations requires clear information shared between the Fed and the markets to fine-tune monetary policy (Lowenstein 2008a).

While Bernanke has long been a student of rational expectations (Bernanke and Woodford 1997), it is his incorporation of adaptive learning into assessments of the future that both grounds and advances the concept of rational expectations and motivates his emphasis on transparency (Bernanke 2007). Theory aside, the public does not have all of the information needed to perfectly predict the condition of the economy or the actions of government in the future. Nor do the expectations that members of the public hold remain stable. Experience, additional information, conflicting information, anxiety about the future, and so on, will result in adjustments of expectations and adjustments of behavior that, when acted on, may contradict or run counter to the expectations and efforts of government policy makers; the result may be the economic "stagflation" in the 1970s (Bernanke 2007) and, more to the point, today's financial crisis. What was deemed a "real estate bubble" by the Fed under Chairman Greenspan, best managed by maintaining the federal funds rate at 5.25 percent, was experienced as foreclosures, credit downgrades, declining values of mortgage backed securities, a decline in capital, and a growing credit crisis by the public. The plummeting confidence (adaptations in public assessments) in real estate-backed securities cascaded through the financial system.

The implications of adaptive learning, Bernanke has argued, suggest even more ardently the need for transparency at the Fed, particularly the transparency of the decision-making practices of the Federal Open Market Committee. The FOMC consists of the seven members of the Federal Reserve Board of Governors of the Federal Reserve System, the president of the Federal Reserve Bank of New York, and four of the remaining 11 Federal Reserve Bank presidents, who rotate every year. The dynamic of broad, shared authority on the FOMC, which can slow decision making and limit the authority of the chairman, has resulted in a governing style of forced consensus by Bernanke's predecessors, and a narrowing of focus to the federal funds rate as the primary target of discussion and action (Harris 2008). Both trends have changed under Bernanke. Meetings are described as open, oriented toward building consensus through discussion, and broad in focus, with opportunities and the expectation for every member to share a perspective (Irwin 2009; Johnson and Kwak 2009). Reflecting on the decision-making processes of the FOMC, Bernanke described it as a "consensus-based system . . . with a leader." Rather than forcing decisions or dictating responses, Bernanke continued, "I have to be comfortable with the outcome of the process, and as chairman I aim to shape a process that produces the best outcome" (Irwin 2009).

Thinking out of the box—finding creative ways beyond interest rate targets to accomplish the mission of the Fed during this time of crisis—is the context Bernanke seeks to establish. The open encouragement to think broadly and creatively goes beyond the work of the Federal Open Market Committee. Staff across the Fed report receiving "blue sky" e-mails from Chairman Bernanke, encouraging their participation in creative efforts to address the financial crisis (Irwin 2009). Public disclosure of Fed actions and easy access to the decisions and financial condition of the Fed is also a goal. In May 2009, Chairman Bernanke established an internal group with Federal Reserve Board vice chairman Donald Kohn at the helm to review the Fed's disclosure policies, or the information made available to the public on a routine basis. According to Bernanke, monthly reports detailing a range of Fed activities, including borrowing activity at Fed facilities and updates of the Fed's financial statements, will soon be available (Bernanke 2009b).

The emphasis on transparency, however, draws skepticism from those who point primarily to the secrecy surrounding the Fed's role in prompting Bank of America to merge with the failing brokerage company Merrill Lynch in late 2008. A 2009 document issued by New York attorney general Andrew Cuomo reports that then-Treasury Secretary Hank Paulson and Chairman Bernanke unduly pressured the executives of Bank of America to complete the merger with Merrill Lynch in December 2008, despite revelations that Merrill's fourth-quarter losses would far exceed the losses reported prior to the merger agreement (Cuomo 2009). According to Bank of America chief executive Ken Lewis, this request also included keeping the actual losses of Merrill Lynch a secret until the merger was complete (Cuomo 2009, 4). In testimony before Congress, Bernanke denied the accusations that he or the Fed put pressure on Bank of America, particularly by threatening to unseat the company's management and board if the merger did not go through (Bernanke 2009a). Instead, Bernanke provided his own account of the events, beginning with the point that he did not play a role in arranging the September 2008 decision to merge, in the first place, and that Federal Reserve assistance was not promised at that time. In December 2008, when Bank of America sought to exit the agreement, Bernanke did resist—in light of the volatility of the markets and the concern for further volatility if the deal did not go through—concerns that the market may have about the decision capacity of Bank of America, and the legality of exiting the deal (Bernanke 2009a).

Bernanke's testimony on the subject was widely viewed as a defense of his reputation as the leader of the Fed and of his efforts to enhance transparency. While the testimony brought the behind-the-scenes decisions and logic to the public, it also demonstrated the tremendous difficulty of pursuing transparency in the midst of economic crisis and market volatility. It is perhaps the conundrum for any financial regulatory leader whose every word is read as an indication of possible market direction or trends, and consequent market reactions can be swift and painful. The traditional critique of regulatory systems is that quick action and innovation are limited. Bernanke's bold moves throughout the crisis to utilize the Fed's resources in ways to prevent collapse, stop the bleeding, and bolster confidence challenge that perspective, but swift action in a dynamic market does not lend itself readily to transparency. In the midst of this quandary, Bernanke has focused on the congressional and administrative challenge of changing the current regulatory framework to "promote financial stability" and to enhance the capacity for supervisory oversight (Bernanke 2009a).

## EXPERIENCE IN THE REAL ECONOMY: A SENSE OF "WHAT IS GOOD"

Bernanke's unprecedented accessibility to the financial and mainstream press, and his frequent speeches and appearances around the country, provide an open window onto the daily activities of the Fed. The connection between the actions of the Fed and its arcane language, and the daily lives of Americans—their ability to secure a loan for a home or business, or the failure of wages to keep up with the cost of living—is not explicit. The urgency of the financial crisis confronting the country, and the role the Fed can play in making it right and making it matter for individual Americans, is central to Bernanke's developing leadership at the Fed. In a recent interview with *60 Minutes,* Bernanke connected the work of the Fed and his leadership to the immediate challenges facing Americans:

> I got into economics because I wanted to make things better for the average person. When I see a job loss number, 650,000, like we saw last month, I know that's not just a number. That's 650,000 lives that have been disrupted. Families that have had to move or take children out of school. Houses that may be in danger of foreclosure. I know something about what people are going through. (*60 Minutes* 2009)

He does. Bernanke's connection to the economic experiences of Americans is grounded in his own experience growing up in Dillon, South Carolina. His family operated a small business on Main Street, in the summer he waited tables in the Mexican-themed restaurant the Sombrero Room at South of the Border just outside of town, and he worked on the construction of a local hospital before heading to college (Phillips 2009). The recent foreclosure on Bernanke's childhood home (at the time no longer owned by his family) is representative of the broader challenges currently facing the residents of Dillon, where unemployment is 14.2 percent in the wake of additional layoffs and plant closings (Phillips 2009). Bernanke's continued connection with the town of Dillon, and his efforts to know directly about the economic conditions of Americans, provide a connection to the real economy that is invoked in his efforts to describe his leadership.

## BERNANKE AND THE EVOLUTION OF THE FED

Autonomy in a public agency is a valuable commodity (Carpenter 2001). Agencies that are perceived as having autonomy often have a "distinctive competence," as Philip Selznick (1957) described, that members of Congress rely on, constituents value, and the president is hesitant to mess with (Khademian 1992; Rourke 1986). Many factors play a role in generating agency autonomy, from professional expertise to organizational structure and mandate and constituent influence.

The Fed is rich in these attributes. Structurally, the Federal Reserve System is governed by the Federal Reserve Board of Governors, whose members are appointed by the president and confirmed by the Senate for 14-year nonrenewable terms. The president designates a chairman and vice chairman for four-year terms that begin midway through a president's term and end midway through the following presidential term. The administrative arms of the Federal Reserve System, the 12 Federal Reserve Banks in Atlanta, Boston, Chicago, Cleveland, Dallas, Kansas City, Minneapolis, New York, Philadelphia, Richmond, St. Louis, and San Francisco, are unique public–private entities that implement the Fed's monetary policy. State-chartered and nationally chartered banks that join the Federal Reserve System purchase stock in the Reserve Bank in one of the 12 regions, and as shareholders, they select six of the nine members of their respective Reserve Bank board of directors. Presidents of the Reserve Banks serve on a rotating basis on the Federal Open Market Committee, with the exception of the president of the New York Reserve Bank, who serves continuously. This shared authority between private banks, the Reserve Banks, and the Board of Governors makes tight political control problematic (Forder 2003), though not impossible (Corder 1998; Woolley 1986). The Federal Reserve Board system is also self-funding (not reliant on Congress for annual appropriations), it is rich in the economic expertise required to navigate the complexities of the economy, and its mission to govern the supply of money and credit is understood to be vital to America's economic health (Kettl 1986; Khademian 1996).

Yet agency leaders are central to the cultivation of agency autonomy (Wilson 1989). Kettl (1986) describes the fundamental role of Fed chairmen over the years in building "political support for its decisions." Regardless of the structural, expert, and mission-based components of Fed autonomy, political support is essential, and how leaders cultivate and maintain that support is vital. Today, leadership at the Fed involves a delicate balancing act between autonomy maintained through the exercise of long-standing, politically accepted practices to regulate the supply of money and credit, and the excruciating pressures of the current crisis that demand action. Finding a means to maintain the previous political balance exercised through the cautious adjustments of the federal funds rate is no longer an option. Yet taking bold action to address the crisis risks political backlash in the immediate term, and the potential for reduced autonomy of the Fed in the long term. Charles Plosser, president of the Federal Reserve Bank of Philadelphia, cautioned against the dramatic cuts in interest rates in 2008 by referencing the credibility of the Fed: "The Fed has worked hard for 30 years to develop credibility with the public that we will deliver on low and stable inflation. . . . That credibility is hard to earn, but easy to lose if you're not careful" (quoted in Weisman 2008).

The "conservator" role that Larry D. Terry advocated in his book *Leadership of Public Bureaucracies* (2003) captures the challenge faced by Bernanke—preserving the integrity of the institution while maintaining its relevance when change is needed. Chairman Bernanke's initial close association with the policies of his predecessor and his assurances that early warning signs of financial distress could be contained positioned Bernanke as a cautious leader of the Fed, enhancing its established distinctive competencies, fostering stability, and deemphasizing personality. Yet through the crisis that began in the subprime mortgage market, Bernanke has become an entrepreneurial pragmatist, daily testing the boundaries of Federal Reserve capacity, resources, and autonomy to find an approach that will work to address the challenges of the financial crisis. While the incentive to find what will work—to stimulate lending, to prevent foreclosures, to stabilize the economy—seemed to guide Bernanke early in the crisis, the concern for the institutional integrity of the Fed and the potential for runaway inflation has more recently come to the fore.

This tightly coupled relationship between leadership and institutional integrity, and between responsiveness and institutional autonomy, is made more complex by the increasingly networked context within which financial regulation is conducted. Multiple regulatory agencies with blurred jurisdictions must work in concert on a daily basis and in response to emergencies or crises. The gaps in this networked system have been laid bare by the crisis, yet it is unlikely that any future regulatory reform will eliminate the need for coordination (Corder 2009). Bernanke's emphasis on the future capacity of the Fed as a potential regulator of systemic risk suggests that the Fed could remain the dominant agency in the regulatory network, but issues of speed and transparency will continue to bump up against the individual institutional identities and distinctive competencies of the various network participants.

## CONCLUSION

The Fed has become the go-to institution in the midst of this economic crisis. Recent testimony and discussion on Capitol Hill that has focused on establishing a regulator with the authority to monitor and regulate systemic risk, for example, as well as input from the White House, features the Fed as the implementing or lead agency in a council of regulators (Drawbaugh 2009; Geithner 2008;

Schmidt and Christie 2009). Yet more authority is not necessarily a path to maintaining regulatory autonomy and excellence at the Fed. Additional authority brings additional constituents into the picture, demands new forms of expertise, and requires the reciprocal education between elected officials and experts at the Fed to frame the parameters and tools that would bring the practice of systemic risk monitoring and regulation to fruition. Should Congress give this authority to the Fed, Bernanke's emphasis on transparency, learning, and the impact of Fed actions on the daily lives of Americans would no doubt guide the development and implementation of the authority. Yet it is the emphasis on these same leadership priorities that will alter the Fed fundamentally as an institution in the wake of the current crisis. Bernanke's working model seems to be an elastic institution, able to scale back the wide range of tools currently invoked to expand the supply of money and credit when the crisis is over, perhaps returning to the more restrained central bank model. But greater transparency in Fed decision making, an ongoing effort to incorporate learning into the policy decisions of the Fed, and a close connection to the daily impact of Fed policy on the lives of Americans may replace mystery and power with transparency and competence—perhaps a more workable model, but certainly not the stuff of political celebrity.

## NOTES

1. This statement was widely cited in media news outlets from NPR to *Face the Nation* and the *New York Times*. See http://www.nytimes.com/2008/09/21/ business/21paulson.html.

## REFERENCES

Andrews, Edmund L., David Leonhardt, Eduardo Porter and Louis Uchitelle. 2005. At the Fed, an Unknown Became the Safe Choice. *New York Times,* October 26.
Bajaj, Vikas, and Julie Creswell. 2008. A Lender Failed: Did Its Auditor? *New York Times,* April 13.
Bernanke, Ben S. 1995. The Macroeconomics of the Great Depression: A Comparative Approach. *Journal of Money, Credit and Banking* 27(1): 1–28.
———. 2000. *Essays on the Great Depression.* Princeton, NJ: Princeton University Press.
———. 2003. Downside Danger: Why the World's Central Banks Must Become More Vigilant about Falling Prices. *Foreign Policy*, no. 139: 74–75.
———. 2004. Fedspeak. Remarks at the Meetings of the American Economic Association, San Diego, California, January 3. http://www.federalreserve.gov/ boarddocs/speeches/2004/200401032/default.htm [accessed September 17, 2009].
———. 2005. Panel Discussion: The Transition from Academic to Policymaker. Remarks at the Annual Meeting of the American Economic Association, Philadelphia, Pennsylvania, January 7. http://www.federalreserve.gov/boarddocs/speeches/2005/20050107/default.htm [accessed September 17, 2009].
———. 2007. Inflation Expectations and Inflation Forecasting. Remarks at the Monetary Economics Workshop of the National Bureau of Economic Research Summer Institute, Cambridge, Massachusetts, July 10. http://www.federalreserve.gov/newsevents/speech/bernanke20070710a.htm [accessed September 17, 2009].
———. 2008. Federal Reserve Policies in the Financial Crisis. Remarks at the Greater Austin Chamber of Commerce, Austin, Texas, December 1. http://www.federalreserve.gov/newsevents/speech/bernanke20081201a.htm [accessed September 17, 2009].
———. 2009a. Acquisition of Merrill Lynch by Bank of America. Testimony before the U.S. House Committee on Oversight and Government Reform, June 25. http://www.federalreserve.gov/newsevents/testimony/bernanke20090625a.htm [accessed September 17, 2009].
———. 2009b. Current Economic and Financial Conditions and the Federal Budget. Testimony before the U.S. House Committee on the Budget, June 3. http://www.federalreserve.gov/newsevents/testimony/bernanke20090603a.htm [accessed September 17, 2009].
———. 2009c. Lessons of the Financial Crisis for Banking Supervision. Remarks at the Federal Reserve Bank of Chicago Conference on Bank Structure and Competition, Chicago, Illinois. May 7. http://www.federalreserve.gov/newsevents/speech/bernanke20090507a.htm [accessed September 17, 2009].

Bernanke, Ben S., and Michael Woodford. 1997. Inflation Forecasts and Monetary Policy. *Journal of Money, Credit and Banking* 29(4): 653–84.

Board of Governors of the Federal Reserve System. 2009a. Credit and Liquidity Programs and the Balance Sheet: The Federal Reserve's Response to the Crisis. http://www.federalreserve.gov/monetarypolicy/bst_crisisresponse.htm [accessed September 17, 2009].

———. 2009b. News release, March 18 (Federal Open Market Committee statement). http://www.federal-reserve.gov/newsevents/press/monetary/20090318a.htm [accessed September 17, 2009].

Carpenter, Daniel P. 2001. *The Forging of Bureaucratic Autonomy: Reputations, Networks, and Policy Innovation in Executive Agencies, 1862–1928.* Princeton, NJ: Princeton University Press.

Cassidy, John. 2008. Anatomy of a Meltdown: Ben Bernanke and the Financial Crisis. *The New Yorker,* December 1.

CNNMoney.com. 2007. New Century Files for Chapter 11 Bankruptcy: Troubled Subprime Mortgage to Cut 3,200 Jobs, Sell Servicing, Seek Funding While It Reorganizes. April 3. http://money.cnn.com/2007/04/02/news/companies/new_century_bankruptcy/ [accessed September 17, 2009].

Corder, J. Kevin. 1998. *Central Bank Autonomy: The Federal Reserve System in American Politics.* New York: Garland.

———. 2009. The Federal Reserve System and the Credit Crisis. *Public Administration Review* 69(4): 623–31.

Cuomo, Andrew. 2009. State of New York, Office of the Attorney General, letter to Chairpersons Dodd, Frank, Shapiro and Warren, regarding Bank of America-Merrill Lynch Merger Investigation, April 23. http://www.oag.state.ny.us/media_center/2009/apr/pdfs/BofAmergLetter.pdf [accessed October 7, 2009].

Drawbaugh, Kevin. 2009. Fed Backing for Panel Seen Boosting Reform Chances. Reuters, October 1. http://www.reuters.com/article/newsOne/idUSN0133725520091001 [accessed October 7, 2009].

Duke, Elizabeth A. 2009. Containing the Crisis and Promoting Economic Recovery. Remarks at the Women in Housing and Finance Annual Meeting, Washington, DC, June 15. http://www.federalreserve.gov/newsevents/speech/duke20090616a.htm#f8 [accessed September 17, 2009].

El-Erian, Mohamed. 2009. Why Bernanke Is Right to Be Worried. *Financial Times,* June 3.

Federal Reserve Bank of St. Louis. 2009. The Financial Crisis: A Timeline of Events and Policy Actions. http://timeline.stlouisfed.org/index.cfm?p=timeline [accessed September 17, 2009].

Forder, James. 2003. Independence and the Founding of the Federal Reserve. *Scottish Journal of Political Economy* 50(3): 297–310.

Frisby, John. 2009. Ben Bernanke vs. the *Journal on Inflation. Lux Libertas,* June 23. http://www.luxlibertas.com/ben-bernanke-vs-the-journal-on-inflation-3/ [accessed September 17, 2009].

Geithner, Timothy F. 2008. Testimony before the U.S. House Committee on Financial Services, July 24, 2008. http://www.newyorkfed.org/newsevents/speeches/2008/gei080724.html [accessed October 7, 2009].

Godt, Nick. 2005. Street Split over Bernanke Appointment. RealMoney.com, October 24. http://www.thestreet.com/p/comment/nickgodt/10249127.html [accessed September 17, 2009].

Harris, Ethan S. 2008. *Ben Bernanke's Fed: The Federal Reserve after Greenspan.* Boston: Harvard Business School Press.

Irwin, Neil. 2009. How Bernanke Staged a Revolution. *Washington Post,* April 9.

Johnson, Simon, and James Kwak. 2009. The Radicalization of Ben Bernanke. *Washington Post,* April 5.

Kessler, E.J. 2005. Fed Nominee Bernanke Was Molded by Upbringing in Small-Town South. *Jewish Daily Forward,* November 18. http://www.forward.com/articles/2273/ [accessed September 17, 2009].

Kettl, Donald F. 1986. *Leadership at the Fed.* New Haven, CT: Yale University Press.

Khademian, Anne M. 1992. *The SEC and Capital Market Regulation: The Politics of Expertise.* Pittsburgh, PA: University of Pittsburgh Press.

———. 1996. *Checking on Banks: Autonomy and Accountability in Three Federal Agencies.* Washington, DC: Brookings Institution Press.

Kudlow, Larry. 2008. My Interview with Senator Jim Bunning. Kudlow's Money Politics, July 16. http://kudlowsmoneypolitics.blogspot.com/2008/07/my-interview-withsenator-jim-bunning.html [accessed September 17, 2009].

Lowenstein, Roger. 2008a. The Education of Ben Bernanke. *New York Times,* January 20.

———. 2008b. Triple A Failure: The Ratings Game. *New York Times,* April 27.

Mankiw, Gregory N. 2006. A Letter to Ben Bernanke. *American Economic Review* 96(2): 182–84.

McRae, Hamish. 2005. Bernanke's Appointment Is a Good One. *The Independent,* October 27.

Pender, Kathleen. 2009. Net Worth: Rising Interest Rates Start to Worry Investors. *San Francisco Chronicle,* June 9.

Peters, Jeremy and Vikas Bajaj. 2007. Fed's Focus and Rate Unchanged. *New York Times,* April 22.

Phillips, Michael. 2009. Fed Chief's Boyhood Home Is Sold after Foreclosure. *Wall Street Journal,* February 15.

Pirsig, Robert M. 2005. *Zen and the Art of Motorcycle Maintenance: An Inquiry into Values.* New York: Harper Perennial Modern Classics.

Rourke, Francis E. 1986. *Bureaucratic Power in National Policy Making: Readings.* 4th ed. Boston: Little, Brown.

Schmidt, Robert and Rebecca Christie. 2009. Geithner Signals Openness to Council of Regulators in Shift. Bloomberg, June 9. http://www.bloomberg.com/apps/news?pid=2 0601087&sid=aSo.cw4af5l0 [accessed October 7, 2009].

Selznick, Philip. 1957. *Leadership in Administration: A Sociological Interpretation.* Evanston, IL: Row, Peterson.

*60 Minutes.* 2009. Ben Bernanke's Greatest Challenge. http://www.cbsnews.com/stories/2009/03/12/60minutes/main4862191_page5.shtml [accessed September 17, 2009].

Teather, David. 2005. Bush Names Bernanke to Succeed Greenspan. *The Guardian,* October 25.

Terry, Larry D. 2003. *Leadership of Public Bureaucracies: The Administrator as Conservator.* 2nd ed. Armonk, NY: M.E. Sharpe.

U.S. Department of the Treasury. 2009. *Financial Regulatory Reform: A New Foundation.* http://www.financialstability.gov/docs/regs/FinalReport_web.pdf [accessed September 17, 2009].

Weisman, Steven. 2008. With Bold Steps Fed Chief Quiets Some Criticism. *New York Times,* May 28.

Werner, Richard. 2009. Bernanke's Speech Shows Where BOJ Failed. *Bill Wotten's Blog,* January 29. http://billtotten.blogspot.com/2009_01_01_archive.html [accessed September 17, 2009].

Wilson, James Q. 1989. *Bureaucracy: What Government Agencies Do and Why They Do It.* Basic Books.

Woolley, John T. 1986. *Monetary Politics: The Federal Reserve and the Politics of Monetary Policy.* New York: Cambridge University Press.

Wray, Randall. 2007. A Post-Keynesian View of Central Bank Independence, Policy Targets, and the Rules-versus-Discretion Debate. Working Paper no. 510, Levy Economics Institute of Bard College.

# 15

# BILL GIBSON AND THE ART OF LEADING ACROSS BOUNDARIES

## RICARDO S. MORSE

If public administration is about governance, then it is fair to say that the orientation of the field today is toward *collaborative* governance. Indeed, the term "collaborative governance" is seemingly everywhere (Ansell and Gash 2008). Precise definitions are more difficult to come by, but in all cases, the emphasis is on solving public problems or creating public value through collaboration across traditional boundaries. These boundaries include jurisdiction (e.g., interlocal or regional collaborations), organization (e.g., public service networks), and sector (e.g., public-private partnerships). Major streams of research in the field, such as intergovernmental management, public management networks, and civic engagement, all fall under a broader model of collaborative governance. Cases are made for collaborative governance on both normative and descriptive fronts (Sirianni 2009). In other words, there are many who argue that collaborative governance is how public administration *should* work, while at the same time, there are many others who are finding that, increasingly, this is how things *do* work.

The big problems that the public sector is concerned with today are almost without exception the kinds of wicked, boundary-crossing problems that require collaborative work (Luke 1998). Put in a more positive light, collaborative governance is about opportunities. There are opportunities (to solve problems or otherwise create public value) that lie in working across boundaries that otherwise are not there within a single agency. This emerging paradigm of collaborative governance presents public administration with many challenges, not the least of which is whether and how communities can better realize opportunities for collaboration. Public organizations are still very much defined by hierarchy and a command and control mind-set. They are in many ways ill equipped to realize "collaborative advantage" (Huxham and Vangen 2005). While there are many admirable examples of boundary-crossing work in the public sector, one wonders how many opportunities for significant value creation are never realized because of the inherent difficulties of collaboration (Linden 2002).

It is within this milieu that we examine an administrative leader whose life's work has been, and continues to be, helping local governments in his region realize collaborative advantage.[1] Bill Gibson has been a champion and facilitator of collaborative governance in western North Carolina for more than three decades. His leadership is collaborative and facilitative. He is a boundary spanner who leads "from the middle" rather than the top (Luke 1998). His work highlights the

From *Public Administration Review*, 70, No. 3 (May/June 2010): 434–442. Copyright © 2010 American Society for Public Administration. Used by permission.

importance not only of boundary-spanning individuals, but also of boundary organizations, for the advancement of collaborative governance in practice.

Gibson was born and raised in Jackson County, North Carolina, in the far western part of the state, near Great Smoky Mountains National Park. After receiving his master's degree from Western Carolina University (also located in Jackson County) and also serving with the U.S. Army in South Korea, he took a position as a regional planner with the Southwestern Commission in 1973. Two years later, Gibson was appointed executive director of that organization, the position he holds to this day. Spending one's whole career with the same organization and in one's hometown certainly is exceptional. Perhaps this explains some of Gibson's success. Having a strong sense of place can be a strong motivator. It is also important to understand the organization Gibson works for.

The Southwestern Commission is a regional council of governments (often referred to as simply regional councils). It is one of 17 "lead regional organizations" designated in the North Carolina General Statutes. Regional councils are unique public agencies. The National Association of Regional Councils defines a regional council as "a multi-service entity with state and locally-defined boundaries that delivers a variety of federal, state and local programs while continuing its function as a planning organization, technical assistance provider and "visionary" to its member local governments. As such, they are accountable to local units of government and effective partners for state and federal governments" (see http://narc.org/regional-councils-mpos/what-is-a-regionalcouncil.html).

There are more than 500 regional councils in the United States. About a third of them also function as the metropolitan planning organization for their region. While some regional councils have evolved from regional organizations that date back to the 1920s, most were created in response to federal legislation in the late 1960s and early 1970s that required regional planning and intergovernmental cooperation in exchange for federal funds (Atkins, DeWitt, and Thangavelu 1999). In the 1980s, federal funding to regional councils declined sharply; nevertheless, regional organizations "have carved out a valuable niche for themselves as reliable agents and many operate more independent of federal funding." Some states have statutorily created a formal role for regional councils. The National Association of Regional Councils reports that approximately 90 percent of all general-purpose local governments in the United States are served by regional councils (see http://narc.org/regional-councils-mpos/what-is-a-regional-council.html).

The Southwestern Commission (http://www.regiona.org) was created in 1965 by a joint resolution of the seven westernmost counties in North Carolina, along with their constituent towns. The region is almost wholly rural, with a population of about 175,000 spread across 3,100 square miles. The commission's staff of 16 is small relative to other urban regional councils in the state, but has "built a reputation of versatility and excellence." Three staff members (including Gibson) are trained mediators, and several more have taken courses in group facilitation (Gibson, personal communication with the author, October 2009).

The commission's governing board comprises elected officials from member jurisdictions. While the board has never conducted a formal evaluation of Gibson's performance, an informal evaluation occurs each year during budget time. Most of the organization's funding comes from federal grant programs, with additional operating funds coming from the member jurisdictions and a small annual state appropriation.

Regional councils are prime examples of *boundary organizations*. Carr and Wilkinson describe boundary organizations as forums in which "multiple perspectives participate and multiple knowledge systems converge" (2005, 261). While research on boundary work and boundary organizations has focused primarily on the boundary between science and nonscience, it is being extended as a way to understand a variety of cross-boundary interactions. Cash et al. (2006) explain that whether as formal organizations specifically charged to play an intermediary role, or as organizations that have "broader roles and responsibilities," boundary organizations have several important characteristics and institutional functions that enable boundary work: "(1) accountability to both sides of the boundary; (2) the use of "boundary objects" such as maps, reports, and forecasts that are co-produced by actors on different sides of the boundary; (3) participation across the boundary; (4) convening; (5) translation; (6) coordination and complementary expertise; and (7) mediation."

Bryson, Crosby, and Stone's research on cross-sector collaboration likewise identifies the importance of what they call "brokering organizations" (2006, 46) that act as conveners, as well as "prior relationships or existing networks" as antecedent conditions that increase the likelihood of partnership formation. Boundary organizations "offer sites for collaboration, the formation of new relationships, the infusion of research and scientific information into policy, and the exercise of innovative leadership. They have the potential for creating new ways of knowing the problem that may lead to better solutions than any of the institutions would have reached acting alone" (Schneider 2009, 61).

As executive director of a regional council, Gibson is in a unique position to be a catalyst for collaboration in his region. Gibson explains that his organization is accountable to the towns and counties in its seven-county region: "We are in effect owned by them, we work for them." Therefore, he and his organization work toward the objectives expressed by those local governments, "but altogether on a regional basis, a multi-county basis." Gibson's position allows him to think about what is good for the region first, whereas local government board members tend to (rightfully) think of their jurisdiction first. There are numerous examples in this region of North Carolina of significant public value being created as a result of multijurisdictional, and often multisectoral, collaboration. It is no coincidence that Gibson is often a key player in those collaborations. The three cases that follow illustrate the kind of boundary-spanning leadership that Gibson provides.

## RURAL SEWER SERVICE AGAINST THE ODDS

In urban areas, sanitary sewer service is a taken-for-granted public service. Rural areas are a different story, however. In mountainous rural North Carolina, many small communities are without sewer service, a fact that often presents environmental problems and limits economic development opportunities. One such place was Whittier, an unincorporated community straddling Swain and Macon counties and immediately adjacent to the Eastern Band of Cherokee Indians (ECBI) Reservation. Many of the homes had been "straight piping" sewage directly into the Tuckasegee River, which runs through the heart of the community. The neighboring campus of the Church of God's Western North Carolina Assembly was looking to expand but was already past capacity for its septic system. The nearby Smoky Mountain Elementary School likewise was in dire need of sewer service, having surpassed the capacity of its septic system years ago. The ECBI also owned property in the Whittier area, and wanted to develop a portion of it with a golf course and dozens of housing units. But, again, these plans would require sewer service.

While there clearly were many stakeholders in the Whittier community with a strong interest in sewer service—those just mentioned, plus the Economic Development Commission and the regional Tuckasegee Water and Sewer Authority (TWSA)—there was no movement to do anything about it because the costs seemed insurmountable. A sewer utility for a community of only 90 households would still cost several million dollars. Gibson, recognizing the community's need and the stakeholders' shared interests, initiated a process to explore options for getting a sewer treatment facility in Whittier. The four initial partners—the Economic Development Commission, the tribe, Jackson County, and the water authority—each agreed to pay one-fourth of the cost of a $26,000 feasibility study.

The study led to a grant application that was developed by Southwestern Commission staff. A $3.0 million grant from the North Carolina Rural Economic Development Center (Rural Center) was awarded to the Whittier Sanitary District in 2000, to be leveraged against Jackson County, the tribe, and the TWSA, each contributing $40,000 toward the project. With the funds secured, the permitting process commenced, but soon the project was facing major roadblocks.

The permitting process ended up taking two years to complete. There were environmental issues concerning threatened species in the river, as well as the discovery of a Native American archeological site on the would-be location of the plant. By the time the permitting process was complete, the total cost of the project had increased by about $1 million. Three years into the effort, and the project was essentially in a holding pattern. During that time, Gibson scrambled to find additional funds and was able to make up part of the difference with new grants from the Appalachian Regional Commission ($200,000), the U.S. Department of Agriculture ($99,000), and the Cherokee Preservation Foundation ($45,000). That still left a $750,000 deficit. At this point, Gibson's skills as a "multilateral broker" (Mandell 1988) were particularly valuable. The ECBI tribe, Jackson County, and the Church of God each eventually agreed to fund one-third of the deficit ($250,000 each).

With those commitments in hand, the project finally went out to bid five years after the initial grant award. The result was another setback—the lowest bid showed a cost overrun of about $1 million. The future of the project was again in question. The Rural Center gave a deadline to have all funds raised and long-term operating costs secured, or the plug would be pulled from the project altogether. Gibson again returned to the primary stakeholders "with his hand out" in search of funds to fill the funding overrun gap. The Rural Center agreed to an additional $200,000, for a total commitment of $3.2 million. Then the county, the tribe, and the church agreed to up their portions another $250,000 and the county and tribe agreed to underwrite a portion of the expected operating losses for the first three years. With Jackson County, the tribe, and the church now invested at $1,500,000, or approximately $500,000 each, and with the county and tribe agreeing to underwrite the expected initial operating losses, the project again was a go.

The long and arduous process is now paying off, with an outcome that will benefit multiple communities economically and environmentally. Gibson's leadership and brokering role in particular helped the partners not only sustain, but also increase their commitment. Larry Blythe, vice chief of the Tribe, notes that "Bill [Gibson] and his office has been a major pushing player in this thing . . . [not only from] a funding standpoint [obtaining and managing the grants] . . . [but also] facilitating groups" (interview with the author, July 2007). It was a remarkable result to all involved, not only in that the project was a unique public–private partnership, but also in that the water authority ultimately agreed to manage and operate the system. The authority board originally had instructed the authority director to "steer clear" of any commitments to the Whittier sewer project. But the board gave the director the go-ahead to begin negotiations, because "Bill [Gibson] asked instead of maybe someone else" (Joe Cline, interview with the author, July 2007).[2]

## PRESERVING AN ECOLOGICAL TREASURE

The story of the preservation of the "Needmore Tract," 4,500 acres of pristine riverfront land encompassing 26 miles of Little Tennessee River frontage and 37 miles of tributary streams, is a remarkable example of collaboration across many different kinds of boundaries (jurisdiction, sector, and worldview). This tract of land is referred to as the "Noah's Ark of Blue Ridge Rivers." It is part of "the most species-rich river system outside of the tropics on earth, [and Needmore] is the most ecologically intact region of the . . . system" (Paul Carlson, interview with the author, July 2007).

The area has been known as Needmore since the first settlements were established in the 1820s. Beginning in the early twentieth century, the Needmore lands were owned by power companies, possibly to be used as the location of another dam in the area. Through all that time, a majority of the land was in use in farm leases. A dam was never built, but the threat was ever present, at least in the minds of those who lived, farmed, hunted, and fished in the area. Duke Power eventually acquired the property, and in 1999, the company announced that it was transferring the Needmore Tract to Crescent Resources, its property development arm. News of the transaction quickly became a source of public concern among the local people. The transfer to Crescent took the threat of a dam off the table permanently, but replaced that fear with one of development of the Needmore Tract.

While the notion of development was threatening to the traditional users of the Needmore lands—farmers, hunters, and fisherman—it is important to note that most people in Swain and Macon counties historically have been very pro-growth. Nearly half of the land in Macon County is in federal ownership, and 87 percent of Swain County is either federal or tribal lands. So for many, Needmore represented a potential boost in the tax base for the respective counties.

Naturally, the environmental community immediately called for complete preservation of the land. Local residents of Needmore, though not typically aligned politically with environmental interests, found common cause with the environmental community. They soon organized themselves as Mountain Neighbors for Needmore Preservation. Many others voiced similar sentiments, and the stage seemed to be set for a clash between pro- and no-development advocates.

By this time, Gibson was working behind the scenes in a mediator-type role. Crescent Resources, in consultation with the Nature Conservancy, announced that it would embark on a two-year study to gather information about and ideas for the Needmore property. Gibson had many conversations with elected leaders in Macon and Swain counties during that time, which resulted in a critical turning point in the process. Macon County Commission chair Harold Corbin decided that complete conservation of the Needmore was the way to go, contradicting his earlier position supporting development. He presented a pro-conservation resolution for the preservation of the Needmore Tract and was able to convince his fellow board members to go along with it. To the surprise of many, the board put forth a unanimous resolution stating that "the conservation of the Needmore Tract in Macon County represents the best opportunity this county will ever have to protect floodplain, farmland and open space."

After many more discussions with Gibson, Paul Carlson of the Land Trust for the Little Tennessee, and others, and after public meetings indicating strong community support for preservation, the Swain County commissioners, working collaboratively with Macon County's board, gave a major boost to the preservation effort by passing a resolution similar to the one that Macon County had passed a year before. It called for 100 percent preservation of the Needmore lands and supported using the property for public purposes in the future consistent with traditional use (farming, fishing, hunting, etc.). At the same time, like Macon County, Swain County appointed Gibson as the county's representative in the process of seeking a solution consistent with the interests expressed in the resolutions. At that point, Gibson worked in an official capacity, as the counties' agent, with the relevant stakeholders to develop a workable solution for the Needmore Tract.

Having a broad consensus was a major first step, but there would have to be enough funds to purchase the land from Crescent. Agreements would also need to be reached to place the land in public trust, while still allowing for farming, fishing, hunting, and so on. At this stage, the process shifted from public consensus building to negotiation. This is where the experience, expertise, and relationships of Gibson (along with other boundary-spanning leaders such as Carlson) were indispensable. Several grant applications were prepared while negotiations with Crescent over the price for the tract ensued. The Nature Conservancy also became an important broker in the process, and in the end, three years after the transfer of the property to Crescent Resources, an agreement was reached for the purchase of the entire tract for $19 million and for the land to be managed by the North Carolina Wildlife Resources Commission (WRC).

At that time, the plan was for the state's Clean Water Management Trust Fund to contribute $13 million, with the balance coming from other agencies and grant sources. About this same time, the state government was entering into a serious budget crisis, which affected the trust fund's appropriation, dropping its commitment to less than half. Gibson and his colleagues (including Carlson and Katherine Skinner of the Nature Conservancy), again, through their expertise in negotiations, grant writing, and simply through connections that had been built up over time, were able to cobble together a large portion of the $19 million from a variety of sources. Still, about $2 million was left that needed to be raised privately. By December 2003, the funds had been raised, and on January 15, 2004, the purchase was made official and the property was transferred from Crescent Resources to the North Carolina Wildlife Resources Commission. The commission had agreed to manage it for public use, continuing the farm leases, hunting, fishing, paddling, and other traditional uses. A public event was held to celebrate the transaction. The *Smoky Mountain News* noted that "up to 10 different organizations and individuals played a key role in the effort that led to the Needmore purchase. Many others worked in peripheral roles" (McLeod 2004).

The Needmore story does not end with the purchase in January 2004. Gibson, Carlson, and Mountain Neighbors for Needmore Preservation, now a 501(c)(3) designated nonprofit, are working with the WRC to develop a campground on the site. This will be a unique venture, as the WRC does not operate facilities. A new nonprofit will manage the campground in partnership with the WRC. The planning, negotiations, and collaboration involved in getting the campground completed and operating is another story itself. But the arrangement that has been made only underscores the deeply collaborative effort that went into preserving, and now managing, this tract of land, which is an ecological and cultural treasure. Behind the scenes throughout the process was Bill Gibson. He was not the only leader in the community who helped make this remarkable outcome a reality. Carlson, Skinner, the political leaders in Swain and Macon counties, and the citizen activists with Mountain Neighbors, all deserve ample credit. But in looking at how events unfolded, it is clear that Gibson was indispensable.

## THE WESTERN NORTH CAROLINA EDUCATION NETWORK

The Western North Carolina Education Network (WNC EdNET) is a partnership made up of the six westernmost counties in North Carolina, the Eastern Band of the Cherokee Indians, two community colleges, a four-year college, two regional agencies, and several grant-making organizations, to bring broadband access to the 70 schools in the region. The broadband network, and the interorganizational network supporting its development and use, will "open up learning opportunities not currently available or imagined" for local students (WNC EdNET 2007). It is a prime example of a broad, regional, multisector collaboration that creates significant public value.

The project was initiated when Gibson learned of an initiative by the Golden LEAF Foundation to support technology in schools; being familiar with other technology-related initiatives in the area, he saw the potential to make something happen. The first partnership formed was between Gibson's Southwestern Commission and the Western Region Education Service Alliance (WRESA)—another regional organization that serves school districts. In the spring of 2005, Gibson and his counterpart at the WRESA, Roger Metcalf, got together to explore next steps. Gibson and Metcalf had worked together on other efforts before, and both brought significant skills and professional networks to the table.

A key precondition that made the EdNET idea possible was the formation in 2003 of BalsamWest FiberNET, LLC, a public–private partnership formed by Drake Enterprises Ltd. and the Eastern Band of Cherokee Indians to develop a fiber-optic backbone connecting the six westernmost counties of the state. Drake and the EBCI initially invested $14 million in BalsamWest with the idea of leveraging those funds to attract additional private and public investments in the future. But the costs of connecting specific locales to a backbone is often a major barrier, particularly in rural areas (the so-called middle mile problem), and even more so in mountainous regions such as western North Carolina. With Golden LEAF expressing interest in helping enhance technology in rural schools, plus potential for other funding sources, Gibson, working with his colleagues at the WRESA, saw an opportunity and provided the spark to bring the relevant stakeholders together to take the next steps.

The school superintendents, technology coordinators, and representatives from the three area colleges were brought in early on. By October 2005, the first grant had been awarded by the Golden LEAF Foundation—$2 million to get WNC EdNET started. The majority of the funds went toward fiber-optic infrastructure and equipment to start connecting schools. The initial Golden LEAF grant was then leveraged to obtain several additional grants.

From the early stages of the effort, the group recognized the need not only to procure the infrastructure, but to also form a network that would assist educators in using it. This recognition of the need to develop two types of networks—broadband and interorganizational—is reflected in the stated objectives of the project, which include establishing a partnership "for the purpose of collaboratively enhancing the development and use of technology as a tool for improving learning opportunities" and facilitating "capacity building and use of broadband technology for the enhancement of teaching and learning" (WNC EdNET 2007). In the few years since the initiation of the project, there has been a great deal of progress toward these objectives, attributable in large part to the strength of the collaboration and the level of support from funding agencies.

Gibson and other project leaders continually reached out to relevant business and nonprofit organizations and used them to help develop the technical plans. This enabled the group to not only come up with better plans, it also formed and strengthened important linkages that are crucial to successfully accomplishing the objectives set forth at the beginning. The collaboration on the EdNET effort has been extensive, both on the "implementation side," through the various school districts, colleges, regional and state agencies, nonprofits, and for-profit vendors, but also on the "funding source side," meaning that the many different "funding agencies have worked together in a rational and sequential manner to insure coverage, quality, and consistency in the WNC EdNET resource procurement process" (Byrd 2007, 5). At the end of 2008, approximately $5.7 million had been secured in grants, with an additional $1 million-plus from local and corporate sources.

Although the network is quite new when one considers that the initial exploratory meeting was held in August 2005, it represents a dramatic example of the value of boundary-spanning leaders such as Bill Gibson. The potential was there, but in order for the potential to be realized, there needed to be a spark to initiate the process and the expertise (in facilitation, network building, and grant management) to see it through. Because of that leadership, schools across the network are already benefiting from the new technology. What is more, a network is now in place to help build individual and organizational capacity to fully realize the potential across all schools. The network will continue to develop and undoubtedly adapt to changing needs and circumstances. WNC EdNET recently incorporated as a 501(c)(3) organization and is realizing the potential to become a "major collaborative, coordinating body" in the region, again, thanks in large part to the boundary crossing leadership of Bill Gibson (Byrd 2008, 22).

## BOUNDARY-SPANNING LEADERSHIP

These stories are illustrative of the work that Gibson has been doing for the past 30 years in his region. Many more could be recounted, such as the consolidation of five water utilities into the successful regional water authority that exists today in Jackson County, or a more recent extensive regional planning effort called the Mountain Landscapes Initiative. Though the subject matter varies (from fiber-optics in schools to land preservation), there are some common threads in the way Gibson adds value to his region. First, the examples all represent latent opportunities to create significant public value that could not be realized without bringing together a variety of stakeholders to act collaboratively. Second, in each case, Gibson was in a unique position to act as a broker or agent given his position working for all of the governments in the region. Third, trust and relationships are Gibson's primary currency.

In interviewing Gibson and several of his colleagues associated with the foregoing cases, four important lessons about boundary crossing leadership stand out.[3] The first three have to do with interconnected personal characteristics: being a social entrepreneur, developing and utilizing "relationship capital," and having ego strength. The fourth lesson has to do with Gibson's leadership platform. Operating from the vantage point of a boundary organization offers Gibson significant advantages in enabling boundary work in his region.

### Social Entrepreneurship

Boundary-spanning leaders such as Bill Gibson are entrepreneurs who create public value. Rather than the business entrepreneur whose success is defined in market terms, social (or civic or public) entrepreneurs[4] define success in terms of public value created. This is not a new insight, of course, but it is a characteristic that Gibson so clearly exemplifies.

In these three cases, Gibson "[saw] opportunity, and mobilize[d] others in the community to work toward their collective well-being" (Henton, Melville, and Walesh 2004, 209). *Opportunity* is a key thread running throughout all three cases. Gibson saw in the set of conditions in front of him an opportunity to do something different. He saw an opportunity for significant value creation through collaboration. This perhaps lies at the core of what it means to be a catalyst (Luke 1998). In order for collaboration to be possible, someone has to envision the process of coming together to create something new. Thus, the vision of public value is often dependent on individual leaders such as Gibson—the entrepreneurial boundary spanners, unsatisfied with the status quo, who are willing to take risks to realize something better.

Consider Henton, Melville, and Walesh's description of civic entrepreneurs: "They are risk takers. They are not afraid of failure. They possess courage born of strong convictions. They are passionate and energetic. They are people of vision and persistence" (2004, 209). Gibson explains that this sensibility means "a willingness to operate outside of my comfort zone. . . . The longer that I operated out of my comfort zone the larger that zone became. Success bred comfort and thereby expanded my zone" (personal communication with the author, October 2009).

In addition to seeing opportunity and taking risks, the social entrepreneur must be persistent in facilitating change, which often is a long-term process. EBCI vice chief Larry Blythe, in discussing the back-and-forth negotiations to get the Whittier sewer project accomplished, explained, "I'll be honest with you, Bill and his office have been a major pushing player in this thing. . . . they kept pushing us to get to the table" (interview with the author, July 2007). Note, however, that the drive is not about getting people to *follow* (per traditional conceptions of leadership). Nor is it a passion for collaboration for collaboration's sake. Rather, it is a *dogged pursuit of public value*, or the common good, that is the driver. It produces a passion and energy directed toward getting people to the table, and once there, helping them envision the opportunity that is there.

## Relationship Capital

Another notable aspect of Gibson's leadership is his notion of "relationship capital." It is not enough to have the passion for results and the vision of possibility. Partnerships often involve conflicting interests, perspectives, cultures, and values. A key boundary-spanning role, therefore, is to be able to sustain commitment through inevitable conflicts and setbacks. The key, according to Gibson, is what he calls "relationship capital."

As Gibson explains it, relationship capital is accumulated over time, and it is absolutely critical during those times when people may need to be pushed or challenged in the process (interview with the author, July 2007). Practitioners usually point to fiscal, physical, and human capital as the ingredients of success for programs and projects. Gibson explains that several years ago, he started hearing references to relationship capital,[5] and as he began to understand what the term meant, he realized that it is the fourth "and *most* essential factor in the project development equation . . . it is the lubricant that smoothly meshes the other three gears/ingredients together. It eases friction and facilitates the assemblage of common interests with fewer incidents of friendly fire" (personal communication with the author, October 2009). Relationship capital is now viewed as the Southwestern Commission's primary "currency" (see http://www.regiona.org/commission/history.htm).

It is relationship capital that, according to TWSA director Joe Cline, factored into his board's decision to reconsider playing a larger role in the Whittier sewer project (given Gibson's extensive history with TWSA). Leonard Winchester, one of the leaders of the WNC EdNET effort, points out that it was this relationship capital that often provided the glue as the network was forming. Speaking of Gibson, he commented on "how he treats people and how people trust him and how they can count on him . . . the gears really spin on that" (interview with the author, July 2007). Additionally, it was evident that the funding agencies' representatives developed relationship capital with EdNET partners, which greatly assisted in keeping things moving forward. Relationship capital factored into the information sharing that occurred throughout the Needmore effort between Gibson and Fred Alexander, a manager at Duke Energy who had been assigned to work with the community on the Needmore situation. Reflecting on the four-year process, Alexander noted that he and Gibson often exchanged information that helped both parties (Crescent Resources and the community) be more effective in the negotiation process and ultimately led to a win–win outcome. He felt that those exchanges were only possible because he "trust[s] Bill Gibson as much as I trust anyone" (interview with the author, July 2007).

Trust is the key to understanding relationship capital. It is about being trustworthy oneself, but equally about "consistently exud[ing] trust in others." Gibson explains that if one fails to "exhibit trust of others' motives, actions, and words, one defines them—by inference—as untrustworthy . . . Once distrust is projected, at that point working together in partnership toward common interests becomes . . . immensely more difficult" (personal communication with the author, October 2009). The notion of trust being at the heart of productive relationships is described well in Stephen Covey's *The 7 Habits of Highly Effective People* (2004).

## Ego Strength

The characteristic of being a social entrepreneur, being one who doggedly pursues the public good, according to Luke, "cannot occur without first shifting one's attention away from a preoccupation with oneself and toward looking outward to relationships and interpersonal networks" (1998, 226–28). This observation is certainly reflected in Gibson's attention to relationship capital. It also speaks to an attribute that Russ Linden describes as a "strong but measured ego" (2002, 154). Boundary-spanning leaders "don't have to grab the headlines for every success. Quite the opposite, they seem to take great satisfaction when they can share credit for accomplishments with many others. Their ambitions are directed more toward organizational success than personal glory" (Linden 2002, 154).

To be sure, Gibson is ambitious and driven. Yet at the same time, there is a certain humility underlying the way he operates. Luke (1998) connects this to what psychologists call "ego strength." Persons with ego strength "don't have the internal motivation to be in charge of everything . . . [there is a] willingness to share credit, which is crucial in forging agreements and sustaining action" (Luke 1998, 230–31). It also means, according to Gibson, that "one not take oneself too seriously and that one avoid taking things (negative or positive) too personally" (personal communication with the author, October 2009).

This does not mean Gibson is always in the background, or that he is a shrinking violet in any way. On the contrary, he is an animated promoter of the Southwestern Commission and its work. Gibson likes to get the word out about the Southwestern Commission's accomplishments. But that is the key: the promotion is about the work and the organization, not about himself.

## Working for a Boundary Organization

Besides these personal characteristics, the fact that Gibson leads the Southwestern Commission—a type of boundary organization—as opposed to a county or municipality or even a state or federal agency, is an important factor in the outcomes he has helped achieve for the region. The literature on boundary organizations is primarily in the sciences and natural resources realm. There has been considerable interest in examining organizations that bridge different ways of knowing, such as cooperative extension, which bridges boundaries between farmers and researchers (Carr and Wilkinson 2005). In public administration, scholars have begun to identify these boundary organizations as "sites for collaboration, the formation of new relationships, the infusion of research and scientific information into policy, and the exercise of innovative leadership" (Schneider 2009, 61). Thus, the purpose of boundary organizations is to facilitate integration across boundaries (boundaries of sector, jurisdiction, and so on)—integration that will lead to "boundary actions" (Feldman et al. 2006, 95). Gibson observes that jurisdictional lines by and large promote inertia. If states were starting from scratch and drawing county lines, for example, it is clear that there would be far fewer counties. Yet in most communities, it is "political heresy" to suggest consolidation, so the alternative is to "do it practically" through multijurisdictional partnerships. Regional councils specialize in this kind of cross-boundary work (Gibson, personal communication with the author, October 2009).

Regional councils of government bridge boundaries of jurisdiction to enable member governments to think and act regionally (Lindstrom 1998). They are intended to function as "a regional forum" (Atkins, DeWitt, and Thangavelu 1999), and they are adept at consensus building and creating partnerships (see http://narc.org/regionalcouncils-mpos/what-is-a-regional-council.html). While not all regional councils (or all boundary organizations, for that matter) are equally successful at facilitating boundary work, the Southwestern Commission, under Bill Gibson's leadership, has been exceptional.

## CONCLUSION

Bill Gibson is, in some ways, a special case. Not many public leaders have the opportunity to direct an organization that is based in their hometown for their entire careers. Those who do are unlikely to have the opportunity to have as broad and deep an impact as Gibson has had with the Southwestern Commission. Yet there are important takeaways for any public leader in a boundary-spanning role. In summary, successful boundary-spanning leadership includes the following:

- *Being entrepreneurial:* Seeing opportunities to create public value, being willing to go outside one's comfort zone, and having the persistence required to bring the pieces together to make it happen.
- *Developing relationship capital:* Building trust with partners, both by being trustworthy and by exuding trust in others.
- *Having ego strength:* Being driven by accomplishment of the common good rather than individual credit or accolades.
- *Leveraging boundary organizations:* Understanding the value and purpose of boundary organizations in enabling collaboration across jurisdictional, sectoral, and other boundaries.

These lessons learned raise some questions for the field of public administration. Many observers of the field view collaborative governance as the present and future of the public sector (Ansell and Gash 2008). If this is the case, then we need to consider how to develop leadership competencies in public managers that will contribute to collaboration and partnerships rather than traditional command and control. Gibson's example sheds light on some of these competencies, and others are recounted elsewhere (Getha-Taylor 2008; Morse 2008). The key question, however, is *how* to develop those competencies in the context of public organizations that are, by and large, dominated by a command and control, bureaucratic paradigm. It is not as if bureaucracy is going away anytime soon, and there are many good reasons to have clear lines of authority. But in a posthierarchical world, public leaders need to be adept at leading across hierarchies as well as within them. Most public leaders do not work in boundary organizations, and yet they will be required to act in boundary-spanning ways. A key question for leadership development going forward is how to achieve this both/and, realizing that it is not either/or.

Gibson's special advantage of leading a regional council of governments raises another question for public administration: are we investing enough in boundary organizations? Boundary organizations relevant to public administration are everywhere. Regional councils, cooperative extensions, and other regional entities (such as education alliances or many economic development councils) are boundary organizations that are established to facilitate boundary work. Yet in many cases, these organizations struggle to secure adequate funding and, as a result, find it difficult to attract (or keep) talented leaders like Gibson. Do the principals of these organizations (often local government boards) appreciate the value of having a regional forum? What could be done to give boundary organizations greater prominence and support so that more opportunities to great public value could be realized?

Finally, while there are many exemplary cases of boundary-spanning leadership and effective boundary organizations in the public sector, there are many more (which we usually do not read about) that are not successful. Why is this the case, beyond a lack of resources? It may be that in some cases, the principals do not demand that kind of leadership. Often, public boundary organizations are reduced to grant management agencies because this may be all that is expected of them. As public leaders realize the importance of collaboration across boundaries, perhaps they will realize the value of boundary organizations beyond grant management or service delivery. As the case of Bill Gibson demonstrates, these organizations provide a platform for the kind of boundary work that is necessary to address today's public problems and otherwise create significant public value.

## NOTES

1. Other administrative profiles in *PAR* have spotlighted boundary-spanning, collaborative leaders such as Gibson. Cooper and Bryer's profile of William Robertson (2007) highlights "the necessity of building trust and collaboration" in successfully serving the citizens of Los Angeles. Naff's profile of San Francisco's Nancy Alfaro (2009) likewise demonstrates "collaborative public management" in action as Alfaro worked to build the city's Call 311 network. These profiles highlight the political savvy, commitment to public service, and deep integrity of boundary-spanning leaders in the public sector—all prominent themes in this profile of Bill Gibson. What is unique about this profile, however, is Gibson's institutional home—a regional council—a type of organization that provides a unique platform for facilitating boundary crossing collaboration.

2. It is important to note here that Gibson and his organization "conceived and facilitated the formation of TWSA in the early 1990s." Gibson explains that the work to consolidate four water systems and four sewer systems into a regional authority "may very well have been the most difficult of the ultimately successful collaborative that I have ever taken on." By all accounts, the TWSA has been a success, and therefore Gibson's "significant history with TWSA" was not lost on the board members when the Whittier project materialized (Gibson, personal communication with the author, October 2009).

3. For several decades, organization theorists have recognized the role of so-called boundary spanners as "key agents managing within interorganizational theaters" (Williams 2002, 103). Boundary spanners "engage in networking tasks and employ methods of coordination and task integration across organizational boundaries" (Alter and Hage 1993, 46; see also Aldrich 1979). More recently, public administration scholars are paying attention to the important role of boundary-spanning leadership in the context of collaborative governance (Linden 2002; Noble and Jones 2006; Williams 2002).

4. For contemporary research on social entrepreneurship, see Schneider, Teske, and Mintrom (1995) and Light (2008).

5. The literature on collaboration and partnerships in the public sector almost uniformly highlights the importance of trusting relationships (see, e.g., Bardach 1998; Linden 2002), though the exact term "relationship capital" is rarely used. In the general management literature, however, there are some explicit references to relationship capital as a critical factor for successful partnerships and alliances (see, e.g., Cullen, Johnson, and Sakano 2000; Sarkar et al. 2001).

## REFERENCES

Aldrich, Howard E. 1979. *Organizations and Environments.* Englewood Cliff s, NJ: Prentice Hall.

Alter, Catherine, and Jerald Hage. 1993. *Organizations Working Together.* Newbury Park, CA: Sage Publications.

Ansell, Chris, and Alison Gash. 2008. Collaborative Governance in Theory and Practice. *Journal of Public Administration Research and Theory* 18(4): 543–71.

Atkins, Patricia, John DeWitt, and Jennifer Thangavelu. 1999. *The Emerging Regional Governance Network: A National Survey of Regional Organizations.* Washington, DC: National Academy of Public Administration and National Association of Regional Councils.

Bardach, Eugene. 1998. *Getting Agencies to Work Together: The Practice and Theory of Managerial Craftsmanship.* Washington DC: Brookings Institution Press.

Bryson, John M., Barbara C. Crosby, and Melissa Middleton Stone. 2006. The Design and Implementation of Cross-Sector Collaboration: Propositions from the Literature. Special issue, *Public Administration Review* 66: 44–55.

Byrd, Robert R. 2007. *WNC EdNET—Final Report*. Report submitted to the Golden LEAF Foundation, November 15.

———. 2008. *ARC Final Report for Contract #NC15443–06*. Report submitted to the Appalachian Regional Commission, October 30.

Carr, Anna, and Roger Wilkinson. 2005. Beyond Participation: Boundary Organizations as a New Space for Farmers and Scientists to Interact. *Society and Natural Resources* 18(3): 255–65.

Cash, David W., W. Neil Adger, Fikret Berkes, Po Garden, Louis Lebel, Per Olsson, Lowell Pritchard, and Oran Young. 2006. Scale and Cross-Scale Dynamics: Governance and Information in a Multilevel World. *Ecology and Society* 11(2). http://www.ecologyandsociety.org/vol11/iss2/art8/ [accessed February 11, 2010].

Cooper, Terry L., and Thomas A. Bryer. 2007. William Robertson: Exemplar of Politics and Public Management Rightly Understood. *Public Administration Review* 67(5): 816–23.

Covey, Stephen R. 2004. *The 7 Habits of Highly Effective People: Restoring the Character Ethic*. Updated ed. New York: Free Press.

Cullen, John B., Jean L. Johnson, and Tomoaki Sakano. 2000. Success Through Commitment and Trust: The Soft Side of Strategic Alliance Management. *Journal of World Business* 35(3): 223–40.

Feldman, Martha S., Anne M. Khademian, Helen Ingram, and Anne S. Schneider. 2006. Ways of Knowing and Inclusive Management Practices. Special issue, *Public Administration Review* 66: 89–99.

Getha-Taylor, Heather. 2008. Identifying Collaborative Competencies. *Review of Public Personnel Administration* 28(2): 103–19.

Henton, Douglas, John Melville, and Kim Walesh. 2004. *Civic Revolutionaries: Igniting the Passion for Change in America's Communities*. San Francisco: Jossey-Bass.

Huxham, Chris, and Siv Vangen. 2005. *Managing to Collaborate: The Theory and Practice of Collaborative Advantage*. New York: Routledge.

Light, Paul C. 2008. *The Search for Social Entrepreneurship*. Washington, DC: Brookings Institution Press.

Linden, Russell M. 2002. *Working across Boundaries: Making Collaboration Work in Government and Nonprofit Organizations*. San Francisco: Jossey-Bass.

Lindstrom, Bonnie. 1998. Regional Cooperation and Sustainable Growth: Nine Councils of Government in Northeastern Illinois. *Journal of Urban Affairs* 20(3): 327–42.

Luke, Jeffrey S. 1998. *Catalytic Leadership: Strategies for an Interconnected World*. San Francisco: Jossey-Bass.

Mandell, Myrna P. 1988. Intergovernmental Management in Interorganizational Networks: A Revised Perspective. *International Journal of Public Administration* 11(4): 393–416.

McLeod, Scott. 2004. Mission Accomplished: Needmore Efforts Lauded by State Officials. *Smoky Mountain News*, January 21.

Morse, Ricardo S. 2008. Developing Public Leaders in an Age of Collaborative Governance. In *Innovations in Public Leadership Development*, edited by Ricardo S. Morse and Terry F. Buss, 79–100. Armonk, NY: M.E. Sharpe.

Naff, Katherine C. 2009. Nancy Alfaro as an Exemplary Collaborative Public Manager: How Customer Service Was Aligned with Customer Needs. *Public Administration Review* 69(3): 487–93.

Noble, Gary, and Ann Robert Jones. 2006. The Role of Boundary-Spanning Managers in the Establishment of Public-Private Partnerships. *Public Administration* 84(4): 891–917.

Sarkar, M. B., Raj Echambadi, S. Tamer Cavusgil, and Preet S. Aulakh. 2001. The Influence of Complementarity, Compatibility, and Relationship Capital on Alliance Performance. *Journal of the Academy of Marketing Science* 29(4): 358–73.

Schneider, Anne S. 2009. Why Do Some Boundary Organizations Result in New Ideas and Practices and Others Only Meet Resistance? Examples from Juvenile Justice. *American Review of Public Administration* 39(1): 60–79.

Schneider, Mark, Paul Teske, and Michael Mintrom. 1995. *Public Entrepreneurs: Agents for Change in American Government*. Princeton, NJ: Princeton University Press.

Sirianni, Carmen. 2009. *Investing in Democracy: Engaging Citizens in Collaborative Governance*. Washington, DC: Brookings Institution Press.

Western North Carolina Education Network (WNC EdNET). 2007. WNC EdNET: A Project to Enhance Learning Using Broadband Techniques. Project brochure, November 20. http://www.wresa.org/wncednet/wncednetinfo.htm [accessed February 11, 2010].

Williams, Paul. 2002. The Competent Boundary Spanner. *Public Administration* 80(1): 103–24.

# 16

# PROSECUTING NAZI COLLABORATORS AND TERRORISTS

Eli Rosenbaum and Managing the Office of Special Investigations

## JEROME S. LEGGE, JR.

Since the attack on the World Trade Center on 9/11 and the increased concern with immigrants entering the United States illegally, the protection of U.S. borders has become a paramount objective of the federal government. Yet government has been involved with illegal entries into the United States for some time. In particular, with the postwar discovery that many Nazi collaborators entered the United States illegally and in fact became citizens,[1] Congress passed legislation to create a mechanism for stripping them of their U.S. citizenship and residency. The purpose of this essay is to describe this effort.

In particular, the focus is on the career of Eli Rosenbaum, the director of the Office of Special Investigations (OSI) in the U.S. Department of Justice. This Administrative Profile focuses on Rosenbaum's management philosophy and his mission-specific recruitment and team building, which are based on cognitive and emotional leadership and management skills. The next focus is on OSI performance in comparison to similar prosecutorial agencies in other nations concerned with Holocaust perpetrators. Also examined is the transition of the OSI in response to the laws generated by the 2004 Intelligence Reform and Terrorism Prevention Act. This law broadened the function of OSI to prosecute cases beyond the Holocaust. Finally, this essay explores the implications of Rosenbaum's management and leadership for public sector practitioners.

In the immediate postwar period, U.S. government agencies did not have a coherent or consistent policy regarding Nazi collaborators who entered the country illegally. To further complicate the situation, the wartime activities of many of these individuals were unknown to federal officials. Indeed, many collaborators attained U.S. citizenship during the 1950s and 1960s and lived "quiet" lives, unsuspected by their neighbors (Ryan 1984). These include former Croatian minister of the interior Andrija Artukovic, who was responsible for the murder of tens of thousands of Serbs and Jews; Karl Linnas, commandant of the Tartu Concentration Camp in Estonia; and John Demjanjuk, a Ukrainian American who previously was prosecuted by Israel and presently is on trial in Germany for crimes in the Sobibor Death Camp in occupied Poland. These are but a few examples; the list of those entering the United States illegally and obtaining citizenship is much longer.[2]

Past inaction of U.S. government agencies, such as the Department of Justice and the Immigration and Naturalization Service, can be attributed to several factors. First was the reluctance

---

From *Public Administration Review*, 71, No. 2 (March/April 2011): 276–284. Copyright © 2011 American Society for Public Administration. Used by permission.

to extradite U.S. citizens to communist nations when blocking their expansion was a keystone of U.S. foreign policy. Second, most Holocaust survivors, many very young or in middle age, were more interested in starting new lives and raising families than they were in holding elusive collaborators accountable. Many of those responsible for World War II crimes melted into the U.S. population easily and without detection. Almost without exception, they became "model" citizens who worked productively, raised families, sent their children to local schools, and joined civic organizations. Ironically, what the victims and perpetrators shared, in many instances, was a desire to leave the war years behind and to begin a new life in America. More extensive discussion of accountability only began during the 1970s.

## REFORM: THE HOLTZMAN AMENDMENT

The principal legislation on which the OSI has based its prosecution of Nazi collaborators is the Holtzman Amendment to the Immigration and Nationality Act. During the 1970s, after the initial failure to bring individuals such as Artukovic and Linnas to justice, the U.S. government became increasingly aware of the possibility that many more Nazi collaborators had entered the United States under the 1948 Displaced Persons Act. The major objective of the act was to aid those who had been persecuted during the war by the Nazi government or other Axis-occupied nations in Europe. But U.S. officials lacked the means to document the wartime activities of many, leading to inappropriate entries into the country.

The Holtzman Amendment was led through Congress by Representative Elizabeth Holtzman of Brooklyn, New York, who served as chair of the Subcommittee on Immigration. Holtzman proposed legislation, enacted in 1978, that developed new procedures for prosecuting Nazis and their collaborators who entered the United States illegally, primarily through the DPA. It is important to understand that the practical application of the Holtzman Amendment by OSI does not involve criminal prosecution. Rather, the procedure is civil and targeted at the stripping of citizenship and removal from the United States. The Holtzman provisions make the following persons ineligible for admission to the United States. If already admitted, the amendment makes possible their deportation and citizenship removal. Citizenship removal applies to those who fall within the following categories:

1. Those who served in the Nazi government in Germany
2. Those who served in any area occupied by the military forces of Germany
3. Individuals who served in any government that was established with the assistance or cooperation of Germany
4. Those who served in governments that were allies of Germany or "otherwise ordered, incited, assisted, or otherwise participated in the persecution of any person because of race, religion, national origin, or political opinion."

A key aspect of the Holtzman Amendment was ending "discretionary relief." This legal concept increased the probability of avoiding deportation. Prior to Holtzman, discretionary relief could consist of circumstances ranging from having a spouse who was a U.S. citizen to the display of good behavior since entering the United States (Legge 2010, 34). Under the new legislation, discretionary relief was denied to those who fit the foregoing definitions. With the passage of the Holtzman Amendment, the United States became fully equipped legally to move against resident Nazi collaborators. All evidence indicates that OSI and its leadership under Eli Rosenbaum have been up to this difficult task.

## OSI AS AN ORGANIZATION IN THE DEPARTMENT OF JUSTICE

As documented by the U.S. Holocaust Memorial Museum (2010), both the museum and the OSI were conceived in the same moral and political environment of the 1970s. During those years, U.S. citizens gained a renewed interest in the Holocaust, prompted in great part by the willingness of many survivors to share their experiences for the first time. While the museum was not established until 1993, the OSI began its work immediately during the Jimmy Carter administration.

The OSI was created after a special team established in the Immigration and Naturalization Service in 1977, the Special Litigation Unit, failed in its mission to bring collaborators to justice. Subsequent testimony on the ineffectiveness of the unit resulted in its transfer to the Department of Justice and its renaming as the OSI (Rosenbaum 2006, 2).

For the duration of its history, the OSI has been a relatively small unit within the larger Department of Justice. It is located within the Criminal Division under the leadership of a deputy assistant attorney general. In terms of both budget (adjusted for inflation) and staff size, there has been little to no growth in the OSI. Nor has the priority or attention given to the OSI varied by presidential administration (Rosenbaum 2009).[3] The small size of the OSI, combined with its modest position within the Department of Justice bureaucracy, has made its accomplishments all the more impressive.

The staff is composed of both attorneys and historians. Recent data indicate that eight prosecutors and 10 historians make up the staff (Rosenbaum 2006, 2). The most important criteria for the selection of attorneys are interest in OSI work and prosecutorial experience in the federal government. The historians, almost without exception, are PhD graduates of the most outstanding history departments in the United States and have significant language skills. All are fluent in German and also have competencies in other languages that are germane to the Holocaust experience, including Russian, Polish, Czech, Italian, and French. As the OSI has moved in the direction of prosecuting war criminals other than Holocaust perpetrators, more languages have been added to the staff inventory, to include Kinyarwanda (the official language of Rwanda), Croatian, and Bosnian. How the attorneys and historians work in tandem will be covered when discussing Rosenbaum's management of the agency.

## ELI ROSENBAUM: HIS BACKGROUND AND EARLY YEARS

Rosenbaum has spent a great deal of his life immersed in the Holocaust. His most direct experience relates to his parents, who were refugees from Hitler's Germany. Rosenbaum's father, Irving, came to the United States in 1939. Like many Jewish German refugees who became American citizens, Irving joined the U.S. Army and returned to his native land as a wartime soldier. One of Irving's orders was to inspect the Dachau Concentration Camp near Munich the day after its liberation by the U.S. 7th Army on April 29, 1945. The senior Rosenbaum was unable to speak about the experience; his eyes filled with tears when attempting to explain to Eli what he had witnessed.

Still, young Eli did not anticipate that his future would involve either the prosecution of Nazi war criminals as an attorney or the administration of a complex government office bringing such cases to court. Irving and his father (Eli's paternal grandfather) became owners of a retail store chain on Long Island, with branches extending into the South and the Midwest, and it was Eli's first ambition to become part of the family enterprise. He enrolled at the University of Pennsylvania in 1972, receiving his undergraduate degree four years later. Rosenbaum then followed with a master of business administration degree from the Wharton School in 1977. By this time, he had become interested in a career as an attorney and entered Harvard Law School.

Among his many memorable experiences, Rosenbaum was influenced by Professor Alan Dershowitz, who taught a professional ethics class. It was Dershowitz who helped Rosenbaum decide whether to follow his first ambition in the family business or to go "where his heart was" and return to the Department of Justice, where he had spent the summer of 1979 as an intern in the Office of Criminal Investigations. While a student at Harvard, Rosenbaum, representing Jewish law students, met with German chancellor Helmut Schmidt, who was on campus to deliver a lecture. Rosenbaum's purpose was to advocate a time extension for the West German statute of limitations for war crimes. The Bundestag did extend the law, although Rosenbaum did not claim credit for influencing this action. After his 1980 graduation, he returned to the Office of Criminal Investigations, where the OSI was then located. From 1980 to 1984, he worked as a litigator for the OSI, prosecuting Nazi war criminals and collaborators.

Public administration and organizational development scholars have investigated the problem of "burnout" in public agencies. Golembiewski et al. (1998) utilize a "phase model" to investigate where an individual fits on a burnout continuum. They argue that large numbers of public employees across the globe fall into advanced stages of burnout, often with symptoms of "emotional exhaustion." While Rosenbaum did not use the term "burnout" to characterize the first four years of his career, the hours were long and demanding. The new litigator experienced frustration with the slow pace of the appeals process once an individual was denaturalized, and he witnessed a lack of cooperation by many foreign governments in accepting former citizens or acknowledging their crimes. Still, it was the litigation of his early career that, paradoxically, was the most rewarding

Rosenbaum's advice to young people who are unsure about a career in the public sector is to try private employment as well. The director bases this recommendation on his own experience. Rosenbaum's 1984 departure from the OSI was followed by a one-year stint as a litigator in a private firm in Manhattan. He then accepted the general counsel position of the World Jewish Congress (WJC), a nonprofit organization in New York. Unexpectedly, it was Rosenbaum's time at the WJC that propelled him back into the center of postwar Holocaust issues. In 1985, the former secretary general of the United Nations, Kurt Waldheim, became a candidate for president in his native Austria, a primarily ceremonial but highly visible position. In the postwar period, including his time at the United Nations (1972–82), Waldheim (1985, 15–20) consistently misrepresented his World War II military service. The diplomat stated that after being wounded on the Eastern Front in December 1941, he convalesced and then spent the remainder of the war obtaining a law degree in Vienna. Waldheim also contended that he had never been a member of a Nazi organization.

But documents unearthed by the WJC and others determined that Waldheim had joined a Nazi youth organization prior to the war and subsequently became a member of the Sturmabteilung (sometimes abbreviated as the SA and known as the Brownshirts)—Hitler's paramilitary force during his rise to power. More serious was the time that Waldheim spent in Yugoslavia as a Wehrmacht officer. At that nation's request, Waldheim's name was placed on the Central Registry of War Criminals and Security Suspects. The specific charge listed was "murder." The registry document also contained an identification number indicating that Waldheim was a suspect of the UN War Crimes Commission, a list of possible war criminals compiled shortly after the war (Rosenbaum and Hoffer 1993, 129–31). Waldheim also served in Greece as an intelligence officer, and although he was not present for the entire period during the major deportation of Greek Jews from Salonika to Auschwitz in July 1943, it strains credulity that he was unaware of the deportations, as he stated consistently. Regardless, he was heavily involved in events surrounding the deportations from the Greek Islands (DOJ 1987).

One analysis of Waldheim's activities undertaken when Rosenbaum was not working at the OSI was conducted primarily by OSI historians and released to the public on April 9, 1987. The report is based on evidence from the U.S. National Archives and documents from the government of Yugoslavia. The analysis concludes that Waldheim's activities during the war "fit within the so-called Holtzman Amendment." More specifically, it found that

> Lieutenant Waldheim "assisted or otherwise participated" in the following persecutorial activities: the transfer of civilian prisoners to the SS for exploitation for slave labor; the mass deportation of civilians to concentration and death camps; the deportation of Jews from Greek Islands and Benja Luka; anti-Semitic propaganda; the mistreatment and execution of Allied prisoners; and reprisal executions of hostages and other civilians. (DOJ 1987, 3)

Although Rosenbaum was working for the WJC at this time, he became involved in a separate investigation of Waldheim that resulted in the book *Betrayal: The Untold Story of the Kurt Waldheim Investigation and Cover-Up* (Rosenbaum and Hoffer 1993). In addition to revealing Waldheim's past, the book asserted that Simon Wiesenthal, an Austrian citizen who had pursued the prosecution of Nazis since the end of the war, conspired with Austrian government officials to conceal Waldheim's crimes. In the end, Waldheim was elected and held the president's office for one term. But as a consequence of the WJC and OSI investigations, and a letter from Rosenbaum to then-Attorney General Edwin Meese (Rosenbaum and Hoffer 1993, 391), Waldheim was placed on an Immigration and Naturalization Service "Watch List" compiled by the OSI that is designed to keep undesirable persons from entering the United States. Included are those who served in military units that participated in persecution of civilians or in other war crimes.

Rosenbaum returned to the OSI in 1988 as principal deputy director, a position in which he supervised the attorneys. The years during which he served as deputy director were very busy, both for Rosenbaum and for the organization. The primary reason is that as the Soviet Union and its satellites had begun to collapse, more archival material became available from behind the former Iron Curtain, and OSI historians were able to investigate previously very difficult cases. Despite the declining numbers of suspects still living, OSI's caseload began to increase during the 1990s because of the newly available evidence. In addition to the disintegration of the Soviet empire, other changes that occurred during Rosenbaum's time as deputy director included improvements in OSI management information systems and increased cooperation by many foreign governments in war crimes investigations (Rosenbaum 2009). The new archival material, coupled with a drastic increase in Holocaust interest and its scholarship, made it easier to comprehend previously unknown or underresearched Nazi military and killing operations.

## ROSENBAUM AS OSI DIRECTOR: COGNITIVE MANAGEMENT AND LEADERSHIP

In analyzing Rosenbaum as a leader and manager, the focus is first on the cognitive and technical aspects of his position, so necessary for successful prosecutions. Later in the essay, especially in discussing team building, the focus will shift to the affective and emotional aspects of administration, which can be particularly acute when working with the Holocaust and its aftermath.

Rosenbaum was appointed OSI director on February 10, 1995 (DOJ 1995). By the time he assumed the directorship, 42 collaborators or war criminals who had entered the United States illegally had been deported, and another 50 had lost their citizenship and, for the most part, were in the appeals process to avoid deportation. In the last year of Rosenbaum's deputy directorship (1994), OSI filed seven new cases, the highest annual total in a decade. While the deputy director position involved some administrative responsibilities, such as writing performance appraisals,

Rosenbaum, as the new director, assumed total supervision of the prosecution of Nazi collaborators in the United States. Of course, past experience as deputy director and as a litigator gave him a thorough knowledge of the operations and the political subtleties of the OSI. When one examines his cognitive leadership and management approach, it is apparent that it is based more on the culture of the OSI and his past experiences in the organization than any formal education in administration or belief in a particular management style.

Harvard Law School was superb training for his future as a prosecutor, but from the beginning, Rosenbaum never imagined that he would be an administrator, nor was it a role that he sought consciously. Management was learned through government experience, not taught (Van Wart 2003). Much OSI work is cognitive in that it is highly specialized and technical. Attorneys must have a high level of proficiency in prosecutorial skills, and historians need foreign-language competency and expertise in historical investigation. In probing Rosenbaum for a management philosophy embedded in the public administration literature, academic models do not emerge. Part of the reason is that the OSI is a very specialized agency with highly qualified and focused individuals, including attorneys and historians.

Yet Rosenbaum does have a management philosophy that is rooted in the skills needed to lead the highly educated and capable personnel of the OSI. One public sector leader whom Rosenbaum admires a great deal is General Colin Powell, former secretary of state in the George W. Bush administration. While Rosenbaum does not accept all of Powell's principles uncritically, the general and the director are in agreement that "theories of management don't much matter" (Powell 2007, lesson 8). Furthermore, both are skeptical of the latest "management fads" (Powell 2007, lesson 9), and believe that it is the mission of the unit that must be the central focus in leading.

Rosenbaum places the "people" aspect of an organization in the highest esteem, as does Powell. Only with the attraction of the "best" people can "great" deeds be accomplished (Powell 2007, lesson 8). Thus, specialized personnel recruiting is vital to accomplishing the OSI mission. Rosenbaum cannot accomplish the mission on his own, but must hire good people and allow them to perform their specialized tasks. In following Powell's approach, Rosenbaum is interested in hiring talented individuals who are not overly concerned with hierarchy. Compared to most public organizations, the OSI is flat in its structure. The director relies on two deputies: one who supervises historians and a second who directs attorneys. Goals are set by Rosenbaum in consultation with his supervisors in the Criminal Division and with the lawyers and historians on staff. Yet again, compared to other government agencies, the goals are well understood and relatively straightforward as set forth in the Holtzman Amendment: to prosecute those who entered the United States illegally because of their actions during World War II. As developed later in this essay, the goal has been expanded under the Intelligence Reform and Terrorism Prevention Act (IRTPA) of 2004. By virtue of the Watch List (White 2006), it also is a central OSI objective to keep perpetrators from entering the United States in the first place. The director's most important function is to obtain the tools and resources for the staff to accomplish the prosecutions effectively.

Personnel management is a key to OSI success. As a New York native, Rosenbaum is a lifelong New York Yankees fan, and he utilizes the wisdom of one of his folk heroes, Casey Stengel, who managed the Yankees from 1949 until 1960, a period when the team won seven World Series championships. The director is fond of quoting Stengel's answer when he was asked the secret to being a good baseball manager. Stengel replied, "give me good players." (Rosenbaum also brought to mind another Yankee folk hero, Yogi Berra, who stated, "it's true, you could look it up" in commenting about Stengel.)

Like Stengel, Rosenbaum believes that "good players" are essential to the OSI's success. According to the director, the assembly of legal talent in the OSI has been remarkable. He noted that his attorneys could earn several times their salaries in the private sector, but instead are attracted to the unique mission of the OSI. Because of this, some of Powell's motivational techniques (especially with regard to troops) are unnecessary in the OSI. The same may be said in supervising the historians who have forsaken less fast-paced and possibly more lucrative academic careers to focus on this difficult and, at times, emotionally exhausting work. So, for Rosenbaum, it is a matter of finding the "right" people, watching their performance, and giving them feedback. This can occur formally through performance appraisals (usually by deputy directors), or less formally through his advice, morale boosting, and coaching, based on Rosenbaum's own experience as a litigator.

The director has some principles of his own that he regards as central to his leadership style. First, both attorneys and historians within the OSI have to know that they will be "backed" by Rosenbaum. Again, one of General Powell's principles is that the judgment of the commander in the field should be given precedence over the "rear echelon," unless proven false (Powell 2007, lesson 16). Within OSI, the working historian or attorney can expect similar support. Although Rosenbaum admits to being something of a "micro manager," he is cautious in second-guessing an investigation. Delegation is, of course, necessary, and he has high confidence in the caliber of the OSI professionals. The director also believes that it is necessary for him to participate in investigations and, at times, to question suspects. This gives him a continued feel for the work of others within the OSI.

Rosenbaum holds that a manager must have the ability to reward outstanding individuals for their performance, but this is sometimes difficult in the public environment, where pay increases are not maintained as in the private sector, especially for the OSI attorneys. The promise of high pay raises is not the motivator within the OSI; rather, it is the mission itself. According to Rosenbaum, the most productive at the OSI feel the mission "in their hearts." Finally, the leader not only must be transparent with the public and with subordinates, but also must make oneself "dispensable." This includes taking risks for the organization and keeping in mind that it is the organization's general welfare and not the individual leading the agency that is paramount.

Having described Rosenbaum's management philosophy and the primarily cognitive aspects of personnel management, discussed next is his leadership in structuring investigative teams, which involves affective as well as cognitive skills.

## TEAM BUILDING AND AFFECTIVE LEADERSHIP AND MANAGEMENT

Rosenbaum's job does not end with recruiting the "right" personnel. Staff must be molded into a team. The idea of a leader being a member of a team has gained traction in the public administration literature. Especially important is the leader's ability to offer support, to instruct, or to teach (Smaliukiene 2008). Team building is a vital concept within the OSI, and it is enforced and encouraged by the director. The mission of the OSI cannot be accomplished without the constant cooperation of historians and attorneys. While the attorneys prosecute, the historians conduct the relevant research for the investigations and must provide the documentation that is crucial to the World War II cases, as many key witnesses are no longer alive. When speaking of this relationship, Rosenbaum draws on the wisdom contained in the Reverend Martin Luther King's essay "Letter from a Birmingham Jail," in which King calls for a tension that is "necessary for growth" (King 1963). While King was referring to the tension between segregationist oppressors and African Americans in the civil rights movement, Rosenbaum believes that creative tension is often necessary in the organizational environment to accomplish its stated mission. A "friendly rivalry" exists in the OSI, as the historians sometimes chide the attorneys for not having a firm grasp of the overall conflicts involved in some investigations. The attorneys similarly jest that the historians do not always understand the subtleties and legal principles in prosecuting a case. Attorneys can generally work across cases regardless of where they originate geographically, but historians most often concentrate on a particular genocide. This is because of the historians' focused specializations as developed in graduate school and OSI work; language skills also are not equally distributed among historians. While all historians who work on World War II cases are skilled in German, today, with the emergence of more recent genocides, many have competencies in African tongues and Balkan-rooted languages. Thus, the OSI attorney must work with the historian who has the greatest substantive and linguistic capability in a particular geographic locale; the partnering shifts depending on the case.

The OSI's unique mission necessitates that special managerial and leadership skills be present for both the director and the agency employees in team building. Cognitive and technical skills are necessary for the OSI to be successful. Staff must have superior technical proficiency in historical investigation and prosecution. But directing and working for the OSI also demands coping with the *emotional* aspects of administration (Newman, Guy, and Mastracci 2009). In working for the OSI, emotion can be both an energizing (e.g., to attain justice for Holocaust victims in the first place) and a draining force on the individual worker as the details of genocidal crimes are encountered in everyday experiences. As director of the OSI, Rosenbaum must practice an "artful affect" in which emotion, as well as technical and cognitive skills, assumes a central role (Newman, Guy, and Mastracci 2009, 14). On a daily basis, both prosecutors and historians are exposed to documents that do not elevate the human spirit; simultaneously, the director and staff must maintain a level of detachment so that they can make objective judgments about whom to investigate or prosecute. The director and his attorneys also use much sensitivity in questioning witnesses, who are likely to become upset when reminded of their ordeals.

As the focus of the OSI began to shift from World War II prosecutions, Rosenbaum underwent some self-examination as cases were considered other than Nazi perpetrators. While the cognitive and technical skills required in prosecuting newer human rights cases are similar to the Holocaust-related trials, the emotional aspects of leadership again came into play for Rosenbaum. At least one journalist questioned whether the director would be able to bring the same level of dedication to prosecuting the new offenders compared to the tenacity that he exhibited in bringing legal procedures against those who had annihilated or helped to exterminate fellow Jews (*Washington Jewish Week* 2010). Rosenbaum admits to some soul searching as the content of the cases changed. After all, Rosenbaum (2009) is a public servant who, in the early days of the OSI, was anxious about losing a single day of work "lest some mass murderer" go free. While the director admits that it is perhaps "human nature" to identify more closely with members of one's own religious or ethnic group when confronting genocide, he finds the new cases as "compelling and moving" as the Holocaust cases.

Rosenbaum experienced deep empathy when he began to meet with newer victims such as Gladys Monterroso, the spouse of Sergio Morales, Guatemala's human rights ombudsman. Monterroso was abducted and tortured the day after her husband issued a human rights report on violations that occurred during Guatemala's civil war. Observing the cigarette burns on her arms and rope burns on her ankles, Rosenbaum states that he was "change[d] forever." Documents are the primary investigative tool in Holocaust cases, but the need for emotional management and leadership may intensify with contemporary human rights violations as staff meet face to face with victims and witnesses and rely on their testimony.

Another emotional aspect of administration for the OSI is external politics. Much of the difficulty that the OSI has faced comes from forces outside the bureaucracy and requires that Rosenbaum exercise political prudence (Dobel 1998). One might believe that Nazi hunting and the prosecution of such perpetrators would be popular and uncontroversial. But the OSI and Rosenbaum have faced criticism from Eastern European and American ethnic organizations, who see the OSI as catering primarily to "Jewish" interests (Legge 2010, 41).[4] Other criticism has come from commentators such as Pat Buchanan, a defender of both Demjanjuk and Linnas. Buchanan has characterized the OSI staff as "hairy-chested Nazi hunters" (Langel 2010).

Given outside political criticism, the emotional challenge of prosecuting human rights and Holocaust cases, and the more lucrative economic opportunities for staff (especially the lawyers), Rosenbaum must devote considerable effort to maintaining skilled personnel. A certain amount of "charismatic" leadership (Javidan and Waldman 2003) is necessary to keep employees enthusiastic. What is important here is not the considerable charisma of Rosenbaum, but the mission of the organization. While the ability to offer financial reward is limited, Rosenbaum holds that the intrinsic rewards of Holocaust work and other genocide cases and attaining justice for victims outweigh the financial gains available elsewhere.

## EVALUATING THE IMPACT OF THE OSI

As someone with experience in the private sector, Rosenbaum is interested in the unit's effectiveness in terms of its objectives. These objectives are relatively straightforward. The attorney general order that created OSI placed on the agency "all of the prosecutorial activities of the Department involving individuals who, in association with the Nazi Government of Germany and its allies, ordered, incited, assisted, or otherwise participated in the persecution of any person because of race, religion, national origin, or personal opinion between 1933 and 1945" (Rosenbaum 2006, 2).

How well has the OSI fared? First, the director is thoroughly familiar with the difficulty of evaluating public programs compared to those in the private sector. According to Rosenbaum (2006), the OSI is no exception, in that dollar figures cannot be placed on the prosecution and conviction of Nazi collaborators. In addition, it is difficult to develop "performance measures" on which government can base the allocation of resources. Rosenbaum (2009) believes that the OSI has been successful in its mission, although its effectiveness is not always rewarded with an increase in funding or recognition. He further states that OSI "has achieved a measure of justice on behalf of more murder victims" than other federal agencies such as the Federal Bureau of Investigation (FBI) and larger municipal police departments such as New York and Los Angeles.

Objective measures of success do exist, especially if one compares the OSI's achievements to similar units in other nations. In making comparisons between nations, one must be cautious because prosecution in the United States does not involve criminal procedures. That is, the primary objective is to determine whether the accused entered the United States illegally and is eligible for deportation. This approach is uncommon except for Canada, which in the 1990s also adopted the civil procedure.

The Simon Wiesenthal Center prepares an annual status report on the persecution of Nazi war criminals. The report, authored by Efraim Zuroffi, encompasses a system whereby individual nations thought to harbor war criminals are rated. First, some nations "fail" either "in principle" or "in practice" to develop a program to prosecute Nazi war criminals. Governments failing in principle include Norway, Sweden, and Syria. In the case of the first two nations, statutes of limitations make the prosecution of war crimes impractical. Syria, which is suspected of harboring Alois Brunner, who was convicted in the deportations of Jews from Austria, Greece, France, and Slovakia, simply has not cooperated with France, where Brunner was sentenced in absentia to life imprisonment. Failure in practice involves nations that have no legal restrictions for prosecuting suspected Nazi war criminals but lack the "political will and/or the requisite resources and/or expertise." Such nations include Australia, Austria, Estonia, Hungary, Lithuania, and Ukraine.

Slightly better, in the eyes of the Wiesenthal Center, are nations with "insufficient and/or unsuccessful efforts" (Category D), where there is some activity but few, if any, tangible results. These include Canada, Denmark, and the Netherlands. Category C includes nations with "minimal success which could have been greater; additional steps urgently required." The only nation in this category is Poland, which has opened far more new cases than any other country since the Wiesenthal Center began its monitoring during 2001–2002, but all of the investigations have resulted in only one conviction and one indictment. Category B comprises nations with an "ongoing investigation and prosecution program which has achieved practical success," including Germany, Italy, Serbia, and Spain. Germany has gained notoriety during the past year through its prosecutions of Demjanjuk and Heinrich Boere, a member of the Dutch Waffen-SS, who admitted in court to killing Dutch civilians and currently is serving a life prison term in Germany.

As represented by the OSI, the United States is the only nation to attain Category A—"a highly successful proactive prosecution program." Regarding Rosenbaum and OSI performance, the report states,

> Since its establishment in 1979, the OSI, currently headed by Eli M. Rosenbaum . . . has conducted the most successful program of its kind in the world, and has been a model of proactive investigation and prosecution of Holocaust perpetrators for the past three decades. Its outstanding performance has earned it unique status, as the only agency to have ever been given the highest grade awarded by this report and to have achieved this honor every single year since the report was launched in 2002. (Simon Wiesenthal Center 2009, 27)

The 2008–2009 grade was received during a year in which the OSI did not record a single denaturalization or deportation; nevertheless, the agency was lauded for its primary role in the extradition of Demjanjuk to Germany and for cooperating with Spanish attorneys and their government's recent efforts to prosecute war criminals. One of the problems that the OSI has faced is an unwillingness of nations to accept those ordered deported because of their behavior during the war. Spain, a nation that sheltered collaborators during the Francisco Franco era, is now interested in receiving perpetrators who served in the Flossenbürg, Mauthausen, or Sachsenhausen concentration camps. During the war, these ghastly facilities held Spanish Republicans as well as Jews, Gypsies, Poles, and German dissidents.

## ORGANIZATIONAL TRANSFORMATION: THE INTELLIGENCE REFORM AND TERRORISM PREVENTION ACT AND THE OSI MERGER

On December 17, 2004, President George W. Bush signed the Intelligence Reform and Terrorism Prevention Act (IRTPA). While many provisions were created in response to 9/11 with the purpose of preventing future national security catastrophes, aspects of the legislation target participants in recent genocidal crimes. These include persons who committed torture or acts of extrajudicial killing (Gordon 2006, 24–26). Criminal prosecution is possible within the United States, unlike the Nazi cases. Such violations could include making false statements to a federal agency or torture and/or the commission of war crimes. Under IRTPA, denaturalization has been pursued not only by the OSI, but other federal prosecutors as well. Such is the case of Kelbessa Negewo, who attained U.S. citizenship in 1995 and was charged in the United States with torture and murder during the 1974–91 military dictatorship in Ethiopia (Gordon 2006, 25–26; Rosenbaum 2007). The prosecutor was the U.S. Attorney's Office in Atlanta. Recognized by a past victim at work in an Atlanta hotel, he was tried and deported to Ethiopia under the provisions of IRTPA and currently is serving a life sentence in his native country, where he was tried in absentia.

Another application of the IRTPA was the Domestic Security Section's prosecution of Charles "Chuckie" Taylor, Jr., the son of Liberian warlord Charles Taylor, who served as president of that nation from 1997 to 2003. The regime was particularly brutal, and the younger Taylor, who was an American citizen (born in the United States when his father was a student in Boston), was convicted under a provision of IRTPA that forbids U.S. citizens from taking part in genocidal acts while overseas. As head of the paramilitary "Anti-Terrorist Unit" in Liberia, Taylor, Jr., committed torture involving burning victims (with molten plastic, lit cigarettes, boiling water, candle wax, and irons), beating victims with firearms, cutting and stabbing, and, utilizing electric shock. After trial in Miami, he was sentenced to 97 years for participation in murder, torture, and the toleration of sexual abuse (DOJ 2008).

Another non-Holocaust case concerns the joint OSI/U.S. District of Kansas prosecution of Kansas resident Lazare Kabaya Kobagaya (*Hays Daily News* 2010). U.S. Immigration and Customs Enforcement cooperated in the investigation as well. Kobagaya was charged with "naturalization fraud and misuse of an alien registration card." In this regard, he was arraigned for participating in the 1994 conflict in Rwanda, where he allegedly incited attackers to commit murder and arson. Like Nazi war criminals before him, he failed to disclose these activities during his naturalization process, claiming that he was in Burundi between 1993 and 1995. His prosecution is of great interest because it is the first time in U.S. history that the government is attempting to prove genocide in court (DOJ/ICE 2009).

One important consequence of the IRTPA and the reorganization of the U.S. intelligence agencies is that government organizations concerned with immigration and illegal entry began to cooperate more closely. Objectives are a bit different as one crosses agencies. For example, the FBI is concerned with individuals transporting terror into the United States in the manner of 9/11, while the OSI mission remains focused on illegal entry by those who have participated in genocide and other atrocities. Still, the IRTPA resulted in considerable agency cross-fertilization. For example, the Departments of Justice and Homeland Security have created an ad hoc interagency working group to coordinate federal law enforcement to prosecute human rights violators who have obtained U.S. citizenship. The OSI is included among the Department of Justice units working as part of the task force, along with other elements of the Criminal Division and the FBI. The Department of Homeland Security is represented by Citizenship and Immigration Services as well as Immigration and Customs Enforcement staff. Also participating are the Central Intelligence Agency and State Department, which also includes the Office of Ambassador at Large for War Crimes Issues (Paskey 2006, 31–32).

The passage of the IRTPA placed Rosenbaum in an internal working group within the Criminal Division that includes the OSI, the Domestic Security Section (DSS), the Counterterrorism Section, and the Office of International Affairs. Any legal matter that comes to the attention of one unit is shared with the others. This has resulted in smoother working relationships and has the advantage of joint consultation when deciding whether to prosecute cases.

The IRTPA gave the OSI opportunities to expand its jurisdiction, but the close working relationship and shared objectives between the agency and other units, especially within the Criminal Division, eventually raised the question of whether the OSI should continue to exist on its own or whether it should be merged with other units within the Criminal Division. This issue first was raised by Lanny Breuer (DOJ 2009, 2010), assistant attorney general for the Criminal Division, who proposed the possibility of a merger between the OSI and the DSS. This suggestion became a reality on March 30, 2010, when Breuer announced the arrangement. The DSS and OSI merged to form a new organization, the Human Rights and Special Prosecutions Section of the Criminal Division (DOJ 2010).

The DSS, founded in 2002, had within its jurisdiction international human rights violations, crimes of violence outside the United States, including those of U.S. citizens involved in genocidal acts abroad (as in the Taylor case), and "complex" immigration and border crimes (DOJ 2010). In addition to Taylor, Jr., DSS also played a part in the prosecution of former U.S. soldier Steven

Green, convicted of rape and murder while he was part of a combat unit in Iraq. Green currently is serving a life term without the possibility of parole.

It is of great interest that the OSI, an organization that since its beginning has been concerned over-whelmingly with cases involving Jewish victims, will in future years, in all probability, conduct many prosecutions involving atrocities against Muslims. While cases have been few thus far, OSI staff (under the new organizational arrangements) are investigating genocidal crimes against Muslim victims, pri-marily in Bosnia. A prominent example concerns Bozo Jozepovic, a member of the Croatian Defense Council, a paramilitary organization responsible for the "ethnic cleansing" of the civilian population in Bosnia (DOJ 2007). Jozepovic is thought to have been responsible for the murders of seven male Muslim Bosnian civilians in Kakanj in the Republic of Bosnia/ Herzegovina in 1993. After fleeing Bosnia and attaining Canadian citizenship in 2004, Jozepovic attempted to enter the United States in his new occupation as a truck driver. He was detained by the Customs and Border Patrol twice and eventually was banned from entering the United States for life by an immigration judge on December 16, 2007 (*Bosnian News* 2007). The OSI developed and investigated the case, and an OSI historian provided key expert testimony linking Jozepovic to the Croatian Defense Council and the murders.

The chief of the new Human Rights and Special Prosecutions Section is the former director of DSS, Teresa L. McHenry. Eli Rosenbaum is the director of human rights enforcement strategy and policy. As the mission of the former DSS is focused on human rights violations comprehensively, Rosenbaum (2010) views the merger as a "good fit."

## MANAGERIAL LESSONS LEARNED

Into the foreseeable future, border security will continue to be a major government objective. Vigi-lance must be maintained to prevent future terrorist attacks and to remove potential perpetrators from the United States. But what about the law-abiding, nonthreatening citizen who creates no immedi-ate danger but was involved as a past collaborator or actual participant in atrocities removed from American soil? U.S. law as specified in the Holtzman Amendment establishes that such individuals have no future in the United States and are unacceptable as citizens. Rosenbaum (2009) made an interesting comparison, contending that it is "hypocritical" for the government to vigorously pursue Latin American immigrants who enter the United States illegally, and simultaneously ignore those who lied to the government in both their immigration and citizenship applications because of past criminal behavior related to either the Holocaust or more contemporary genocides.

The OSI and Rosenbaum's leadership offer important insights into public management with implications for practitioners. A first lesson is that for an organization such as the OSI, with personnel of high quality and sharply defined tasks, an overarching "management" or leadership philosophy may not be necessary. In many ways, the OSI is unique for a public organization. It is an extremely small agency with well-defined objectives and a staff of highly specialized, educated, and motivated individuals. Rosenbaum's devotion to the mission and his recruitment of others with similar enthusiasm for the organizational goals have helped make OSI extremely effective. Thus, innovative motivation techniques and organizational approaches are not necessary to ac-complish its basic but essential mission, regardless of location in the Department of Justice. The "charisma" of the task is sufficient (Javidan and Waldman 2003).

The OSI also offers the important managerial lesson that government goals can be measured and, indeed, realized. In addition, in evaluating the OSI, it is not necessary, or even useful, to conduct a multivariate or other sophisticated analysis to determine effectiveness. More importantly, the OSI offers the lesson that an agency's goals have to be clearly specified legislatively (in the case of OSI, the Holtzman Amendment) in order to fulfill them. There is no doubt that it has been extremely successful in accomplishing its goals, especially if we compare it to other nations involved in the prosecution of Nazi war criminals. In the future, some attention must focus on how evaluation will proceed as the population of Nazi collaborators in the United States dwindles and more attention is given to contemporary genocides. In particular, it may be more difficult to develop a system that makes comparisons across nations, as does the Wiesenthal Center method.

The final, and probably the most important, lesson for practitioners in public service is that cognitive management frequently has to be balanced by affect and emotion, especially when one considers topics as intense and draining as the Holocaust and other genocides. The public administration literature demonstrates that "emotional exhaustion" and "burnout" are symptoms that characterize bureaucrats worldwide, regardless of field specialization (Golembiewski et al. 1998). In addition to OSI personnel, these problems probably are most intense for frontline human services professionals dealing with problems such as the neglect and abuse of children and/ or elderly citizens, alcohol and drug addiction, and mental health services. Public safety workers (police officers, firefighters, and emergency medical service personnel) are also vulnerable to extreme stressors. In this regard, this Administrative Profile contributes to a growing literature on affective management, which is characterized by recognizing the emotional stress that many public service workers face on a day to day basis (Denhart and Denhardt 2006; Goleman, Boyatzis, and McKee 2002; Guy, Newman, and Mastracci 2008; Newman, Guy, and Mastracci 2009).

## NOTES

1. The distinction between a Nazi "collaborator" and "war criminal" is somewhat difficult to define. In general, one would think of a collaborator as someone who was not directly responsible for atrocities, but who worked with Nazis in Germany or in occupied nations to make crimes against civilian or military targets possible. A war criminal ordinarily would be thought of as one who performed the atrocities personally or ordered others to do so. In actual fact, U.S. law enforcement officials are able to prosecute and remove citizenship of both categories of individuals under the Holtzman Amendment. In this essay, the more conservative term "collaborator" is employed, although the term "criminal" fits many.

2. Trial transcripts of persons prosecuted by the OSI are available at the U.S. Memorial Holocaust Museum (2009), Center for Advanced Holocaust Studies.

3. Information on Rosenbaum's OSI directorship was acquired during a July 27, 2009, interview at his Washington, D.C., office. Unless otherwise cited, this is the primary source of information.

4. According to Rosenbaum, less than half of the OSI staff is Jewish.

## REFERENCES

*Bosnian News.* 2007. Croatian War Criminal Bozo Jozepovic to Be Deported to Canada. December 16.

Denhardt, Robert B., and Janet V. Denhardt. 2006. *The Dance of Leadership: The Art of Leading in Business, Government, and Society.* Armonk, NY: M.E. Sharpe.

Dobel, Patrick. 1998. Political Prudence and the Ethics of Leadership. *Public Administration Review* 58(1): 74–81.

Goleman, Daniel, Richard Boyatzis, and Annie McKee. 2002. *Primal Leadership: Realizing the Power of Emotional Intelligence.* Boston: Harvard Business School Press.

Golembiewski, Robert T., Robert A. Boudreau, Ben-Chu Sun, and Huaping Luo. 1998. Estimates of Burnout in Public Agencies: Worldwide, How Many Employees Have Which Degrees of Burnout, and with What Consequences? *Public Administration Review* 58(1): 59–65.

Gordon, Gregory S. 2006. OSI's Expanded Jurisdiction under the Intelligence Reform and Terrorism Prevention Act of 2007. *USA Bulletin* 54(1): 24–29.

Guy, Mary E., Meredith A. Newman, and Sharon H. Mastracci. 2008. *Emotional Labor: Putting the Service in Public Service.* Armonk, NY: M.E. Sharpe.

*Hays Daily News.* 2010. Kansas Man Seeks to Dismiss Genocide-Related Charges. February 23.

Javidan, Mansour, and David A. Waldman. 2003. Charismatic Leadership in the Public Sector: Measurement and Consequences. *Public Administration Review* 63(2): 229–42.

Langel, Allen. 2010. Justice Dept. Prosecutor Eli Rosenbaum Still Hunting Nazis. 2010. http://www.ticklethewire.com/2010/04/06/justice-dept-prosecutor-elirosenbaum-still-hunting-nazis/ [accessed June 1, 2010].

King, Martin Luther, Jr. 1963. Letter from a Birmingham Jail. http://abacus.bates.edu/admin/offiic/dos/mlk/letter.html. [accessed March 16, 2010].

Legge, Jerome S., Jr. 2010. The Karl Linnas Deportation Case, the Office of Special Investigations, and American Ethnic Politics. *Holocaust and Genocide Studies* 24(1): 26–55.

*New York Times.* 2009. As Old Nazis Die Off, Pursuit Goes On. August 26.

Newman, Meredith A., Mary E. Guy, and Sharon Mastracci. 2009. Beyond Cognition: Affective Leadership and Emotional Labor. *Public Administration Review* (1): 6–20.

Paskey, Stephen J. 2006. Intra- and Inter-Agency Cooperation in the Investigation and Litigation of Cases Involving Modern Human Rights Violators. *USA Bulletin* 54(1): 30–35.

Powell, Colin. 2007. *A Leadership Primer from Colin Powell.* Dayton, OH: HR Challey Group. http://www.chally.com/enews/powell.html [accessed March 1, 2010].

Rosenbaum, Eli. 2006. Introduction to the Work of the Office of Special Investigations. *USA Bulletin* 54(1): 1–8.

———. 2007. Concerning Genocide and the Rule of Law. Statement before the U.S. House Committee on the Judiciary, Subcommittee on Crime, Terrorism, and Homeland Security, 110th Cong., 1st sess., October 23.

———. 2010. Personal communication with the author, February 25.

———. 2009. Personal interview with the author, July 27.

Rosenbaum, Eli, with William Hoffer. 1993. *Betrayal: The Untold Story of the Kurt Waldheim Investigation and Cover-Up.* New York: St. Martin's Press.

Ryan, Allan A., Jr. 1984. *Quiet Neighbors: Prosecuting Nazi War Criminals in America.* San Diego, CA: Harcourt Brace Jovanovich.

Simon Wiesenthal Center. 2009. Worldwide Investigation and Prosecution of Nazi War Criminals, An Annual Status Report, April 1, 2008–March 31, 2009. http://www.wiesenthal.com/site/apps/nlnet/content2.aspx?c=lsKWLbPJLnF&b=4441467&ct=6929435 [accessed December 11, 2010].

Smaliukiene, Rasa. 2008. Leadership in Public Administration: Theoretical Aspects. *Public Administration* 2(18): 34–41.

U.S. Department of Justice (DOJ). 1987. In the Matter of Kurt Waldheim. http://www.justice.gov/criminal/osipress/osi-reports/1987/1987Waldheim.pdf [accessed December 11, 2010].

———. 1995. Eli Rosenbaum Named Director of Office of Special Investigations. News release, February 10. http://www.justice.gov/opa/pr/Pre_96/February95/81.txt.html [accessed December 11, 2010].

———. 2007. Executive Office for Immigration Review, Immigration Court, Seattle, WA. In the Matter of Bozo Jozepovic. File no. A95–421–365.

———. 2008. Roy Belfast, Jr. A/K/A Chuckie Taylor Convicted on Torture Charges. News release, October 30. http://www.justice.gov/opa/pr/2008/October/08crm-971.html [accessed December 11, 2010].

———. 2009. Statement of Lanny A. Breuer, Assistant Attorney General, Criminal Division, before the U.S. Senate Committee on the Judiciary Subcommittee on Human Rights and the Law. 111th Cong., 1st sess., October 6.

———. 2010. Assistant Attorney General Lanny A. Breuer Announces New Human Rights and Special Prosecutions Section in Criminal Division. News release, March 30. http://www.justice.gov/opa/pr/2010/March/10-crm-347.html [accessed December 11, 2010].

U.S. Department of Justice, and U.S. Immigration and Customs Enforcement (DOJ/ICE). 2009. Kansas Man Charged with Immigration Crimes in Connection with 1994 Genocide in Rwanda. News release, April 23. http://www.ice.gov/news/releases/0904/090423washington.htm [accessed December 11, 2010].

U.S. Holocaust Memorial Museum, Center for Advanced Holocaust Studies. 2009. Record Group 06.029, War Crimes Investigation and Prosecutions.

———. 2010. Office of Special Investigations. Holocaust Encyclopedia. http://www.ushmm.org/wlc/en/search_result.php [accessed April 4, 2010].

Van Wart, Montgomery. 2003. Public-Sector Leadership Theory: An Assessment. *Public Administration Review* 63(2): 214–28.

Waldheim, Kurt. 1985. *In the Eye of the Storm: A Memoir.* Bethesda, MD: Adler & Adler.

*Washington Jewish Week.* 2010. End of an Era at OSI. February 17.

White, Elizabeth B. 2006. Barring Axis Persecutors from the United States: OSI's Watch List Program. *USA Bulletin* 54(1): 19–22.

# CONCLUSION

## What Are the Ingredients of Effective Performance Among Public Servants?

This book presented a series of profiles of public servants who have promoted the public good in some capacity. This broad spectrum of cases introduced administrators from a host of sectors and illustrated their accomplishments in environments that are immensely political. The table that follows provides a summary of the qualities of these public servants along with the various factors that contributed to their effective performance in their policy domains. Those factors, discussed in the Introduction, include: political skills; management and leadership skills; experience; strategy; and personality. It should be noted that as editor of the series rather than author of the profiles, I present summaries in the table that represent my interpretations of the administrators' skills and characteristics. In deference to the authors, this is not an exhaustive list, but it is intended to provide the reader with a snapshot of the work, skills, personalities, and styles of effective public servants. Thus, key elements of administrative behavior are captured. In addition, while some characteristics may be shared between or among administrators, each public servant profile here is unique. In other words, there is no cookie-cutter approach to effectiveness among public servants.

As seen in the table, there are some commonalities between and among the public servants in several of the categories. For example, all of the administrators exhibited such management and leadership skills as good communication and interpersonal skills, fostering participation and ability to motivate staff. Other attributes stem from the particularized environment within which the administrators operate. For example, Lillian Borrone's ability to maneuver in a male-dominated profession contributes to her managerial and leadership effectiveness. Similarly, the ability of Colleen Jollie, a Native American, to operate effectively within white cultural institutions contributed to her success as a manager and leader. The administrators' understanding and awareness of their particular environment catalyzes certain management and leadership skills.

There are also a number of personality traits that are common among the public servants. For example, honesty, open-mindedness, ethical behavior, and trustworthiness are traits shared by all and certainly contribute to their efficacy in their respective policy arenas. Not surprisingly, there is some overlap between personality and management and leadership style. For example, open-minded administrators are democratic; ethical administrators promote a sense of ethics and morality in the workplace; and a loyal public servant will demonstrate loyalty toward the agency mission as well as staff.

Also noteworthy is that overall, every administrator spent most of his or her career in public service. Whether bringing some experience from higher education (e.g., Donna Shalala and Sean O'Keefe), law (e.g., Eli Rosenbaum), or volunteerism (e.g., Viola Baskerville), these administrators share a lifelong commitment to promoting the public good, which serves as an important attribute of effective performance.

Table

## Summary of Administrators and Characteristics of Effective Performance

| Name, title, and agency | Featured accomplishment/ activity | Political skills | Management and leadership skills | Experience | Strategy | Personality |
|---|---|---|---|---|---|---|
| **Elmer Staats,** Comptroller General, U.S. GAO | Organizational reform to promote transparency and accountability | Understanding of Washington's political and bureaucratic establishment; excellent rapport on Capitol Hill; good relationship with President Johnson | Good interpersonal skills; commitment to fairness and equity; good planner; effective communicator; inspired loyalty and followership; participative style; emphasis on professionalism; consensus builder; visionary | Entire career in government | Introduced program evaluation; promotion of good, honest, fiscally responsible government; revamped organization structure and workforce; eliminated fragmentation | Strong sense of honesty and loyalty; optimistic; strong work ethic; trustworthy |
| **Charles Rossotti,** Commissioner, IRS | Organizational reform to improve services to taxpayers and agency image | Good relationship with White House, Congress, tax groups, and federal employee unions | Visionary; open and honest communicator; coalition builder; fosters transparency; good listener; consultative; participative style | Mostly government career | Modernizing IRS's computer and information system; customer service priority; changed organizational culture to balance enforcement with service to taxpayers; involvement of internal and external stakeholders | Honest; open; sincere; energetic; reflective; optimistic; determined |

| | | | | | | |
|---|---|---|---|---|---|---|
| **Burtell Jefferson**, Chief, Washington D.C. Police Department | First African-American Police Chief in D.C.; improvement of policing procedures and practices; reduced discriminatory practices in police department | Fostered collaborations between and among community residents, local business leaders, and community-based organizations | Shared vision; good motivator; open and fair; morale booster; patient; innovative; fostered equality and equity; collaborative; emphasis on professionalism; change agent | Entire career in policing and investigations | Networking; coaching and mentoring young officers; fostering cultural change; promotion of community-oriented policing practices; creation of management intern program; reducing crime rate | Dynamic; inspirational; strong sense of integrity; perseverant; courageous; dedicated; strong sense of cultural identity |
| **Donna Shalala**, Secretary, Health and Human Services | Promoting sound, effective health care policy | Excellent relationship with career officials; excellent relationship with White House; good working skills with Congress | Good listener and communicator; willingness to listen; open; culturally sensitive; good analytical skills; politically astute; setting clear goals; democratic; pragmatic | Government and higher education | Balancing fiscal, equity, political, and implementation perspectives in health policy design; building public support for health policy; coalition building | Loyal; personable; trustworthy; flexible; even-tempered; honest |
| **William Robertson**, Director, City of Los Angeles's Bureau of Street Services | Community Action Research Project (improving service delivery) | Collaborative relationship with elected officials, neighborhood leaders, citizens, employees, and management peers | Leads by example; politically astute; democratic; ability to delegate; bridges politics and administration; good motivator; provides mentoring; strategic planner; technologically astute | Military and mostly Los Angeles city government | Collaborative governance; citizen empowerment; promotion of transparency and technical efficiency; respect for stakeholders | Loyal; respectful; honest; dedicated; humble; patient; good sense of humor; strong sense of integrity |

(continued)

Table (continued)

| | | | | | |
|---|---|---|---|---|---|
| **Lillian Borrone,** Director, Port Authority of New York and New Jersey's Commerce Department | Revitalization and recovery of agency operations | Effective working with multiple policy and political players, including governors, federal and state agencies, U.S. Congress, interest groups, and employee unions | Visionary; open; innovative; good listener; "relationally anchored behavior"; good motivator; ability to maneuver in male-dominated environment; good problem solver; good negotiator; egalitarian; consensus builder; coaching and mentoring women (to work in male-dominated field) | Federal and state government | Creative marketing; coalition and network building; respect for stakeholders | Courageous; energetic; enthusiastic; determined; respectful; perseverant; maverick and pioneer (in male-dominated field) |
| **Sean O'Keefe,** Administrator NASA | Vision for Exploration (returning to the Moon and then to Mars) | Strong connections to Bush administration, especially Vice President Cheney; effective use of "politics inside the beltway"; good relations with international space partners | Entrepreneurial; nonideological; transformational; innovative; team builder; effective negotiator; good listener; visionary; participative style | Mostly federal government and higher education | Promotion of science-driven objectives; reorganize and reprioritize; creation of technology development program; emphasis on process in decision making (linking policy and budget) | Compassionate; hardworking; steady; subtle; loyal |
| **George Tenet,** Director, CIA | Rebuilding the CIA | Good relationship with Congress; loyalty to Bush administration | Hands-on; ability to prioritize; institutional building; investment in workers (e.g., training) | Lobbyist; congressional staffer | Coalition building; improving the execution of intelligence collection and analysis | "Blunt, straightforward and totally loyal!"; gregarious; energetic; affable |

| | | | | | | |
|---|---|---|---|---|---|---|
| **Colleen Jollie,** State Tribal Liaison, Washington State Department of Transportation | Forging positive relationship between American Indian tribes and Washington State government | Ability to cultivate ties with federal, state, and local governments; effective working with multiple policy players | Transformational; optimistic; cooperative; collaborative; good listener; "trickster"; culturally astute and sensitive; good facilitator; ability to maneuver in white cultural institutions; good interpreter; strong sense of social justice and equity | State-level Indian affairs | Create culture of cooperation; link power and resources to people; promote intergovernmental relations; civic activism | Honorable; determined; integrity; trustworthy; maverick; pillar; healer; perseverant; strong-willed |
| **Viola O. Baskerville,** Secretary of Administration, State of Virginia | Promoting civil rights and well-being of children, women, and families | Good relationship with governor and other cabinet secretaries; networking with political allies | Risk taker; integrative (power sharing); strong work ethic; attention to detail; pragmatic; good interpersonal skills; fosters equity and equality; sense of social justice; goal oriented; empowering workers; provides mentoring | Voluntary and elected posts | Coalition building; empowerment of constituents; working collaboratively; consensus builder | Trailblazer; dedicated; integrity; graceful; dignified; strong-willed; steadfast; strong sense of cultural identity |
| **Admiral James Loy,** U.S. Coast Guard and Department of Homeland Security | Leading during the "new normalcy" | Good relationship with key political actors and with industry officials | Values-based leadership; visionary; good listener; inspirational; good motivator; team builder; shared values; respect for staff; openness | Military and federal government | Coalition building; partnering with stakeholders; consensus builder | Determined; loyal; respectful; genuine; honest; personable |

*(continued)*

Table *(continued)*

| | | | | | |
|---|---|---|---|---|---|
| **Nancy Alfaro**, Director, San Francisco's 311 Customer Service Center and County Clerk | Overseeing gay marriages; leading the 311 network | Effective at harmonizing political officials, agencies, and the public; good relationship with mayor | Collaborative; empowers employees; open; clarity; harmonizer; democratic; good motivator; approachable | Mostly city government | Building partnerships and cross-government alliances; networking; citizen engagement; customer service first | Dedicated; honest; determined; unassuming; strong sense of integrity |
| **Chrik Poortman**, Vice President, World Bank | Serving and assisting developing countries | Good working relationship with and respect for client countries; good working relationship with international and local staff | Strategic planner; diplomatic; nonpartisan; technocrat; good communicator; hands-on; commitment to staff; political sensitivity; risk taker; integrative; ability to delegate | Government, mostly World Bank | Building bridges (donors, clients, and factions); commitment to development; understanding and respect for political milieux; diplomacy | Dynamic; charismatic; dedicated; honest; "no nonsense"; humble; respectable; "levelheaded"; passionate; trustworthy |
| **Ben Bernanke**, Chair, Federal Reserve Board | Response to financial crisis | Ability to maneuver in political settings (Congress, President, and media) | Promoting a "learning organization"; selfless; detailed; knowledge of law; regulatory expertise | Higher education; federal government | Regulation of subprime mortgage market; lowered federal funds rate; central bank swaps; lowered discount rate; extended loan terms | Dedicated; hardworking; rational; open-minded; resolved; straightforward |

| Bill Gibson, Executive Director, Southwestern Commission (North Carolina) | Leading across boundaries | Partnering with local government officials, community leaders, and private enterprise | Entrepreneurial; good facilitator and mediator; leads from the middle; risktaker; consensus builder; good negotiating skills; good coordinator; visionary; change agent | Public service; nonprofits | Collaborative governance; boundary spanning; brokering and partnering with organizations | Dedicated; open-minded; understanding; committed; trustworthy; selfless; civic minded |
|---|---|---|---|---|---|---|
| Eli Rosenbaum, Director, Office of Special Investigations, Department of Justice | Targeting and prosecuting Nazi collaborators and global terrorists | Good relationships with OSI deputies and Criminal Division supervisor; good relationships with relevant attorneys and historians | Acute cognitive and affective skills; team builder; charismatic; risk taker; promotes transparency; mission-specific recruiter; morale booster; democratic; effective use of intrinsic rewards; good motivator; conflict resolver; good goal setter; "people" oriented | Public service; law | Gaining support and cooperation of foreign governments; improvement of agency's MIS; exercising political prudence | Steadfast; high moral and ethical character; perseverant; focused; sensitive; committed; honest |

*Note:* The more neutral term "good" is used here rather than such terms as "effective" and "outstanding."

The specific political skills employed by public administrators also contribute to their effective performance, and these skills are domain sensitive. That is to say, for some administrators, fostering good relationships with elected officials is important, for others it is not relevant. For example, it is critical for federally appointed administrators such as Donna Shalala, Elmer Staats, Charles Rossotti, and George Tenet to develop good working relationships with the White House and Congress. Similarly, for Viola Baskerville, a state-appointed administrator, good relationships with the governor and cabinet secretaries are critical for her successful performance. For Nancy Alfaro, a mayoral appointee, close ties to the mayor are obviously critical. For Bill Gibson, director of a regional council in North Carolina, partnering with local government officials, community leaders, and private organizations is essential. In short, the particular sphere within which the public administrator works requires political skills relevant to that particular sphere.

The specific strategy relied upon by the public servant also contributes to his or her success. For example, one goal of Burtell Jefferson, the first African American police chief in Washington, D.C., was to increase the ranks of African Americans in the D.C. police force. An important strategy for doing so was coaching and mentoring not just African Americans but all races and ethnic groups. For Eli Rosenbaum, gaining support and cooperation from foreign governments was vital in his efforts to hunt, prosecute, and deport Nazi criminals from the United States. William Robertson empowered citizens and promoted collaborative governance in his efforts to improve service delivery to communities in Los Angeles. For Chrik Poortman of the World Bank, diplomacy and building bridges between donors and clients was paramount.

In addition, with some notable exceptions (e.g., high-level political appointees such as Shalala, Tenet, and Bernanke), public administrators such as those profiled here are rarely credited for their work or placed in the limelight. A good example can be seen in Rosenbaum of the Office of Special Investigations (OSI), who has been extremely effective and instrumental in bringing a number of Nazi and other war criminals to justice. Most recently, John Demjanjuk was convicted of murdering thousands of Jews while a guard at the Nazi death camp Sobibor in 1943. It was Rosenbaum who led Demjanjuk's prosecution in the United States, but his name is not mentioned in the *New York Times'* (Ewing and Cowell 2011) reporting of the conviction. Rosenbaum can also be partly credited for rooting out Lazare Kobagaya, 84, of Rwanda, for his participation in genocide. Kobagaya, who is being prosecuted for illegally obtaining U.S. citizenship and misusing an alien registration card, was indicted for ordering the massacre of Tutsis during the 1994 civil war in Rwanda. The *New York Times* (Stumpe 2011), reporting on Kobagaya's trial, never mentions Rosenbaum or any other official from OSI. Again, the public servants who work behind the scenes to promote the public good are rarely acknowledged publicly for their hard work.

In sum, a number of factors contribute to successful performance on the part of public servants, as seen here. An important goal of this book was to not only illuminate these factors but also to present accounts of the significant work performed by individuals dedicated to promoting the public interest.

## REFERENCES

Ewing, Jack, and Alan Cowell. 2011. Ex-Guard at Nazi Death Camp Is Found Guilty by German Court. *New York Times*, May 13, A4.

Stumpe, Joe. 2011. Kansas Trial Will Recall Genocide in Rwanda. *New York Times*, April 26, A18.

# ABOUT THE EDITOR AND CONTRIBUTORS

## EDITOR

**Norma M. Riccucci** is Professor of public administration at Rutgers University's Newark campus. She has published extensively in the areas of public management, affirmative action, and diversity management in the public sector. Some of her books include *Public Administration: Traditions of Inquiry and Philosophies of Knowledge; Managing Diversity in Public Sector Workforces; Public Personnel Management: Current Concerns, Future Challenges;* and *How Management Matters: Street Level Bureaucrats and Welfare Reform.* Dr. Riccucci is the recipient of several national awards including ASPA's Charles H. Levine Award for excellence in teaching, research, and service to the community; ASPA/NASPAA's Distinguished Research Award; the ASPA Section of Women in Public Administration's Rita Mae Kelly Award for Research Excellence; ASPA's Section on Personnel Administration and Labor Relations' Scholarship in Public Human Resources Award; and APSA's Herbert Simon Book Award. She has received a number of university awards as well, including the Board of Trustees Award for Excellence in Research. In 2005 she was inducted into the National Academy of Public Administration.

## CONTRIBUTORS

**Megan Beeby** is from the Snoqualmie tribe and works as the environmental tribal liaison for the Washington State Department of Transportation. She has a bachelor's degree in liberal arts with an emphasis in Native American studies and a master of public administration degree in tribal governance, both from The Evergreen State College.

**Thomas A. Bryer** is Assistant Professor in the School of Public Administration at the University of Central Florida and Director of the Center for Public and Nonprofit Management at UCF. His research and teaching focuses on public participation, cross-sector collaboration and governance, and bureaucratic responsiveness.

**Kathe Callahan** is the associate director of the Center for Executive Leadership in Government at Rutgers, the State University of New Jersey. She publishes on the topics of citizen participation, government performance, and accountability.

**Deirdre M. Condit** is an associate professor of political science in the L. Douglas Wilder School of Government and Public Affairs at Virginia Commonwealth University. Her research interests in feminist political theory and ethics broadly encompass issues of gender within electoral politics, the politics of reproductive technologies, and maternal theory and public policy. Her recent work on reproductive technologies examines the potential impact of "androgenesis" on feminist theories of identity and maternalism and intersects with a parallel foray into feminist and transgender theory and complexity. She teaches courses in Political Science, Women's Studies, and the Honor's College. Her recent publications include an article on the language of sex and gender in transgender aging theory, an article on androgenesis in a collection entitled, *Twenty-first Century Motherhood*, and various articles in the journals *Sex Roles, Rhetoric and Public Affairs,* the *Journal of Medical Humanities, Policy Sciences, Women and Politics*, and with Dr. Hutchinson, in *The American Review of Public Administration*.

**Terry L. Cooper** is the Maria B. Crutcher Professor in Citizenship and Democratic Values at the University of Southern California. His research centers on citizen engagement and public ethics. Currently, he is the director of the USC Civic Engagement Initiative. Cooper is the author of *The Responsible Administrator: An Approach to Ethics for the Administrative Role*, and the author or editor of three other books and numerous articles in scholarly journals.

**Heather Getha-Taylor** is an assistant professor in the School of Public Affairs and Administration at the University of Kansas. Her research and teaching interests focus on public and nonprofit management, with special emphasis on public personnel administration, executive leadership, and organizational behavior. She received her PhD in public administration from the Maxwell School of Citizenship and Public Affairs at Syracuse University.

**Janet R. Hutchinson** is Professor of Public Policy and Chair of the Department of Gender, Sexuality and Women's Studies at Virginia Commonwealth University. She holds a dual appointment with the L. Douglas Wilder School of Government and Public Affairs and is codirector of the Virginia Family Impact Seminars. Her research and publications focus on theoretical feminisms and their influence on matters of public policy.

**J. Edward Kellough** is a Professor and Head of the Department of Public Administration and Policy at the University of Georgia. He specializes in public personnel management, public administration, and program evaluation. Recent books include *Understanding Affirmative Action* (2007); *The New Public Personnel Administration* (2007), with Lloyd G. Nigro and Felix Nigro; and *Civil Service Reform in the States* (2006), edited with Lloyd G. Nigro. His research has appeared in numerous academic journals.

**Anne M. Khademian** is a Professor and Director of Virginia Tech's School of Public and International Affairs. She is the author of *The SEC and Capital Market Regulation: The Politics of Expertise* (1992), *Checking on Banks: Autonomy and Accountability in Three Federal Agencies* (1996), and *Working with Culture: How the Job Gets Done in Public Programs* (2002), as well as numerous articles focused on inclusive management, homeland security, and financial regulation.

**Cheryl Simrell King** is a member of the faculty in public administration at The Evergreen State College. She is the coauthor of *Transformational Public Service: Portraits of Theory in Practice* (2005), *Government Is Us: Public Administration in an Anti-Government Era* (1998), and editor of *Government is Us, 2.0* (2011), as well as articles in other trade press and academic journals. She writes and practices in the areas of democratizing and transforming public administration, accountability, sustainability, and the relationships among and between citizens and their governments.

**W. Henry Lambright** is Professor of public administration and international affairs, and political science in the Maxwell School at Syracuse University. He is the author or editor of seven books and more than 250 articles, papers, and reports. His books include a biography, *Powering Apollo: James E. Webb of NASA* (1995). His current research focuses on leadership and change at NASA since the end of the Cold War.

**Jerome S. Legge, Jr.,** is associate dean of the School of Public and International Affairs and a professor of public administration and policy at the University of Georgia, where he has taught since 1980. His research on European support for privatization (with R. Paul Battaglio, Jr.) appeared in the August 2009 issue of *Public Administration Review*. Currently, he is examining bureaucratic responses to the entry of Nazi collaborators into the United States in the 1940s and 1950s to include the Federal Bureau of Investigation and Immigration and Naturalization Service. A recent article on Estonian collaborator Karl Linnas appeared in the spring 2010 issue of *Holocaust and Genocide Studies*.

**Ricardo S. Morse** is an assistant professor of public administration and government in the School of Government at the University of North Carolina at Chapel Hill. His research focuses on leadership and collaborative governance. He is lead editor of *Transforming Public Leadership for the 21st Century* (2007) and *Innovations in Public Leadership Development* (2008).

**Katherine C. Naff** is a Professor of public administration at San Francisco State University. Her primary areas of teaching are human resource management, public law, diversity in public administration, and public management. Her research specialties include equal employment opportunity and affirmative action in the United States and South Africa. Previously, she served as a senior research analyst with the U.S. Merit Systems Protection Board in Washington, D.C.

**Beryl A. Radin** is a member of the faculty of the Public Policy Institute at Georgetown University. A past editor of the *Journal of Public Administration Research and Theory*, her work has emphasized issues related to federal management. She served as a special adviser to the Assistant Secretary of Management and Budget in the Department of Health and Human Services during the Clinton administration. Her most recent book is *Federal Management Reform in a World of Contradictions* (2012).

**Hal G. Rainey** is Alumni Foundation distinguished professor in the School of Public and International Affairs at the University of Georgia. His research concentrates on organizations and management in government, with an emphasis on performance, change, leadership, incentives, privatization, and comparisons of governmental management to management in the business and nonprofit sectors. The fourth edition of his book *Understanding and Managing Public Organizations* was published in 2009. He received the John Gaus Award in 2011 from the American Political Science Association. He was recently elected a fellow of the National Academy of Public Administration.

**Hindy Lauer Schachter** is a professor in the School of Management at the New Jersey Institute of Technology. She is the author of *Reinventing Government or Reinventing Ourselves: The Role of Citizen Owners in Making a Better Government* (1997), *Frederick Taylor and the Public Administration Community: A Reevaluation* (1989), and *Public Agency Communication: Theory and*

*Practice* (1983). Her articles have appeared in *Public Administration Review, Administration & Society, International Journal of Public Administration,* and *Public Administration Quarterly.*

**James R. Thompson** is associate professor and head of the Department of Public Administration at the University of Illinois–Chicago, where he teaches courses in public personnel management, information technology, and public management. Topics on which he has written include civil service reform ("The Federal Civil Service: Demise of an Institution," *Public Administration Review*, 2006) and human resource management innovation ("Personnel Demonstration Projects and Human Resource Management Innovation," *Review of Public Personnel Administration*, 2008).

**Patrick Weller** is Professor and Director of the Centre for Governance and Public Policy, Griffith University, Australia. He recently coauthored *Governance of World Trade* (2004), *Inside the World Bank* (2009), *Westminster Compared* (2009), and *Learning to be a Minister* (2010).

**Richard D. White, Jr.,** is the Marjory Ourso Professor for Academic Excellence and Associate Dean of the E. J. College of Business at Louisiana State University. He is the author of *Kingfish: The Reign of Huey P. Long* (2005), *Roosevelt the Reformer: Theodore Roosevelt as Civil Service Commissioner 1889–1895* (2003), and *Will Rogers: A Political Life* (2011). His twenty-four-year government career includes service in the White House, State Department, Central Intelligence Agency, and the U.S. Coast Guard.

**Brian N. Williams** is an assistant professor in the Department of Public Administration and Policy at the University of Georgia. His research explores race, policing, and the coproduction of public safety and public order. He is the author of *Citizen Perspectives on Community Policing: A Case Study in Athens, Georgia* (1998). His research has appeared in *Public Administration Review, Teachers College Record, Police Quarterly*, and other academic journals.

**Xu Yi-chong** is a Professor in the Centre for Governance and Public Policy, Griffith University, Australia. She currently coauthored *Governance of World Trade* (2004), *Inside the World Bank* (2009), and authored *The Politics of Nuclear Energy in China* (2010).